SOUTHERN SHOCK AMERICANA

Thank you so much Elinor!

Copyright © 2014
All rights reserved. No part of this book may be reproduced commercially without permission of the author and publisher.
First Printing

Thank you.
Bruce Eric

SOUTHERN SHOCK AMERICANA

The LIFE and EXECUTION of JOHN MILLS, JR.

Herb Donaldson

For my mother, Rachel;
my grandmother Blonzie;
my father, Herbert, Sr.;
my grandfather, John, Sr.;
my family, both first and second;
for L.J. Lawhon;
for my Uncle;
and for those who are not writers of books by profession,
but still have a truth to tell.

The FAMILY TREE of...

Yuhanna Abdullah Muhammad
(Formerly)
John Mills, Jr.

<u>John Mills Sr.</u> *(Father)*   <u>Blonzie Mae (Booth Ransom) Mills</u> *(Mother)*

⬇   *(Brothers and sisters)*

Floyd, Lloyd, Rachel, and Jesse, Jr.

<u>Charlie & Susie (Simmons) Mills</u>
(Grandparents; John Sr.'s parents)

Arlee 'Pinder' (Bruster) Simmons
(Grandmother; Blonzie's mother)

Betty Jean (Booth) Hines
(Aunt; Blonzie's sister; Arlee's daughter)

Rachel (Franklin Bruster) Booth   &   **Arza Bruster**
Great–grandmother   *Great-Grandfather*
Blonzie's grandmother   *Blonzie's grandfather*
Arlee's mother   *Arlee's father*

Surrey Booth
Step great-Grandfather (Married Rachel Franklin Bruster Booth)
Grandfather (By way of Rachel's daughter, Arlee; Blonzie's father)

A few reasons why...

A willful blindness of the peculiar, wieldy sort, overtook Wakulla County, Florida almost three decades ago. Something happened in the community of approximately 11,000 that was, according to former circuit judge, the Honorable George L. Harper:

> "...one of the most atrocious crimes committed in this century, in this county, and probably the most atrocious against a male subject of Wakulla."

Judge Harper's observation manages to leave out a multitude of historical sins. Blacks in the county, well into the 1970's, were mowed-down by cars; killed as they walked home from their jobs, the homes of relatives, or the local juke-joints late at night. Some were found beside dirt roads, or along the brackish water creeks flowing throughout the area, with their throats cut. Or worse.

'Nelson Pond', located in Panacea, a small town within Wakulla confines, is said to have gained its name because Mr. Nelson, a black man, was caught fishing in the wrong place at the wrong time. Rumor has it that the cap he wore at the time of his demise was seen for weeks after, floating on the pond's surface, before sinking once again into the watery depths below. Mr. Nelson's very existence has been reduced to nothing more than a backwoods ghost story.

If a cosmic, otherworldly malfunction were to strike the live oak trees that shade Wakulla's lonely dirt-roads with the power of speech, what sordid bedtime tales would they unravel for the children?

Dull ones, perhaps. Wakulla's young have learned early the lessons of human failing, disappointment, and the chill of reality. Foreclosures, poverty, unemployment, bank fraud, wetland ordinances that affect their drinking water, drug exchanges among their peers that filter through the classroom as early as middle school; more than a true-life ghost story is needed to disturb the sleep of their generation.

...

Few facts are known concerning what happened that grizzly Friday afternoon of March 5, 1982. The date is marked as the most horrific in my family's history.

We were not the only ones rocked by 'the nightmare'. Two other families were involved. Their surviving members were also crippled from the collision of justice, faith, and race.

Many in Wakulla stop reading when 'race', that infamous word, makes its guest appearance. This writing is not for them. It is for those who understand and remember what the nightmare did to our community. We no longer cling to trust as if it were the final straw when dealing with our fellow man. To trust is to take a leap of faith; that faith requires that one treat the other equally in word, thought, and action. Trust has become a rarity in our world. Wakulla County is no exception.

Talk of our southern rebel past will end a friendly conversation in this neck of the Forgotten Coast. From our truck-windows to our non-profit institutions run with government funding, we wave our Confederate flag grandly here.

The price for doing so, is the energy we must exert when placing a chokehold on any voice that dares to talk openly – that challenges – that Confederate history or its meaning.

Our neighbors, those not officially proven to be bloodline descendants of the glorified Stars and Stripes, are not our concern, and therefore, not real to us.

It is true that, due to history's grip, the black and white cultures here are married to one another in ways that time can never untangle. A joke runs smilingly from the lips of old-timers (and not-so-old-timers), that everyone in Wakulla is related in one way or another. A veiled allusion, perhaps, to our forefathers' crossing of the color barrier; a line crossed out of a specific need. In similar ways, the present generations have crossed over also. And like our forefathers, denial runs deep.

Like the many flowers of a garden, the cross-pollinizing of our county's people is obvious at a glance. Only for a fleeting moment is it striking to see an older, white grandfather holding the hand of his darkly-hued grandchild as they exit the Family Dollar store; or a school basketball team overflowing with youth who defy the terms 'black' or 'white', and run the gamut of all the unknown in between; or chocolate-toned mothers sitting in church with children whose faces are the color of milk and golden honey, with eyes as green as sea-foam.

Something within the nature of the county has changed these last 30-plus years. And though the familiar trails and landmarks have either been refashioned or become extinct, the majority of Wakulla's people have borne this evolution with a graceful acceptance.

There does remain, however, a certain element throughout the area who hold tightly to what is believed to be the 'traditional' or 'old Wakulla' way. There are those who feel wholeheartedly that certain changes and immoral unions are proof that the county – the nation – is standing in the threshold of demise; lulled into a deep sleep by the melodic overture of an oncoming terror.

...

Nightmares: Only two things are readily agreed upon: (1) That it rained on Friday, March 5, 1982, and (2) that a man by the name of Lesley James Lawhon would eventually be found dead. Murdered, supposedly, by my Uncle.

Through research of appeals; from conversations with family and friends of the victim and the accused; along with my Uncle's own words in the letters and journals he amassed during his 13.92 years on Florida's Death Row, something has begun to sting deep within me: What if justice was not served? What if he didn't do this?

...And what then?

Bitterness: I wonder if that is the inner substance emoting from me as I write these words. I also wonder if I'm purging myself of a poison that Wakulla has fed me far too long.

What if I'm wrong? Am I completely obsessed with my own version of truth that I've turned a quest for answers into a living lie?

Our family has had to ready itself for embracing, good or bad, the painful truth of my Uncle's case. There is always the possibility that we may go to our graves knowing nothing more than we do now.

Something guides me; is preparing me for an answer not based on what I want or hope, but on what facts reveal. And it is this revelation that has become a wide brick wall on the narrow road of my journey.

With revelation, the messenger is quick to find that those within hearing range can only bear and accept so much. Will the writing of these notes be accepted and understood by my larger family: Wakulla County?

I do not wish to place my home in a poor light. But I do have a right to examine it, at least, for my Uncle's sake, and for the man who was supposedly his victim. This is a story that has been misunderstood by our Wakulla family, and was an incident that very nearly tore the safety of our quaint little dwelling apart.

After the storm, we were left to sift through the valley of broken relationships; left to repair the brutality of words spoken in anger during a whirlwind of accusations; left to salvage only that which was necessary to reconstruct the frail fortress of a broken home.

...

In early 2013, I gave my very first eulogy. Less than two weeks later I gave my second. During the first tribute – my Grandmother's – I looked out on the front rows where loved ones and friends had gathered.

Beside the pews, sitting in his wheelchair, was my Uncle Jesse James Ransom III. He was no longer the big, bearded man with dancing eyes, gentle smile, and boyish laughter. Cancer had entered his flesh and snatched away the bits and familiar pieces of his terrific beauty.

Two weeks later I stood in a different church, behind another podium, staring down at another casket. And there lay Uncle Jess. Only months before we had lost one cousin in a car accident, and another, barely a teenager, died from pneumonia.

The links that held our family together seemed to be crumbling before my eyes. I found myself absent of the odd, curious presence of mind that allows the mourner to pick up the pieces and rebuild.

Destruction, in its varied forms, is normal for any family. Though a number of relatives on my Mother's side are still alive, that's about all that can be said for their existence.

Few are surviving and even fewer have managed to stay away from the excesses of alcohol, drugs, or stints in jail. The desire to escape, by whatever means available, the unending pains of daily life, remains the most vibrantly colored fabric within our family's patchwork.

While preparing Grandma's eulogy I felt the need to confront who we were as her descendants. When attempting to atone in such a manner, even those you love are bound to hate you. And if your family is southern, though the dislike may seem subtle for the moment, it will grow to be painful, and in time, complete. It is seldom expressed to one's face, but flourishes with comfort behind one's back.

Although I left Wakulla at seventeen and vowed never to return, I could not fail to recognize a similar pain – the internal features of myself – in the lives of the people I met, in the cities where I lived.

These kindred spirits were from entirely different areas of the United States and from around the world. But the keen sense that something had gone wrong, or that they were somehow damaged, glowed as brightly within them as it did in me. One friend, older than I, told those who inquired of his background that his family was 'killed in the riots'. If you didn't know him, as I did, you'd leave his presence believing it to be true, even though his parents were less than a 2-hour train ride away.

The accumulation of death and birth among my own is what drew me back into the fold – the hold – of Wakulla County, more than 20-plus years later.

I'd been home only a few months before understanding that one's condition, fortunate or unfortunate, is always being discussed. Where you've been and, more importantly, why you've come back, is up for speculation. People here are dumbfounded as to why you would ever return. Apparently, simply being born in Wakulla sounds the gun that launches the great race of escape; the act of leaving being the first major hurdle. It is to be leapt over sooner, than later.

After Grandma's funeral some relatives kept their distance. And why not? I'd leaked inside information; provided a map, of sorts, that led to family secrets. Yet the issues of our familial history and more, were not being dealt with among us collectively. We and our children were sporting open wounds inflicted by others from generations past; scars that should have healed long ago.

In the attempt to close the lid on death, I opened my eyes. I noticed how common our family's story was. Like us, others in Wakulla expressed their familial pain through actions designed not to heal, but cause greater damage, placing the ones they cared for most in the line of fire.

The state of Wakulla reflects the heart and spirit of its people. Here, we gentle folk, speak around our problems; our true state of affairs. To address our realities head-on shows weakness; you are seen as one who is unable to control both his thoughts and his mouth. The frail mask of a 'stiff upper lip' is more preferable. To lay a fact out plainly is in poor taste and lacks southern gentility. You will be looked upon as a trouble-maker, instigator, and professional 'shit-stirrer'.

Some in our family have adopted these ways and tend to talk around the issue, the person, the conflict – and find great discomfort in addressing things directly. Even love – especially for older males who are 'set in their ways' – is a difficult thing to express, let alone speak.

No one wanted to deal openly with the fact that our Grandma had died of complications due to HIV, and later, full-blown AIDS. And even if they did, there was little comfort zone to do so in ways that were constructive, informative, or educational.

And so, they simply acted as if it wasn't there. As if it were not a truth, or a fact, but instead, a deep, dark secret that couldn't be discussed with or around our Grandmother. So present was this hidden secret that many forgot that it was she who rose daily with it on bright mornings; and she who lay beside it – like a lover – as it whispered words of fear into her soul on dark nights. What a lonely place for an elderly black woman.

Although the world may have come to understand this disease, it does not mean that small 'country' towns like ours have followed suit. The virus, race, sexuality, mental illness, suicide, rape, incest, and more, are not to be spoken of here. If so, it is done with shame, pity, and the mockingly judgmental sucking of self-righteous, God-chattering teeth.

...

I wonder at the loneliness Grandma must have felt. All of us, to some degree, know that loneliness. Families are built and children are made in an effort to avoid it.

This brand of exile was also felt by her youngest son, John Mills, Jr., who we called 'Boone'. I was born the next child after him in our family line. The world knew very little about him; only a small portion, a fleeting event in his life. And they assumed this to be the whole.

The bits and pieces contained herein are just that: Fragments of one man's 42-year existence in Wakulla County, in the State of Florida, and on this earth. These words are not meant to be divisive, but it is likely that some will view them as being so. To this I can only say that I've made my peace with being disliked. I have not made peace with the clues my Uncle left behind, nor the justice my Grandmother went to her grave seeking.

Therefore, I approach these notes regarding Boone, Grandma, our family history, and 'the nightmare', as if the whole of Wakulla County was my own flesh and blood (for it is); as if every man and woman who resides in it, my brother and sister (for they are); as if all things held precious to them, were equally as precious to me.

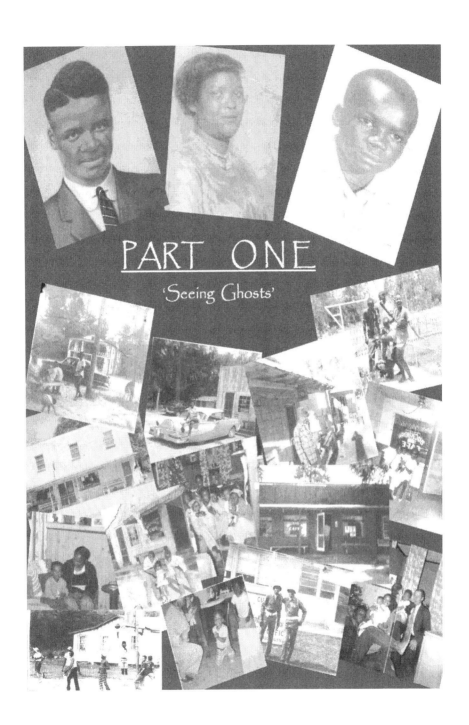

PART ONE
'Seeing Ghosts'

Chapter One

'The Black Mayor'

Wakulla is a mystery. Its very name remains, for most, unsettled. Legend tells us that the term 'wakala' was thought to be Creek Indian/Native for 'spring of water', or 'mysterious waters'. Others say it refers to an aquatic bird called the 'loon', while some claim it means 'mist' or 'misting'. And chances are, somewhere, out there, is a historian clamoring to tell you that you've got it all wrong.

Officially established March 11, 1843, Spanish conquistadors like Panfilo Narvaez and Hernando de Soto traveled this area as early as the 1700's, in search of treasure, power, and all the other lethal abominations that lead to domination. Andrew Jackson, before becoming U.S. President, slaughtered a host of Native populations here.

Confederate Negro soldiers fought bravely alongside their white brethren during a turning point of the Civil War called the Battle of Natural Bridge, just up the road.

Wakulla Negroes made their share of strides during the late 1800's. Amos Hargrett, a former slave, is said to have gained his freedom after his master died. However, he chose to help the master's widow maintain the property. She, in return, taught black children to read and write, Amos' children among them.

Hargrett was appointed Wakulla Co. Commissioner from 1868 - 70, by former Florida Governor, Harrison Reed; he served as Justice of the Peace, and was Wakulla's delegate to the 1885 Constitutional Convention. His descendants created the first school for blacks in the county, and were instrumental in the development of the Shadeville School, established in 1909. Shadeville is currently the oldest school standing in Wakulla.

Although Hargrett's history is known by many, the achievements of other blacks during that period are seldom noted, if at all. Edward Wise, Joseph Poole, Richard H. Hargrett, Isaac Gavin, Robert Braswell, and Anthony Bradham all served as Wakulla Commissioners, at various points, from 1868 to 1877. Bradham was a Justice of the Peace from 1873-77. Another unknown would be Turner Duling, the county's voter registrar from 1867-68.

...

Unlike all but one other community in Wakulla, Sopchoppy is incorporated and referred to as a 'city'.

Sopchoppy's name – again – is a mystery. Some believe it means 'twisted' and 'long'. Others say it was pulled from the Muskogee to mean 'acorn' 'stem'.

It was here that Charlie Mills, tall, gangly bodied, with a long, easy stride to his walk, met and married Susie Simmons in the year 1896.

Susie was a melding of Africa and a native Floridian tribe: High cheekbones and forehead with skin pulled taut, smooth like brown cream; eyes that slanted up toward the edges, as black and wet as the amber-tinted waters of a Sopchoppy creek. In short, she looked like a woman from the Islands.

They were not strangers to hard work and deep affection, evidenced by the small parcel of land they acquired and the cavalry of children they raised. One son, John, born December 1902, would eventually, through a series of odd and 'mysterious' events, become my grandfather.

Stories handed down reveal that when John was approximately thirteen, he planted a tree alongside the dirt road that ran through Sopchoppy. In time, the tree grew so large that he built a wooden table around it, complete with benches at the base and on the outskirts. The community – friends, family, strangers, musicians, and workers that passed through – were the ones who made the spot popular.

During the summer months, the heat of Wakulla isn't so much hot, as it is humid. Something in the air pulls and draws out the very essence of the body. The large old trees, with their widespread branches and marvelous wigging of Spanish moss, become a haven for the drained and parched throughout the burning season.

And here, beneath the shade of the John Mills Tree, as it was now called, is where they all gathered: Black, brown, and white assembled for a game of 'tonk', 'spades', or 'rummy 500'.

The eldest of the men and women who had (for what seemed like centuries, from the state of their worn faces and beaten hands) spent their working lives pulling fishnets in at the seine yards, grunting in the baitwoods, shucking shells and breaking claws at the crab-houses, or – at the most backbreaking places of all – the turpentine camps, sat like a band of worldly sages beneath the tree to watch, reflect, and remember.

Blacks in the county had numerous softball teams back then for both men and women. After the game they would pile in, dressed in their jerseys. Two teams may have played, but everybody won, and now was a time for celebration.

On the farthest corner of the bench, a young man could always be found waiting patiently, holding close his quiet secret. All would be revealed as a young lady came strolling down the dirt road, summer dress dancing lightly on the breeze as though she had all the time in the world to spare. Sheepishly, the young man would rise, amble towards his date, as the elders watched, and remembered.

But none of it was complete without the sinners; those who had nothing better to do on hot Sunday afternoons than relive – loudly – their Saturday night escapes. And, oddly enough, the ones they enjoyed sharing their newfound knowledge with most, were the saints.

For the anointed, too, would congregate beneath the tree's protection after service. And though they'd heard tell of Jesus and the multiplication of fish that morning, the more pressing obligation lay at their fingertips; picking delicately at the fried mullet, hushpuppies, coleslaw, 2-piece white bread, and packet of hot-sauce on the paper plate in front of them – fresh from the Buckhorn Café.

In later years, when I, my brother, sister, and cousins came onto the scene, all we needed on such afternoons were Peach Ne-Hi sodas, RC colas, push-up ice-cream, gingerbread Stage Plank cookies, and Moon Pies.

Eventually, as the night rolled in and fireflies twinkled in midair, the men who had spent hours getting high on southern spirit, began to think themselves well-versed on all things right – and wrong – with the American way. By dark, someone was sure to be drunk and emboldened enough to pick a fight.

But the even more surreal beauty of it all, was that even though the area was predominately black, the white community was always around, engaging with Buckhorn residents as if all were kissing cousins. In a few cases, they actually were.

To this day people tell me of their times spent in the Buckhorn Café, and how my Grandfather served them their very first beer; how they won or lost money during a card game under the tree. It was not uncommon to walk into my Grandfather's store and see a white child sweeping the floor for extra change. When the job was done, they'd have spending money in their pocket, and the pick of any soda or sweet that they wanted – on the house.

Though race played a large role in the realm of social politics, Buckhorn was a familiar ground that all could stand on to talk and associate with each other as human beings. Not colors.

The flip side of this is that – just up the road from my Grandfather's store, in the heart of Sopchoppy – Klansmen (KKK) robes were for sale in the front windows of the main grocery store. A friend, white, and well into his 60's, remembers vividly the times when their black neighbors came knocking on their door in the middle of the night. His family would hide them in the back of the house. The job of the white children who lived there was to sit on the front porch and watch as the Klan members rode by. The children were instructed to wave now and then, for effect.

...

By the 1930's Wakulla was said to have had the highest rate of educated blacks per capita in all of North Florida. Jim Crow was on the scene, and the only way to not get caught in its lawful grip was to create a place where Crow held no power.

Those who grew up in Wakulla during that period speak frankly about having to walk miles to work for local white families. Tales of being 'allowed' to sweep off the front porch, but having to enter through the back, are common.

Some talk of their relatives who, after doing yard-work for white families, were given tin-plates of food. The tin was placed on the back-porch steps and the person was then called forward to eat, as if the family pet were being, lovingly, fed.

Being friends with white children was no problem. That is, until the white child grew up. Once the child reached a certain age, blacks – old and young – were not allowed to refer to them by their first names any longer. They were to be called 'Mister' or 'Miss'. There were consequences, in Wakulla, if these rules were not followed. *(Throughout the county, a few of the old 'hanging trees' still exist. The most well-known tree is in Panacea, holding more than soil and water at its spirit-root.)*

Even today, grown men and women address folks in this manner. 'Mister', or 'Miss' is used before the first name of the individual being addressed, as opposed to the last. In general, it is a way of showing respect to those who are older, or mature in years. But there's the creeping feeling of history's ghost at one's shoulder when hearing blacks say it to whites here, in this day and age, in this county, with its history.

I'd been away for some time and had begun to view my hometown from a distance. I wouldn't doubt that there was a bit of bias on my part. Yet, it is this strange, unspoken duality within the nature of Wakulla's people that makes the overall birds-eye view of the county's 'family' so odd.

Of Wakulla's current 30,000-plus residents, the white population is around 82 percent. Blacks hover between 14-15 percent, as of 2012. This is no one's fault; its simply the way things have played out. It is the larger view – the turning of the page that bring the other branches of the family tree into focus – that concerns us here.

According to that same 2012 census, black-owned businesses do not meet the required standards to even be listed for publication.

In the realm of finance one is hard-pressed to locate five black bank tellers – those who work in 'front', so to speak – in either bank or credit union in all Wakulla combined.

There have been a total of two, possibly three, black assistant principals in the county's school system throughout the 70's and up to the present day. There have been no black school principals since the days of the Shadeville, and Old Buckhorn schools, which educated black students before the days of de-segregation, more than 50-plus years ago.

There are a handful of black teachers spread throughout the classrooms of the county. And though many of them have knowledge, degrees, and certificates to back them up, it has always been doubtful – and sometimes spoken aloud (in private, one-on-one meetings) – that though the potential for them to rise in their careers may exist in other counties, it will not happen anytime soon in Wakulla.

This has something to do, some claim (for I've sat down with a number of them to ask), with what is termed, the "grooming process".

This occurs when a person of lesser qualifications (Often white and thought to be a close friend or relative of someone in the system) is 'picked' and placed in a certain position for approximately 10 years. Down the line, they are handed a higher, more authoritative role.

In essence, they've leapt over those who have waited in line for 10 years, or more, to be considered for the same position; those that were more than qualified to do the job 10 years earlier and who are now 10 years older, stuck, killing time, until retirement.

Comments like these arise from those who've worked in the system (and seen that system at work) for years; who, even with their stellar achievements have yet to rise, while people from other counties (some with lesser qualifications and white) arrive to be given jobs above them.

And yes, I can hear the thunder roll as I write these things. My response is simple: If one takes the above as mere assumption on the part of bitter complainants – and does not agree – they need only check the track record of Wakulla's school system in order to find out and prove it wrong.

And: Places like the Old Buckhorn School, which should've stood as a historic landmark, was torn apart and remodeled as a church. Only the lunchroom remains, mostly, intact. This revision was done by the blacks. As if the sustaining of their historical monuments should be altered or destroyed, with something shiny and new put in their place that projects a sense of wealth.

This ignores the inward, personal decay that can occur when consciously abolishing all things created by one's forebears. In some cases this is necessary. In others, it is the obliteration of a people's final testimony and historic achievement.

Wakulla had not seen a black county commissioner, it seems, since the days of Amos Hargrett and others during the late 1800's. Many have run for office through the years, but none succeeded until George Nathan Greene (Crawfordville), and Anginita Rosier (Sopchoppy) who served during the turn of the millennium.

Rosier served during the final years of Colleen Skipper's term as Mayor for the City of Sopchoppy. This was a coveted spot that Skipper held for almost 13 years. For many, there was – and is – reason to be extremely proud. She will forever go into the annals of Wakulla history as the First African-American Mayor for the City of Sopchoppy, who happened to also be a woman.

But at what price?

On June 11, Skipper had won the election by a few votes, but a canvassing board decided to throw out three votes claiming certain voters were not within the city limits of Sopchoppy. She lost her post in the 2013 election by one vote.

(There is another story behind this that we need not go into here. I will say that it concerns Ms. Rosier and Ms. Skipper's desire to offer a small stipend to those serving in Sopchoppy office. This was discussed at one of the meetings. It was there that a Sopchoppy resident rose to his feet and informed the two ladies that, if they pursued the issue further, they could expect to lose their positions in the next election.)

Also relieved of duty was Ms. Rosier, who in no way went quietly, amid rumors from residents in her district of voter tampering and ballot fraud. Though her story went national, it may be expecting too much to expect change.

Ms. Rosier's speaking out caused a great deal of upset. Many felt she was making a mountain out of a molehill, or was a sore loser. Her allegations of possible fraud, simply, could not be understood, therefore, they were unwarranted.

What seemed to be overlooked by all was the fact that – historically, in Wakulla County – Ms. Rosier was one of only two blacks chosen to serve in the capacity of commissioner since the 1800's. Blacks make-up more than 14 percent of the county. This is not large, but it is considerable.

The lack of black representation in the political theatre and school system may seem an unimportant issue for those who have seen their faces mirrored in the seats of power for so long. But it would be a mistake to think that Wakulla's black community have accepted this gladly, and swallowed it down whole; a mistake to not realize that black students who attend these schools, or see these faces of 'authority', are not watching closely.

The gap between Ms. Rosier, Mr. Green, and their predecessors, is more than 120 years. This means that – other than former Sopchoppy Mayor Colleen Skipper – in that span of time, there was no one else in office that fully understood, knew, or had lived the experiences of the thousands of black lives they were elected to represent.

No one person can serve all people. All of us are individuals in a nation that peddles individuality from the rooftops, making it difficult for those in any 'group' to agree on almost anything. But when applying for – and taking on – the role of a public servant, one must, somehow, come to grips with the fact that all people must be, in effect, served. There is no way around it.

Race is not the issue. It is nothing more than a shadowy veil thrown over the face of humanity. But once the veil is lifted and we see who we are, the question lies in how we treat one another; how we embrace, avoid, glorify, or repudiate members of the larger family.

There are people in the county, both black and white, who do not for one fraction of an instant, trust the powers that be who 'run' Wakulla, and often with good reason. Many have tried, while in office, to bridge this gap, and many have failed. Some in the county have been too hurt to place their hearts on the line again. But, with coaxing, there is room for growth in any heart. And, with time, a heart can mend, as well as change.

...

Few can offer factual evidence as to how the community of Buckhorn got its name. The most popular tale is that it is in relation to the large deer, or 'bucks', that were plentiful throughout the area in days of old. While fishing in the local 'holes' (creeks), old-timers were said to have remarked on the magnificence of the 'buck's horns'. From this, 'Buckhorn' may have been born.

How it would become a predominately black community is fascinating, but not uncommon. Similar communities once existed in both the Hyde Park, and Panacea areas. Though, how my Grandfather, John, managed to build Buckhorn up while simultaneously making sure his mother, brothers, and sisters would never in their lifetimes be without a house of their own, is mystifying.

Moonshine and corn liquor, or 'buck', may have accounted for some of it. There were 'stills' throughout the county, the fields mainly, and along Buckhorn Creek where residents made their special brand of undercover homemade brew.

But for the most part, John did honest work. He planted, cut and sold the pine on his land to local sawmills, such as one owned by the Raker family. He even had ponds dug and fish put in so those in the area could have their own fishing holes.

As a young man, he was chauffeur to a white doctor. One night, he drove the doctor to a house-call in Franklin County and later delivered him to his hotel room to rest before making the return trip the next morning. Nothing stirred at sun-up when John arrived and knocked on the door: The good doctor had died in his sleep.

...

Again, I must be careful with how I proceed and the people I name because there's still a great deal of unrest that surrounds the past. Yet, I can't help but feel that the blacks here are not necessarily frightened, but have become used to a way of life that makes them, their beliefs, and their culture, practically invisible.

Blacks are seldom seen at county commission meetings. Many black oriented events seem to take place underground and are predominately religion-based.

Religion, faith, and the need to develop a spiritual connection with a higher power are easily understood, given the world in which we exist. But to hide behind it to the point that it is no longer useful, but selfish, defeats the command of becoming 'fishers of men'. 'Fishing' among those in the church who have already been caught is not necessarily an active use of faith.

Nevertheless, the churches are numerous; the dominations many. All following, supposedly, the same God, but in highly separate fashions, in churches that are race divided.

The Wakulla Co. Christian Coalition (having had quite a few missiles fired in their direction since they began) sponsors an annual Martin Luther King, Jr. parade and read-in event. It is unfortunate that the attendance to these gatherings is often quite small. There appears to be only one certain 'happening' for which Wakulla's black population will appear in droves. It was my father who pointed this out, and I have witnessed it myself on more than one occasion: Funerals.

Why is it that death attracts us so quickly, when the moments and events intended to enrich us; to make our lives useful, are seldom attended?

Of the black events, most are prefaced with the desire to be all-inclusive; to draw in every man, woman, and child of the Wakulla community. This leads one to think that to prepare an event specifically designed for black audiences, from a black perspective, addressing black needs – in a county where the black presence is not represented on a political, financial, or educational level – is a type of betrayal.

I recently attended an event that was highly publicized in our local paper, complete with flyers, email campaigns – the works. I arrived at the event in a part of the county that was resplendent in view – complete with horses – and so secluded that I doubted whether I'd be able to find my way home once the sun ran out. There were over 300 people there. Only two were black. One being myself. The other was serving beverages.

Although there was an outreach to all, beneath it sat the sinister reason why blacks in the county remain distrustful of certain gatherings and institutions. We all know the story of Emmett Till, the Scottsboro Boys – even the movie *Birth of a Nation*, where whites felt threatened by the black presence. For many blacks, given the nation's history, especially our southern history, this discomforting sense of 'threat' has almost always been there, working in warped reverse.

In the 20 year existence of the county's historical society, I was their first black board member. I've never cared to be saddled with such a title, especially in the new millennium. Milestones like these should have been reached ages ago. The holders of our county's history knew little, if anything, about Wakulla's black history. This was evidenced by the lack of anything black – more than 10 years into the new millennium – in their museum spaces proper.

I encountered a county resident (black) who attended a few genealogy workshops held by the Historical Society in years past. She mentioned that she was seeking information on John Lovick Crawford, whom Wakulla's county seat of Crawfordville is named for. She believed herself to be a direct descendant, and him a distant relative, by way of her great-grandmother.

According to this resident, instead of getting the assistance she was in search of, she was told that she had nothing that could prove such a statement to be true. She quickly reminded them that this was the reason she sought the assistance of the Society in the first place. She has yet, years later, to receive that assistance, or attend another Society meeting.

One Society member held highly important artifacts pertaining to black culture. One item was a newspaper said to have been compiled in the late 1800's by a small group of blacks in the area. In the same breath, when I asked to see this item, the response was that it was "somewhere in the garage".

To a black southern male, such a find sheds light on one's responsibility to those that came before, and those surely to come after. I admit, I was a little unsettled by being, yet again, the 'only black person'. And it took me a while to realize that no one could see through my eyes, but me. What I knew, what I felt, were my experiences – mine alone – not theirs. And to blame them for what they may honestly have not known or even considered; or had possibly tried their hand at and failed, might prove to be a unfairness on my part.

It was difficult for me to resign from the group because I loved that feeling – that rush – of uncovering something old, yet new, about the past. But like family, something about our past became difficult to discuss. I could not function in that capacity, while simultaneously trying to grip, mold, and maintain my cracking mask of friendship. So I dropped the board position altogether, and chose to remain friends instead.

Instances like these alert me to how mindboggling my grandfather's life must have been in an era where race relations were not the best.

His Mills Grocery Store was a two-level cinder-block set-up offering decent prices and credit when needed. Food, basic staples, and kerosene could be purchased downstairs on the first floor, while clothing, shoes, and jewelry were sold up top, on the second.

Eventually, John built over 30 small houses that he rented to blacks and whites in the area, many who had fallen on hard times. He later built the Buckhorn Café and a community center. He screened 'western' films on Friday nights in what he called the 'showhouse', and his sisters and nieces ran their own beauty shop. There were also the automobile dealership, mechanic shop, and funeral parlor. His brothers, most specifically, Aaron, helped with the building and repairing of the homes.

During an election season, candidates, no matter their party affiliation, were given an honorary fish fry where they could meet and greet with the people of Buckhorn. Once the eating was done, the candidate addressed the community-at-large with a speech delivered from the foot of the tree.

Not unlike the other drinking and eating establishments in Wakulla (and quite probably churches), politicians paid handsomely for the beer and the food provided. The candidate most likely voted in was usually the one who offered rides to the voting booth and, afterwards, a five-dollar 'thank you'. Many blacks from Buckhorn can – and have – attested to this.

When in need of money, or to receive an extension on paying their rent, the townspeople would visit John in his store, or arrive unannounced at his home. They were offered an array of odd-jobs, including clean-up detail, which meant mowing the grass areas of the main thoroughfare; picking up trash around the café and immediate roadside; stocking shelves or cleaning in the general store; lending a hand in the minor repairs of their neighbor's homes.

When a house in the county was being torn down, John recruited those owing back-rent to help gather the wood left behind. The pieces were brought back to the work-shed and the removal of nails from each and every wood-piece began. The nails were then carefully hammered out – to straighten them – so that they could be used for a future project.

Wakulla's maritime industry (fishing, shrimping, oyster-ing, crabbing...) goes back to the days of the Native Americans that used the bounty of the Gulf Coast as a means of survival.

The seafood industry thrived in Wakulla. Charles Barwick Sr., who lived in Panacea, opened his own crab-picking plant there in 1949. During the '60's and '70's, Wakulla's crab-picking / processing business was so strong, that vans were sent to surrounding counties to load-in the 'pickers'. In fact, it was 'Old Man Barwick' who helped my mother get her very first driver's license. She drove one of the vans.

Many residents were raised on worm-grunting, or "pickin' in the baitwoods". Bait were always needed for fishing. The practice of 'worm-grunting' is done all over the world by those who have discovered that if you cause the ground to vibrate, the worms will pop up to the surface. Charles Darwin perfected the method back in the 19th century. For decades, this was how families in Buckhorn made their living.

This came to an abrupt end when the television program, *'On the Road with Charles Kuralt'* came to town. In the episode worm-grunting was highlighted, and a few people spoke a bit too freely about how it helped their finances in hard times. Both the IRS and the U.S. Forest Service were listening. In less than a few weeks the practice was immediately taxed and regulated.

...

Everyone had a hand in the longevity of Buckhorn. So much of it stems from the 'tree' my Grandfather planted and the spirit of those who gathered around it.

How heartening it must have been for the blacks of Wakulla to belong to a society of people whose lives were not much different than their own; no longer ostracized by a nation that they were forced to call home.

And no, you couldn't just "go back to Africa". Thanks to the greed; the cunning of glorified convicts and outcasts arriving on these shores – ages ago – to settle this 'new world', going back to Africa was no longer possible.

You were snatched; often sold into servitude by your own people; forbidden to learn the common English language that would, at least, crack open the door for you to begin to understand the reasons for your subjugation.

With a gun to your temple and a whip at your back, you came to understand that you would never know Africa again. And that Africa would never know or – given all you've become during your absence – fully trust you.

You: Descendant of holocaust that rivals the terrors of the Bible, stand with one foot on American soil, and the other on the grassy plains of a dark continent you barely know. And neither place wishes you to stay.

Chapter Two

The 'Queen of Buckhorn'

Arlee Bruster Simmons was a quiet woman who smoked 'Kool' brand menthol cigarettes and drank way too much. Born in July 1917, to Arza Bruster and Rachel (Franklin) Bruster, young Arlee's lifelong nickname would become 'Pinder'.

When she was about twelve, Pinder's parent's marriage failed. The children stayed with their mother, in Sopchoppy, and their father moved to St. Marks, not far away.

Mother Rachel Franklin was a proud and godly woman who raised her children in a similar fashion. She eventually met Surry Booth, born in March of 1903. He was younger than

Mother Rachel and employed as a logger. Soon, they were married.

This one union would strike the tone of betrayal and mistrust in our family for many years to come. The way in which its course played out serves as an unsettling reminder of how patient, and deeply hidden, is our potential to destroy one another through nothing more than pure selfishness.

...

Within the town of Sopchoppy proper sits a house not far from the roadside. Less than a few yards from Rose Street, hidden behind an old rusted fence and mounting brush, the Lawhon house stands virtually unnoticed. It is historic not for its age, but because of the name of its former inhabitants.

The Lawhon's (and different variations of the name) have been in Wakulla for generations. A friend, himself a Lawhon descendant, said that he was told that once, long ago, two brothers were stopped by a man who asked them their names. One brother replied "Lawhorn"; the other one said "Lawhon". Yes, another mystery...

The old Lawhon house itself is terrific in stature, with its high ceilings, broad windows, and partial wrap-around veranda. Mother Rachel worked as a maid in this house for many years. Her rising days and early nights were spent caring for the Lawhon household. Her own family either worked menial jobs, or stayed home to tend chores and children when Mother Rachel could not.

Mother Rachel expected supper to be cooked, clothes to be hand-washed, and an immaculate house when she came home. If she had to spend her day doing it for her betters, her children could do it for theirs.

...

But, when? How? Why did it happen?

Could it have been one of those nights that Mother Rachel wound her way home through the darkness? Or – maybe – while standing at the woodstove, or smoothing-out the beds; sweeping the wide veranda of the Lawhon home? Is it possible the occurrence took place as she wept in the house of the Lord? Who knows when she first shuddered; found herself caught-up in the ill whirlwinds of revelation blowing past?

And blow they did: Pinder was now fourteen. And pregnant.

Mother Rachel wracked her brain to pull forth a perpetrator. But then, just as quickly, the question side-wound its way to an answer – turned toward the easiest target – and struck.

Pinder was berated for being so foolish. Her wantonness was something Mother Rachel could not – would not – abide in her home. Boiling to the surface were memories of the times that Pinder smiled too easily, or didn't have the wherewithal to sit lady-like, or – in her childishness – laughed too loudly.

And then, as it was relayed to me by Grandma Blonzie, Pinder was stripped naked – there, in front of her brothers and sisters – and shoved out, into the front yard. The door bolted solidly behind her.

Hiding her fear and bewilderment behind the loud voice of authority, Mother Rachel screamed at Pinder to "rake the leaves". In tears and nakedness, Pinder did so, as all the neighbors watched.

However, as Mother Rachel was soon to learn, the evil did not reside in her daughter. Instead, it rested lazily somewhere else, and it was not far from home at all.

In fact, it was there when Mother Rachel was working for the Lawhon's; sat nightly at their dinner table, drinking, belching and breaking – with each one of them – its delicious bread of deceit.

It shared Rachel's bed. It even had a name: Surry.

...

Pride is a tricky thing. It is said to be the blackest of all sins, for it is shrouded, wrapped, and all but drowned in the adoration of one's own perceived excellence.

Mother Rachel was proud. For the rest of her life she would remain at odds with her daughter. Her sense of failure and disgrace when it came to Pinder, seeped out like oil, covering and smothering – till dead – all cries of love underneath.

But still... how can a woman stay with a man that does that to her daughter?

Such questions were hurled towards Mother Rachel's face; thrown with skillful precision behind her back. Her plight was used by local busybodies as a scandalous means to kick-start a dying conversation.

Cloaked in distant, watchful silence, Mother Rachel – on her knees – scrubbed the Lawhon house clean with soap, rag, and prayer. She kept their family rosy-pink and happily fat, as her own home fell to emotional ruin. And, though her children had food in their stomachs, something in their spirits were starved.

A tiny baby girl that Pinder named Betty Jean, was born.

But betrayal seldom ends so easily. Surry, emboldened by his conquest and – in some sycophantic circles – admired by others of his ilk, lay in wait before taking Pinder once again against her will. By the time she turned seventeen, Pinder had two daughters sired by her mother's second husband.

And still, Mother Rachel held fast to her Surry. She would feel the stinging backlash of her decisions years later, when he took up with one of her closest friends. He made his new wife's children his own. And proceeded to have even more.

...

It was after her death that I, along with others in the family, came into the knowledge of all great-Grandma Pinder suffered at the hands of her stepfather, and the rupture it caused between mother and daughter.

Their arguments grew loud and ruthless, yet, there was no doubt that they loved one another.

After the second daughter, my Grandmother, Blonzie Mae, was born in January 1934, Pinder left home. She tended the girls as best she could, but Mother Rachel eventually took control.

Betty Jean and Blonzie were put to work early, cleaning houses with their grandmother. Blonzie cleaned homes on a regular basis when she was only 8 years old.

Betty Jean was taller, somewhat rounder, with a caramel and honey tone to her skin. Blonzie was shorter, more brown in color than her sister, and full of mischief. Betty Jean was the angel. Blonzie was always into something that she had no business dealing.

Whenever the girls were with Mother Rachel, Pinder was in fear. She raged at her mother for letting the girls go anywhere near her stepfather, who she often referred to as 'That Man'. For the rest of her life she continued to despise him.

It was only a matter of time before the girls heard the rumors. Blonzie was the first to address them. Around age twelve, she approached Surry:

"And I said to him – outright – " she told me many years later, *" – is you my daddy? He took his time, but he told me the truth."*

Instead of hating Surry, as her mother did, Blonzie came to care for him. Pinder never got over the anger she harbored. Betty Jean was quiet and non-committal in what she felt. She neither loved nor despised him. But for Blonzie, who would eventually outlive them all, the years would bring her closer to her biological father. Upon his death in 2003, at the age of 103, she referred to Surrey Booth with a sense of romantic nostalgia as *"the only daddy I ever had."*

...

As a child, Blonzie's education was minimal. She was later shipped off to live with her aunt, Ossie Spicer, who she called Mo'dear (Mother, dear). This aunt would remain Blonzie's ideal mother figure. Ossie worked and lived in Aspen, Colorado, where Blonzie spent the early period of her teen years, before later moving to Nashville, Tennessee.

While there, she joined a singing group that performed on local radio stations during Sunday morning programming. It was here that she met a young man – a tenor – who was a member of The Israelite Travelers, and would stand-in, on occasion, with the Fireside Gospel Singers. His name was Jesse James Ransom, II.

Jesse was tall, broad, had freckles, and was 'red-skinned'. Hence, his nickname, 'Red'. The two went on a double-date with others from the singing groups. They became inseparable. In no time, Blonzie was pregnant. Their first child, a boy, was stillborn.

Blonzie must have been very young during this period, for she became pregnant again – with triplets. Again, one of the boys died, but the others, Floyd and Lloyd, survived. Their birth certificates have Blonzie as being 16 years, and Red, 20.

Red enlisted in March of 1951. He was an airman for the U.S. Air Force and fought in the Korean War. Seven months after his departure he became a father once more when his 'baby girl' Rachel, my mother, was born.

During Red's enlistment, Blonzie uprooted herself and the children from the home they all shared with Red's mother and father, Mahaley and Jesse, Sr. She returned to be among her own family in Sopchoppy.

Back home, Blonzie earned her pay by cleaning houses. She was also receiving income from Red's time in the military. One day, the checks stopped coming. Strapped for cash, Blonzie took the withholding of funds as a personal affront, and switched into survival mode by eradicating Red from her thoughts – her life – entirely. To make the severance complete, she cut short any talk or remembrance of him by his three children. Red was officially dead to her.

That is, until the day he arrived in Buckhorn with a brand new Cadillac. By this time Blonzie was working for John Mills, Sr., who, by now, had earned the 'Black Mayor of Buckhorn' title from the community. It was rumored that the two were dating.

When Red appeared – and just as abruptly – vanished, it would be close to 30 years before his daughter, his sons, or Blonzie, would see him again.

By then, Blonzie had another child: A son. Even though his biological father was well-known in the Buckhorn area, she chose to name him Jesse James Ransom, III.

Her decision perplexed more than a few. And it would come to plague Jesse, Jr., himself. Like his mother years before, Jesse, Jr., found out, through rumor, who his biological father was.

In later years, the feeling of disconnect haunted Jesse, Jr., to the point that he drank and drugged a great deal. His methods of controlling and abusing the woman who later became his wife, were legendary. That union would later end in divorce.

...

It is fascinating, almost magical, to review the span of a person's lifetime; how it plays out; how something akin to a hauntingly familiar, distinctly human melody can be heard, and often repeated, in the distant corners of the soul.

To look at the fractured relationship between Pinder and her mother, is to also look into the relations of Pinder and her daughter Blonzie. One can only wonder what Pinder saw in the woman-child who, in so many ways, bore the inherent signature of her father, Surrey.

Pinder babysat the children while Blonzie worked. They were getting along as best could be expected. If the universe saw fit that they be mother and daughter, they, simply, had to accept it.

When little Rachel was around three years old, she wandered away from Pinder's care. Supposedly, while drowning her sorrows in moonshine, it was during one of Pinder's 'spells' that little Rachel got too close to an abandoned well. If not for the lightening-flash reflexes of a neighbor who snatched her to safety, I, the writer of this family chronicle, would not exist in this world as I do now, if at all.

This incident became the push that opened the door for John to ask Blonzie to move into the boarding house. She could work there, cook, clean, watch after the needs of the boarders, while simultaneously keeping an eye on her own children. She followed his advice.

Pinder later married a man named Sam Simmons. This marriage lasted only a short while. Who knows why or how, but Sam was swept away into the arms of another woman. It may have had something to do with Pinder's drinking, which continued through to the end of her life.

Quite possibly, Sam could've been a drinker as well. This may have been the tie that bound them. Then again, the thing that could've broken them apart were the demons; Pinder's vivid memories of her first intimacy, and her first betrayal, at the hands of those who should've been her protectors.

Pinder did love Sam Simmons enough to keep his last name, and statements she made later in life confirmed this. Sam died in 1972. It was his new wife and children that put him to rest.

Years later, Aunt Betty Jean died of cancer. Her daughters and sons I remember well. Her grandchildren I attended school with. One grandchild, Solomon, who became my closest cousin at the time, was to go through his share of hardships. He is in prison now, serving a 15-year sentence, accused of an unfortunate sex incident with a girl (white) from Wakulla. No one cared to discuss the raunchy pictures of the girl, circulating around town long before she and Solomon ever met. No one cared to know about the things – and the people – she'd been involved with before their paths crossed.

Betty Jean's death hit Pinder with terrible force. The world and all things in it could not have proved more painful in Pinder's sights. The feelings of betrayal by her mother, enhanced by her stepfather, a failed marriage, and now, a child lost.

Arlee 'Pinder' Bruster Simmons remained a quiet woman who smoked 'Kool' brand menthol cigarettes, and drank way too much. There is no need to wonder why.

Meanwhile, Blonzie made sure to take care of herself. John Mills, Sr. was older than Pinder. He was more than 30 years older than Blonzie. Yet, when he offered his hand to her in marriage, Blonzie's answer was 'yes'.

It was through this union that in September 1955, John Eugene Mills, Jr. was born.

Chapter Three

"Princes and Revolutions"

In 1969, I arrived and became the firstborn grandson of the 'Black Mayor'. Those in the Buckhorn community became my second family. The memories of 'grown-ups' lifting me in their arms, or bringing their children (my partners in crime) to roam out back by the pond – all, are my uncles, aunts, and cousins.

Night: Gran'daddy John would close down the store and then check the café to make sure things were going smoothly. He would then come home to Grandma Blonzie, cooking him something light to snack on for dinner. I'd be watching television, or, whenever my little brother and parents came over, playing checkers. Cards were a sin in Grandma's house unless they were part of a popular board game.

When it was just the three of us, Gran'daddy would pour out his money-sack and spread the pennies, nickels and dimes onto my little folding table by the fireplace. My job was to separate the coin denominations, count the change properly, and then place the coins into small paper packets that read

'Pennies 50 cents', 'Nickels $2', etc. I would have to wait a few more years before he moved me up to quarters.

My brother and I, along with my little sister to some degree, have never forgotten those days at the Buckhorn Café. There was a room in the back complete with a television, couch, seats, and a small bathroom. We were underage, so, by law, we were not supposed to be on the premises. Though, when my mother and father worked the bar, we were allowed in the back. When Stephen King's *'Salem's Lot'* came out on television, my brother and I sat in the backroom watching, terrified, while the adults played pool, had the loudest conversations, and juked the night away on the dance floor. On special occasions there were dance contests. Once, a female contestant and her partner were working it down to the ground so hard – she broke her leg. No joke.

And though we howl about it with laughter now, CB radios were the thing back then. 'Good buddies', dressed in t-shirts with their 'handles' scripted across their backs, held fundraisers for their groups. The distant scent of fried chicken, shrimp, mullet, and burgers being flipped; the funkiest of soul music blasting all day long in an effort to forget growing up, all of it was magic for a kid to see.

Friday and Saturday nights, along with holidays, were the liveliest. Gran'daddy was born close to New Year's Eve, so the parties that took place at year's end were astoundingly notorious affairs. I remember the big boys, years older than I, who did the unthinkable: They held 'Roman Candles' in their bare hands that spit fire and flung bleeding colors across the midnight sky.

Something in me feels old, yet young, when recalling the men in tight bell-bottoms and wicked platform shoes; or the stunningly made-up women with afros a yard wide; and the music(!), my god – the music. Will we ever feel rhythm and move that way again in life – living instruments in sync –

instead of in syncopated hollow vacuums? The world of disco, down home countrified blues, and ballads of good-lovin'-gone-bad, sung by people who sounded exactly like the men and women in the choir on Sunday mornings. Youth, after having survived it, when remembered, is unbelievable.

...

It was in this familial environment that my Uncle John, Jr. – 'Boone' – came of age. He was 14 when I was born. I was born on the 14th. His birthday was a few days before mine, and my mother's only a few days later.

Of all my family photos, there is one that is very dear to me. It is the only picture of Uncle Boone, Grandma Blonzie, and myself. I couldn't have been more than a year old. Grandma is sitting on the bed in Gran'daddy's room, standing me up for the camera shot. Uncle Boone is on the floor at Grandma's feet, staring up at us both. He is smiling, and his eyes are absolute laughter.

That picture is more than 40 years old and is beginning to show its age. It has begun to flake, wrinkle, and crack in certain places, giving it a look of fine, weathered skin. My memory of my Uncle is similar. Not perfect in some places. Overrun with creases and tears; blurred details in a haze of stinging pain.

His face floats in and out of my memory. I see him over me – over my body – laughing down, tickling greedily the tender spot of my ribs. His presence was that of a kid, very playful. He was the closest thing I've ever known to a big brother. As the oldest grandchild, I've been trying, in the strangest of ways, to fill that void ever since.

...

As the baby of the family, Boone was very much doted upon by his father. He was the one true child of his parents union. I've heard stories of how Gran'daddy John would give Boone a bag of candy from the store, and it was Boone's job to disburse it to his siblings as he pleased. This is not to say Gran'daddy didn't love the others. He showed it in the best way he knew how. It was their mother that he could not go against.

The children did their chores in the house as expected. And although they received an allowance, their mother quickly took the earnings and charged them rent. My mother was a young girl who, having worked the whole year, and managing to save up what little she could to go to the fair, was promptly stopped at the front door while the others loaded into the car.

"You ain't going nowhere. I need you to stay here and watch the house tonight," Blonzie told her daughter. Every dime of little Rachel's earnings was spent on her brothers at the fair.

Blonzie could be cruel. And exceedingly selfish. Maybe it was the fact that as a child she didn't have much. Maybe she felt it was her duty to take all that came her way. Maybe she was truly her father's daughter. Though these things may never be known, there is no doubt that her children suffered for it.

One of the twins she sent to a boy's home for a short time. I'm not sure if anything happened to him there. I asked him about the experience not long after Grandma died.

With a faraway look in his eyes, staring at the television, or at something beyond me, space, or time, all he could say about the home was, *"I didn't like it".*

This was the same home in Marianna, Florida that came up in the news recently. Over 50 graves of young boys were found on the property. It is under investigation how these little boys died in the care of what was, essentially, a halfway house for delinquent young males.

The other twin joined the Armed Forces. He stayed away from home for almost 15 years at a time. No word. No visit. When he moved home for good, his mother was dead, and he was in his sixties. Just this past year his oldest son – whom none of us had known to exist – came to visit us for the first time. We knew he was ours as soon as he walked through the door, for, not only did he favor us physically; he looked exactly like our Grandfather 'Red'. And we proceeded to love him at once.

A hauntingly familiar, distinctly human melody... like the eyes, nose, hands, and feet of parents repeated in the features of their children, it was I who tracked our cousin down and brought him home to meet us all.

Not being cognizant of a pattern, I was following my mother's lead, repeating what she had done more than 30 years earlier. It was she who went on a mission to find her biological father when she was in her mid-thirties. The last time she laid eyes on Grandaddy Red, she was barely 5 years old. And yet, she found him, and brought him home to embrace his descendants.

...

Jesse, Jr. also joined the Army. Any checks that were sent home for their service was properly deposited or cashed, and then politely spent by their mother, Blonzie. When her sons returned home, there was no money to show for their service, and no excuse given them about how their mother had spent their earnings.

It was imperative that the children stick together, because they could never be sure of what their mother would do, or where her mind, when addled, would take her.

When Rachel, Blonzie's only daughter, was blossoming into womanhood, her mother attempted to put her in a girls home. If not for the intervention of her adopted father, John, Sr., Rachel's life would've been very different. She'd already seen how her mother had divided the twins so that they seldom came to agree on anything.

Blonzie also kept Jesse, Jr. at a distance, so that he chose to spend what time he could with his grandmother, Pinder, and his older sister, Rachel. Once, when Jesse was around 5 years old, he was stung by a number of wasps and his eyes became swollen to the point that he could barely see. Years later, days before he died, he shared with his sister from his deathbed how he never forgot the time his sight had left him; how she lifted him – on piggyback – and carried him wherever he needed to go; and that he'd always love her for taking care of him.

Though Boone was the son of John Mills, Sr., and the heir apparent, he was in no way shielded from the burn of his mother's often treacherous warfare.

John, Sr. knew that only he had the means to properly provide for the children. And his manner of doing so was strict, but not abusive. In all the years John spent with Blonzie, he never once let her write a single check. He handled all finances because he became aware, through hard won experience, that whenever money hit her palm – it stung and burned, needing only to be spent to ease the pain.

Keeping an eye on Blonzie's spending was one thing; keeping close watch of her ways, was something else. And for this, John would often make use of the children. Anything they saw that didn't 'seem quite right' was to be reported back to him directly. Especially when it came to the Buckhorn Café, over which Blonzie maintained precedence.

In 1987, Rachel and others were interviewed by Boone's lawyers during his appeals process. She recalls what it was like growing up with her siblings, and her mother Blonzie.

'Uncle John' is how Rachel and her brothers – minus Boone – referred to Gran'daddy John, the man who adopted them all as his own:

"One time when Boone was younger, he was at the store (Mills Grocery) with Uncle John. Uncle John sent Boone over to the café to give a message to Mama (Blonzie). When Boone got to the back of the café he saw Mama kissing another man. Boone ran out and went and told Uncle John, who went over to the café and caught them together, too. There was a real bad scene, and when Mama got Boone home, she beat him all day. Mama never forgave him for that. She always treated him worse than the rest of us.

When any of us kids would misbehave, like kids do, Mama would really beat us. When she said 'jump', you went high. And if it didn't suit her, she'd beat us again. And I mean for the least little thing. She'd hit with a switch, a belt, or whatever was around. It wasn't a spanking. It was a beating. When we got older, and she wasn't big enough to hold us down like she used to, she'd tie us to the bed before she started the whipping."

Of all her children, Boone would grow to be the only one who would ever be so bold as to tell Blonzie exactly what was on his mind, and what she could do with the information received.

And herein lay the strangeness of our family, or of any family, really: They still loved her greatly. Blonzie was their mother. This love; this adoration they had for her is a fact that has never once been denied by any of them. But they were also raised to fear her. And although this troubling element, this subtle terror, would grow smaller as the children grew older, it cannot be said that it has ever been, truly, diminished.

...

Blonzie was not a well woman. Neither was she beyond a display of high melodrama. She carried a pistol, tucked neatly within her bosom, when she went to church. Not every Sunday, but certainly on those holy days when things at the Buckhorn Café had become somewhat tricky the night before. Given her family's history and the means by which she was born into the world, it is not surprising that she felt the need to act out in certain ways. More of Rachel's 1987 interview:

"Our mother would do some really strange, mean things to us. One thing she'd do was to get dressed up all in black – big black hip boots, black clothes, and even a black mask over her face. Then she'd come out and just scare us kids to death. She'd say, "Here comes the devil, you'd better be good or the devil's gon' get you." She wasn't kiddin' or playin' with us. She was serious. Even thinking about it now makes me scared."

My little brother, Kevin, and I, would come to understand this. Kevin was a bit more hip to certain things than I was and, when noticed, would clue me in.

One such incident had been occurring for quite a while. If we got out of hand, playing, running, throwing – the normal kid stuff – there would suddenly appear this 'thing' in our midst. The thing was dressed in black from head to toe, with a hood that drooped down covering most of its face. We got a look at the face once, and it was the mask of a bloodied cow's head.

Needless to say, we were terrified. Our parents never seemed to be around when we saw it, and it always made its appearance at Grandma's house, at the height of our childish antics.

One day, it walked through the neighborhood, dragging one foot, and leaning on a cane. Kevin and I saw it at once and were linked in our collective horror. Without word or signal, we left a trail of dust as we bee-lined for the café to our parents.

We arrived – falling, crawling, screaming – our cries caught in the throat; our words a phlegm-wracked babble. That's when the ruckus really started. Somewhere down the dirt-road, less than a few yards from the café, we heard someone – a man (!) – scream.

Everyone rushed out toward the commotion and saw Big Bud, an older man who lived with this wife, Martha, in the boarding house – wielding an axe, swinging at the thing:

"Run for your life, Martha –" Big Bud hollered – *"Greaa-hht GOD – run for your life!"*

Poor Martha could not go far, for she was blind, and was presently suffering the confusion of where her rocking-chair was – from which she'd just leaped – feeling her way from the windows to the front-door to the side of the house:

"What is it, Bud–" she mewed.

Someone called out for Big Bud to put down the axe; to not do it.

It was then that Bud saw something amiss; that the thing did not possess any obvious superpowers, for – instead of it chasing him – he was chasing it.

Mass confusion set in as the thing hobbled away and into the café. There was the quick screech of verbal fright from the few who'd remained inside, then laughter, and finally, quiet mumbling all along the dirt road.

Kevin and I had seen enough. We moved towards the house to lock doors and select hiding spots. Instead – to our shock and horror – our parents took us with them into the café.

We shook, my brother and I, and the snot we threw about was in large supply. For the moment, the thing was nowhere in sight, but every movement – even that of the air – we quickly detected; every fiber of our being was on red alert.

Once behind the bar, the coast, it seemed, became clear, but it couldn't be trusted – and suddenly... there it was, in the backroom, standing... seeming to wait.

I can only describe this as what must have been felt, ages ago, when the town virgin had been bound and gagged by friends and loved ones, then dragged to the mouth of the volcano, and hurled – without the slightest whiff of mercy – into the pit.

The thing moved toward us – my brother screamed – I tried to run, but to no avail, someone held onto me. My mother had to be close because – in my last ditch effort to bust loose – I remember grabbing for her; lunging out to snatch her from the jaws of certain death. I peered back to see the thing raise its hand and reach out towards us. Again, I turned away, but my brother became deathly silent.

I felt his body stiffen close to mine. Then he just as quickly nudged me in the side with his elbow. Avoiding, on pain of death, the possibility of seeing the thing up close, I somehow managed to glance at my brother. I followed his eyes.

If you have been privileged enough to have grandparents in your life who were there long enough for you to remember and love them, then chances are you recall certain things about them that only a little person can summon when reflecting.

My Grandmother had a ring on her right hand. It was a gold band with two beautiful pearls. That ring is a thing that I will associate with her for the rest of my life. It was there when she dried my tears; there when she served my breakfast, lunch, and dinner; there on my shoulder when she hugged me close.

Apparently, the thing had a similar fetish for this make of jewelry. For when I looked at what it was that had laid my brother silent, I became speechless as well. An invisible bee had, somehow, stung me, and injected me with a poison that numbed my entire body. I could not take my eyes from what I knew to be my Grandmother's ring, on what appeared to be my Grandmother's hand.

I've a feeling the thing recognized what it was my brother and I saw. It withdrew, and slumped out the back door.

My mother said nothing; paralyzed in thought, only her body was cognizant enough to go into autopilot, as it did presently. She moved behind the counter, began wiping it down, and prepared for the rush to come.

My father, on the other hand, has a way of becoming completely silent, expressionless, as his eyes turn steely and vibrant. It is then that you know he is angry. He, too, said nothing, and would look at no one.

Kevin and I were thawing from the chill and, slowly, began to move; two brown little tin-men from a not-so-glittering Oz. We glanced at one another on the sly, our silent communication asking *"Did you see that?"*

I can never know for sure what it was my brother thought in that moment. But I remember clearly what was in my mind. It was not a statement, but a question that re-emerges, now and again, from the depths of a dark place within me. It would surface at intervals throughout my life for almost 40 years afterwards: *'Why would my grandmother do that to me?'*

...

Rachel was among the first group of black students to attend the Sopchoppy Elementary School. She later attended Wakulla High. Back then the high school was known as the Wakulla Rebels.

When you arrived at the front area of the school you were greeted by the huge design of the rebel (Confederate) flag, carved into the main entrance lawn. At the beginning of the school season everyone stood outside as the rebel flag was hoisted up in honor of the new academic year.

Throughout the 1980's, when I was a student at Wakulla High, and well into the '90's, the rebel flag remained at the school's entrance. We were much too clueless back then to understand that the manicured grass-area where we ate our brown-bagged lunches, or held our clique courts, represented the bloodiest era of our southern history. I say 'ours' because, like it or not, our black ancestors were there and had a hand in it, too. These members of our Wakulla family cannot be overlooked.

There was something of a mild outcry – by the students – not many years ago, and the grounds have since been refashioned. But the memories remain.

...

Rachel dropped out of school when she was in the tenth grade. She arrived home from classes one day to find her mother, Blonzie, sitting in the bottom of a closet, naked, with a gun aimed directly at her. Blonzie pulled the trigger three times – the barrel aimed at her daughter's face – with only three clicks as a reply.

Rachel ran and got Gran'daddy John. This led to much confusion in the household for a while to come.

Beginning June of 1967, John petitioned the court of Wakulla and County Judge George L. Harper, for an inquisition of incompetency. An order to summon a committee was put forth and said committee, which included doctors R.L. Anderson, A.D. Brickler, and Mr. R.E. Whaley, determined that Blonzie suffered from 'depressive psychosis'. She was institutionalized at the Chattahoochee Mental Institution, in Chattahoochee, Florida. This would not be the last time she would be admitted into a mental health facility against her will.

My mother Rachel remembers that time well:

"Mama took pills all the time. She always had some ache or pain and lots of doctors gave her pain pills. I don't know what all kinds she had, but she had a real drugstore right there in our house.

Our mother got crazier and crazier as we got older. She'd see people coming in the house when there wasn't anybody there. There was one person she'd imagined that she'd see a lot – a woman with long black hair. Our mother would go hide in places – in closets, out in the woods – and we couldn't find her. She'd take off all her clothes and throw 'em in the fire. She was always getting guns out. In fact, she's already shot herself several times."

The hand, the foot, and the thigh. Those were the places her bullets had entered. All three were separate incidents. What I recall is the 'thigh' affair. She'd come home from the hospital not long after, and I remember her sitting on the edge of the tub in the bathroom.

I peeked in because it was extremely quiet in our old Buckhorn house, yet I knew Grandma was somewhere around. When I looked in, she was just sitting there, staring at nothing in particular. And then she looked at me. I called to her and she just stared. I looked down to see the large white bandage and tape on her upper thigh, knowing that it was the place where something had happened; a thing the adults were keeping from me.

Earlier in these notes I mentioned the cousin that none of us knew about, who visited us for the first time earlier this year. He and I had a moment together to talk about our lives, our families, and the decisions we, as adults, have made along the way.

In the middle of the conversation, out of the blue, he asked if voodoo was ever practiced in our family. I was momentarily taken aback by this and could only stare at him. He looked down, sheepishly, at the floor. I could tell he was embarrassed that he even brought it up. I inquired as to why he would ask such an odd question.

It came out that, as a young person wanting to know more about his biological father, (my Uncle, one of the twins), my newfound cousin would often quiz his mother about what his father was like. Her response, it seems, is that he may have been damaged in some ways, due to his upbringing. She mentioned the fires and other strange things our Grandmother would do in her moments of perceived madness, and how my Uncle spoke to her of these things.

This is the Uncle that would disappear for years at a time, but has now returned home. I can only assume that he, like I when I left Florida, was trying to escape his particular entourage of demons, only to find that the secrets of a family, and very often the shared horrors among its members, can never be escaped; but must be faced, confronted, and dealt with. If not, we run the risk of sharing quarters with these ghastly, grotesque interlopers, for eternity, in the grave.

...

Boone moved in certain circles. From what I've been able to gather through the years, a great number of his friends were white. The blacks he knew and grew up with were right there, in the community, but they were not his only collection of friends. It cannot be known for sure if he felt set apart, given his father's influence, but the majority of his girlfriends that I've met through the years were black. All speak of him with fondness to this day.

A friend who knew him during this period, Clayton Lewis (white), was interviewed in the late 1980's as part of Boone's court appeals process. Lewis resided in St. James, Florida at the time:

"In the late 1960s and early 70s, I lived for several years near Sopchoppy, Florida in the area known as Buckhorn. While I lived there I came to know John Mills, Jr. and his family very well. When I first met him, he was about 14 or 15 years old. He was a quiet, likable young man who seemed to need friends. He didn't have many friends among the black people in the area and preferred the company of white people like me and my friends.

John really didn't have much free time because his father John Mills, Sr., had him at work around the family business most of the time, Mills Grocery Store and Mills Café. But whenever he could get away he came over to my house. He helped me a lot in building my own house.

I visited his family's house many times. His parents, Blonzie and John, Sr. treated us all like family. We ate supper with them and sometimes spent the night there. Even when John was that young, he started drinking and smoking marijuana. It was mostly drinking beer but sometimes, especially on the weekends, hard liquor too. He smoked marijuana nearly every day for the several years I knew him at that time."

Was Boone any different than any other young boy in Wakulla County back then? Or even now? It was the early '70's. With 'free love', Vietnam, the fight for civil rights, assassinations, LSD, Woodstock, the death of the famous three (Morrison, Joplin, Hendrix), would a strong cocktail or a fat joint seem that uncommon? What's even more curious is how others his age could know of it, not to mention being comfortable around it enough for him to use it in their presence.

I conducted an interview in Spring Creek, also in Wakulla, a year or so ago, and the gentleman I spoke with, whom I cannot name because his children own businesses in the county, told me a little bit of what Wakulla was like when he and his wife moved here in 1977:

"It was the wild west when we got down here. I knew this Marshall that was down here at the time, and he told me – and this was years later – that 90% of the cocaine coming into the U.S., was coming through the Spring Creek area of Wakulla County."

That's a whole lotta coke. And a whole lotta smiles. In July of 1973, a few marijuana farms were found in Wakulla. By 1978 there were raids throughout the county on such places. In one instance, several thousand dollars' worth of pharmaceutical drugs were stolen from the town pharmacy in Crawfordville.

Everyone knew about the drugs being sold here and other places, like Dog Island. Uncle Jesse, when working his shifts at the Buckhorn Café counter, mentioned that members of the sheriff's office would bring marijuana into the café, hand it over, and once sold, certain members of the sheriff's department received the greater cut.

As mentioned, Jess had a drug problem. He was arrested numerous times for his illegal use of drugs. But he never did hard time in jail. He'd make a simple phone call and was free again in no time flat. It was always a wonder to us, for he never called anyone in the family to seek his release. He simply reached out to those in certain positions for favors to be returned.

These are his accounts of things he claimed happened at the time, and not my own. And now that he's gone, there's no way to truly verify his statements. It is doubtful that anyone in the county who could confirm it would ever be brave enough to do so publicly.

...

On July 15, 1977 something happened that greatly altered Boone's life:

Tallahassee Democrat
July 17, 1977

DEVELOPER'S SON KILLED IN WRECK

SOPCHOPPY – The son of a Gulf Coast developer was killed late Friday in a one-car accident near here. Jefferson "Jeff" Davis Lewis, Jr. was killed when the truck he was a passenger in hit a bridge. Lewis, 28, was the son of Mr. and Mrs. Jeff Lewis, Sr. of Carrabelle. Jeff Lewis, Sr, is president of Dog Island Company Inc., developers of the Gulf Coast Island on Franklin County. According (to) the Franklin Highway Patrol, the younger Lewis was a passenger in a truck driven by John Eugene Mills, Jr., 24, of Sopchoppy. The accident occurred 2.4 miles east of the Sopchoppy city limits on U.S. 319.

Trooper Ron Surber said the pick-up truck was headed east on the highway when it left the roadway and travelled about 350 feet before hitting a concrete guard-post of the bridge, which crosses Buckhorn Creek, shortly after 11pm...

Lewis was killed on impact and Mills was treated at Tallahassee Memorial Hospital for injuries...

Lewis was a 1966 graduate of Leon High School and a 1971 graduate of Louisiana State University, where he majored in landscape architecture. He was employed with the Dog Island Company.

The Lewis family has owned the 1,850 acre Dog Island since 1956 and has been developing it as a secluded resort...

…

Though Boone's age is incorrect in the article, and Jeff was known to many as 'Jebby', this event would affect Boone's mindset, character, and overall mental state. Clayton Lewis remembers:

"John had a tragic accident and my cousin, who was riding with him and was a good friend of John's, was killed. Jeff was one of the most likable people you'd ever want to know. He was my family's favorite. My family is fairly well known in Wakulla and Leon counties, so when he was killed a lot of people knew about it... Even though his death was an accident and John was never tried for anything about Jeff's death, I know that there was a lot of prejudice against John for that. I saw John once sometime after the wreck, and he was really different. He just wasn't like himself; real nervous and detached. It really surprised me because I hadn't realized he'd been hurt that bad."

Others noticed it too, especially on the home-front. His sister, Rachel:

"Boone was knocked in the head, hurt his ribs, and broke his nose. That really changed him. He felt bad about his friend dying. He stayed by himself all the time after the wreck and got real moody. For months, he'd be asleep and then he'd wake up screaming."

…

By August 4, 1977, Boone, physically and emotionally damaged after the death of his best friend, had to face the county's music:

Wakulla News

SLAUGHTER CHARGED IN AUTO DEATH

John Mills, Jr. driver of the pickup truck involved in a crash here July 15 which killed a passenger, has been charged with manslaughter. Killed in the wreck of the truck was Jefferson Davis Lewis, Jr. of Carrabelle...

Mills, 24, was charged with manslaughter following an investigation by the Florida Hwy Patrol... Mills was arrested by the Sheriff's Dept. Sunday on a warrant signed by Circuit Court Judge George Harper. He was booked at the Wakulla Co. Jail and released on $5000 bond posted by his father, John Mills, Sr., of Buckhorn.

...

Almost a year later (12 days shy of the accident's anniversary), Boone was taken to prison on a completely different matter.

I spoke to Grandma Blonzie about this approximately a year and a half after I'd returned home. In that time, I'd had a terrible falling out with my Grandmother. I had seen a number of things, and had my share of unsettling experiences with her throughout my teens and early adulthood, to suspect something was up. By the time I decided to move back home to Florida, a good 20 years had passed. My senses were dulled, somewhat, to the pings of warning that alerted me to be on my guard.

In time, my intuitions sharpened, came to a point, and led to an outburst. I felt she was attempting to manipulate myself and others with her late night emergency rushes to the hospital, only to find nothing wrong; or her severe pain spells

– when things were not going her way – in order to acquire more medication, or gain our sympathies, which often led to her moving into your house, where you were expected to wait on her hand and foot, as she slipped out back for a quick cigarette. And, even worse, she accused specific relatives of wrongdoing, dropping hints in and outside of the family that led to loved ones turning against each other with no clear reason as to why.

I confronted her about this, rather harshly, when I caught her in a lie. It was a moment I am unlikely to forget because never in my life would I have dreamed of saying such horrible things as I did to my Grandmother that day. I loved her too much to fake the fact that she was hurting us. I am convinced that she suffered a type of illness not fully explained, at least, not to me. I don't pretend to be a scholar in these things; all I knew was that a type of train had jumped track, was running amuck, and needed to be stopped. When dealing with mental illness our love, anger, and confusion are perpetually at war.

When all was over, I left the scene, went into a room and cried. Inside, although I could barely breathe, my body felt as light as a feather. My mother, Rachel, came into the room. It was then that I felt worse. I didn't want to hurt my mother, given the pain that had been poured into her life already.

You can imagine how stunned I was when – with tears in her eyes – she came over and held me in her arms and said "Thank you. You said something we've been wantin' to say all our lives."

I was stunned into silence. Days later, my Uncle Jesse and his second wife came to visit us. Uncle Jess had the biggest grin on his face when he saw me, and grabbed me in a bear hug. I could only assume that he'd gotten wind of the outburst, and that he felt exactly as my mother did.

After this, my relationship with my Grandmother grew. Our bond became stronger due to our honesty. On a deeper, internal level, we had become two real people, capable of a real conversation that was no longer locked into the roles of 'elder' and 'youth'. We'd put down the shovels used to cover things over for so long and had come to a point of mutual respect.

I could speak to her openly about certain things now, such as her condition, her dreams achieved, as well as failed, and the loss of Uncle Boone, her youngest child. I'd been in that mode of recording conversations and gathering information for the book about Uncle Boone that I was threatening to write.

I say 'threatening', because I'd never attempted a book before. I didn't know if it was in me. To some degree, I still don't. I expressed this to Grandma. It was she, along with my mother, who said it needed to be done. How could I look them in the face knowing that I hadn't even tried?

Uncle Boone's auto accident and initial arrest had occurred over thirty years before:

Me: So he (Boone) first got arrested when? – '77, '78 – ?
Blonzie: Yeah, somewhere around then. I think he got arrested with them boys.
Me: The McKinney's?
Blonzie: Yep, both of 'em. They sent him (Boone) up to Cedar Prison. You know where Cedar Prison at?
Me: Cedar Prison –
Blonzie: Yeah –
Me: No –
Blonzie: Way over there on the other side of Monticello. That was the first prison he went to. He stayed there, I think, about 6, maybe 7 months. And this is prison time here, it ain't no jail time.

...

The McKinney's were a family that rented one of the homes (the largest, in fact) on Gran'daddy's property in Buckhorn.

I may have been looking in all the wrong places, but I never found information or a listing for Cedar Prison. I could only get so much of these things from my Grandma because, as time went on, it became harder for her to remember.

She was in her late seventies when this conversation, like many others, took place in my car after we left her doctor's appointments. We talked of how Uncle Boone's first arrest came about. She says it was around the May 20th celebrations that were still popular at the time. In Florida, the 20th of May is celebrated as Emancipation Day. In the south, slaves received the news of their freedom almost two years after it was officially announced.

But, from articles I've read, the robbery incident, for which Boone was arrested, happened closer to the Fourth of July...

...

Me: So everybody was celebrating around that time in Buckhorn?
Blonzie: Yeah, we supposed to had went to fishing.
Me: It was supposed to be you, Uncle Boone, Granddaddy, or what –
Blonzie: Naw, just me and Boone. 'Cause we would do the fishin' an' huntin'. We came back there, them sheriff's had the house surrounded! Boone didn't really know what was happening. He was sittin' up there on the front porch playin' his guitar.

...

The guitar. Grandma held onto this item for the rest of her life. I have it now. It is sitting directly across from me as I pen these words. I'm learning to play...

...

Blonzie: Next thing we know, the sheriff – David Harvey – all of 'em was there. Your granddaddy John walked out there, wanted to know what it was all about. They told him, 'Well, your son went down there and help load-up some stuff, robbed some white folks' houses – about four or five houses on the Ochlocknee River down there'.

...

A Wakulla News article a few weeks after the incident reads:

BURGLAR HANDED 8 YEARS

" H.L. McKinney of Sopchoppy was sentenced to eight years in jail by Circuit Court Judge George L. Harper, July 28, following conviction on four counts of burglary.

McKinney, who was charged with four counts of grand theft and four counts of burglary, withdrew his earlier plea of not guilty and entered a plea of nolo contendere...

McKinney and John Mills, Jr. were charged following the July 3 break-ins of four residences in Wakulla County, including the home of Walter Solburg of Sopchoppy, the James McIver home next to Ace High Stables near Wakulla, the Clayton Whaley home in Crawfordville, and the residence of Lee O. King in Crawfordville... "

...

By this time, Boone had his own house, like the other kids. It was white, with green trim, and a long screened-in porch on the side. My little brother and I used to play on his living room floor with his Doberman Pincher, 'Mojo'.

He had a stereo and records were everywhere. An image on one of the covers always made me feel dirty. There were children my age, naked, climbing over rocks. They looked like white seals. Years later, while sitting with friends in a 9th Avenue bar in Manhattan, I came to know the album as, *Led Zeppelin's House of the Holy*. A few of his records, along with this one, are now in my possession...

Blonzie: They searched all the cars and everything out there – all over the place. And Boone – this is why I say he didn't know – Boone came home with the flowers the boys had give him, and had 'em strung up all on the front porch.
Me: So he didn't know where the other guys got the flowers from?
Blonzie: Naw – he didn't know where they got 'em from!

...

This is the thing I will never understand: Just because someone gives you something – property – does not mean you should accept it. As far as Boone was concerned, I cannot be sure what his thinking was. And this irks me. Hopefully we all know by now that if something looks too 'perfect', there's usually a deadly flaw hidden underneath.

What immediately comes to mind, at least for me, are the messages sent during the Blaxploitation movie era of the '70s, the period in which Boone was a young adult, having just been a teenager during the civil rights uproar of the '60's. A number of the messages seemed to be of the 'get whitey' genre; or crafted around a type of revenge fantasy.

This is in no way a justification for theft, but people wronged for so long, having heard the speeches of Martin Luther King, Jr., Malcolm X, Megdar Evers, and Huey P. Newton – and having heard the response of the white world, their leaders in particular – may have begun to think differently, and to act outwardly.

...

Me: Did they find anything other than flowers?
Blonzie: All the jewelry and stuff they found down to Miss Bertha's house –
Me: The McKinney's –
Blonzie: That's right, the McKinney's. Right behind the house back there.

...

It is here that she discusses 'the nightmare', that occurred in 1982:

Me: Uncle Boone said, from some the statements I read, that it was him, Uncle Jess, and Fawndretta, painting the house, or the café –
Blonzie: They were painting the café –
Me: And Michael Fredrick comes over –
Blonzie: That's right. Michael Fredrick came over. When he came over he got my truck – that old Dodge truck –
Me: Yeah –
Blonzie: Michael wanted him (Boone) to go with him, and Boone said "I ain't got time, man, I'm paintin'"... So Boone told him he could use the truck. So, Michael Fredrick got the truck, went to the river – did all this dirt – and bought a whole truckload back to the house. Boone told him he couldn't leave it there. He said "Mama's house full and she don't want no more stuff in her house". So they ended up taking it to Fawndretta's mama's house in Tallahassee, and that's where they found the stuff at.
Me: Uh – huh –
Blonzie: 'Cause they ain't found nuthin' in my house, no guns or nothin'. And then they come back, they (the sheriff's office) came and got the pick-up truck – I was in Tallahassee – they got the truck from Tallahassee, and took it to the shop to test and see for blood – you know that red paint that Boone had –?
Me: Mm-hm –
Blonzie: They thought it was blood. They took it up there, searched that truck and tore that truck down. And it wa'nt no blood so they brought it back home.

...

Sheriff David Harvey, Fawndretta Galimore, and more specifically, Michael Fredrick, are names that will become familiar to you, as they did our family and most of the county at that time.

Again, my Grandmother mentions a lot and I can't be sure what is truth or what is fiction. Especially the statement that there was nothing found in her house.

But again, we're rushing forward without the groundwork to lead us to the people, truck, blood, and case that all of this is referring to.

It is important that – instead of just hearing about 'the nightmare' alone, one should look at the picture in its entirety. How do you discuss a play, or judge a film, when all you've seen is the movie trailer, or the first five minutes of the second act?

...

Boone's offense date for the Ocklocknee River robberies was July 3, 1978. The offense, noted on his Psychological Screening Report, Gain Time Awards, and Process Reviews, states "BURGLARY WITHOUT A FIREARM". He was sentenced to 8 years. From this incident, he received 4 felony counts that would come back to haunt him later in court.

His sentence date, was August 18, 1978. His first report, from the many he collected and kept in a handmade binder, shows a date of August 28.

His work experience shows "Carpenter training 2 years and store cashier 5 years" and that he is "interested in same".

As far as educational recommendation, it is stated:

"Youthful offender appears to have borderline learning aptitude and read(s) at 3.1 level."

One quote on this page stands out. It looks as if Boone may have been trying to explain something: *"I can't get the words together,"* is all it says.

The reports go on for pages. A psychological screening report from August 28, 1978 states:

"Due to the low functional level, psychometric testing was not administered... Mills' parental home was intact and he claims a positive relationship with his father. However his mother had emotional problems and was in Chattahoochee. He states that his relationship with her was fair but they argued a great deal. Mills was the youngest of five and none of his siblings were full brothers or sisters. He states he left public school because he felt he was not learning enough and the teachers did not have time to explain things to him. He entered the job corps, earned his GED and stated that he completed a course in carpentry. Mills has lived common-law with one woman, this producing one child and states that he intends to marry her. He also admits to siring another child. Mills has also attended a vo-tech school taking cooking. Mills admits to the moderate use of marijuana and alcohol and was under the influence of alcohol at the time of the instant offense."

By February of 1979, Boone was moved to a new location, Apalachee Correctional Institution. The evaluation notes offer insight into how he was functioning in this environment:

INSTITUTIONAL EVALUATION:

"This subject is presently assigned to bunk #77 in E dormitory... describes this subject as being a courteous and friendly individual who appears to be making an above average adjustment... subject puts forth good effort and relates he tries to avoid trouble.

Academically, the subject is functioning at a 3.9 grade level with a tested beta IQ of 71... recommends the subject for Parole and DC Work-Release... a courteous and friendly individual who is alert and reliable... puts forth a good effort and relates he takes pride in his work..."

August, 1979, one year later:

INSTITUTIONAL EVALUATION:

"...described subject as being a courteous and friendly individual, who exhibits good self-control. During this reporting period, the subject incurred a Disciplinary Report for disobeying Verbal Order. However the subject was not disciplined as he was given a Verbal Reprimand... Academically, this subject is functioning at a 4.4 grade level with a tested beta IQ of 71...recommends the subject for Parole, DC Work Release, and the Honor Dormitory...

On June 27, 1979, the subject was interviewed by Mr. L., of the Florida Parole and Probation Commission. Mr. L. recommended a Presumptive Parole Release Date of March 2, 1982, which was approved by the Florida Parole and Probation Commission on July 18, 1979."

October 15, 1979:

TRANSFER:
"It is recommended that the subject be transferred to Tallahassee Road Prison... The subject has expressed an interest in this transfer as it will facilitate visitation..."

June 5, 1980:
Tallahassee Road Prison

INSTITUTIONAL EVALUATION:

"When John first arrived here at the Tallahassee Road Prison, he was assigned to a DOT Road Maintenance squad as a laborer... this inmate was rated as being an

above satisfactory inmate... Subject has been quite active in our religious program. He attends Sunday Chapel service regularly. He also attends our mid-week services regularly. This inmate volunteers for extra work in the dormitory. He spends a great deal of his leisure time working in the woodcraft shop. He also enjoys watching television, reading in his bunk and shooting pool.

TEAM EVALUATION:

"The team has described this inmate as being a well-behaved person. It should be noted that this inmate's father recently passed away and arrangements are presently being made for him to attend his father's funeral."

...

June, 1980: I remember faces. My mother's, father's, and Grandma's, who, while holding my Gran'daddy's hand, stared deep into his eyes, and he into hers. And then he drifted. That simple. That quick; with his eyes wide open.

The house began to hum and, eventually, to weep. The people, our second family, along with the rising sounds of those freshly wounded, were everywhere.

...

A dark blue hearse silently pulled up in front of the Mills Grocery Store, and stopped.

I stepped out from our house to the edge of the chain-link fence. I stared at the long dark car, knowing Gran'daddy was inside.

I'd seen him two days before at the Strong & Jones Funeral Home in Tallahassee. That day, everybody wept: His sister, Evelyn (Aunt Ebb), and all the others, even Uncle Aaron who seldom seemed to possess any emotions at all. They may have continued to weep, inwardly, for years after. The link that connected them all, their relations as well as their fortunes, was gone.

I watched them. I wanted to go up to Gran'daddy and talk to him. I waited until they were in other places throughout the room, or sitting. Then I stepped forward, and just stared at him there. When no one was looking, I reached in and stroked his hands.

Now, standing at the fence, I tore my eyes away from the hearse as it sat for one last moment; allowing the spirit of my dead Grandfather to look upon his work once more, before the world stepped in to pick the bones of all left behind.

When I looked around, I noticed that the community had come outside of their doors – the homes he built for them – to gather and watch also. There we stood, united for that one brief moment, in absolute silence.

Gone was the jukebox music. Gone, the laughter and games of 'spades', or 'tonk' under the tree. No more fish-fries, or dance contests that worked their way from the cafe floor to the parking lot. We all knew, through no words that could have been spoken, what was passing; we knew that the Black Mayor was the key to the locked doors of Wakulla County that we would never again – at least not willingly – be allowed access. We could expect from here on out to be, simply, tolerated. A man like him would never come this way again with the betterment of Wakulla's black people on his mind.

...

Mount Trial Church was packed. There were no seats available, so people stood crouched along the walls, or out of doors.

We climbed from the family car and headed toward the church entrance. A police car pulled up, parked, and my second cousin, Kurdis Donaldson stepped out. There was another deputy (white) exiting the passenger's side.

They opened the back door of the car, and out stepped Uncle Boone in a dark blue suit. My brother and I ran toward him – grabbed him in a hug. The officers were momentarily taken aback. I think they understood. Boone leaned down as best he could, kissed and nudged us, as everyone else made their way over to him.

Inside the church I looked at Gran'daddy one last time before taking my seat on the second row, behind Grandma, my mother, great-Grandma Pinder, and others.

There was something like a quick rush of air, yet, it wasn't the wind. It was the people. For, when I turned back to look, I saw Uncle Boone shuffling down the aisle in his chains; a deputy on either side of him.

It was then that I actually noticed – or became fully aware – of his confining ornaments. Everyone in the room seemed stunned by the painful audacity of the handcuffs and chain that ran downward, from his wrists, to the shackles on his ankles.

He went straight forward, his eyes on the casket as if it called him by name. How he bore the energy in that church – the stares and stormy bewilderment – I do not know.

But the people did. The officers quickly found they were in someone else's home now. A hand reached out to touch him, and another patted him lovingly on the shoulder.

Some, the elder ladies mostly, came towards Boone, kissed him, and whispered words of comfort. He was still a child to them. Their child. Heaven only knows what all they've had to endure in life to be able to stand there and strengthen him as they did.

It was like a ritual; as if preparing him – not for this moment alone – but all that would come later; long after we disappeared from his presence, and could no longer protect him. The officers could do nothing against this son's return, only accept it.

Finally, he arrived at the casket. He and Gran'daddy John seemed to have on the same dark blue suit (Probably Grandma's doing. He would, in less than a few years, don this very same outfit for his court trial).

Boone stood there for a long moment, the officers beside him. The choir sang long enough to let him make it through, and then he took his seat on the front row; an officer to his left, another to his right.

Following the burial at the Buckhorn Cemetery, everyone gathered at our grandparent's home. There was food, family, friends, outside and in. Uncle Boone was there. My father had managed to talk his cousin and the other deputy into removing the handcuffs and shackles.

It was a moment of freedom and joy, not only for Boone, but for the whole community. He looked so tall, handsome and dapper in his suit. He hugged and kissed everyone, and found a different – a spirit-filled – nourishment in the food.

But now it was time to leave. There was no ill will towards the deputies, for they greatly enjoyed themselves also. But they had a job to do. We all said our goodbyes, but it wasn't a feeling of intense sorrow. He was home, if only for a short while. There lingered in his absence, a feeling I won't – can't, attempt to explain.

...

When we went to visit Uncle Boone at the Tallahassee Road Prison, it was usually on weekends, no less than twice a month. Mostly after church, with a quick stop at Kentucky Fried Chicken to load-up and turn it into a Sunday dinner. I recall coleslaw and the greasy feel of the yard-bird from those days. Grandma always made sure I had a chocolate parfait for dessert. And I associate all parfaits that I eat, every now and then, with memories of those visits.

He was never sad or melancholy. Or, at least he never showed it. He asked a lot of questions of both the adults and the kids. It really was the feeling of visiting him on the job. He had to stay there in order to get his work done. And there was someone, like the principal at our school, who was the ultimate authority on his comings and goings.

Colors: His dark skin with hints of copper; the mid-shade blue of his road prison uniforms, that would later become white, and then orange, as he moved closer to the end; the grayish trapped-in-steel hues of the penitentiaries where we often visited. I was small and thin when Grandma and I first went to Starke, Florida. I had to hold my arms out when the officer patted me down for those visits. Something about a strange man in a policeman's uniform, touching me all over, created an oil-slickened, sickening feeling in the bottom portion of my stomach.

To this day I cannot a visit a KFC without asking for one of their parfaits. The electricity that once surged through me as I peeled back the silvery foil lid. And there, waiting for me, were all the great flavors of America in one cup. The foamy white whipped cream, with its dark, chocolaty sprinkles; a golden creamy custard, savory – not too sweet – but so delicious it was not meant to last.

Like life, its flavor would change. And so would my taste for it.

PART TWO
Muslims, Christians, & Murderers

Chapter Four

Cold waves and bitter snowstorms cause more than 300 deaths throughout the United States at the start of the 1982. TIME magazine's February cover features a photo of Steve Jobs. Porn star John Holmes is ordered to stand trial for the 'Wonderland murders'; and a 23-year-old Wayne Bertram Williams is convicted of killing two of the 28 people whose names are forever synonymous with the Atlanta Child Murders.

Meanwhile, in Crawfordville, Florida, two men share a cell at the Wakulla County Jail for 12 days in February 1982.

Man One: John Mills, Jr. (Boone). He was to serve an 8-year sentence for his involvement in the 'burglary' that occurred in 1978. Instead, he is released early on probation.

During his initial incarceration, Boone accepted the Muslim/Moslem faith. He'd also changed his name to Ans Serene. He was now a man uncommon among those in Wakulla who were unfamiliar with anything outside of their own Christianity. Whether the change in his spiritual beliefs altered his friendships is hard to say, but in Clayton Lewis' affidavit, dated April 20, '87, he states:

"I was surprised when John got sent to prison. It didn't seem like him to be out stealing. I remember when John got out of prison, I saw him once at the Oaks (Restaurant). He was real glad to see me, and I was happy to see him, too. He sure didn't seem like he didn't like whites or anything. I think things would have been just the same as ever between us if we'd seen each other around more."

Boone is in the process of building upon his father's legacy. He also has a twenty-two year old girlfriend, Fawndretta Galimore. Fawndretta's family has quite a history of its own. She is the daughter of the former Chicago Bears star running back, Willie Galimore. Her brother, Ron, was the NCAA's first four-year champion in gymnastics. He was the first gymnast to score a perfect 10 in NCAA Championship history; the first African-American to be named to the U.S. Olympic gymnastics team, and was founder and athletic director of the Ron Galimore Athletic Training Center USA, in Tallahassee.

Man Two: Michael Tyrone Fredrick, born Christmas Day, 1961. Michael claims he met Boone in 1976 and again in February '82, when they were cellmates.

With this, Boone disagrees. He says he met Michael in jail that February for the first time and that he introduced himself with a last name other than 'Fredrick'.

Two things about their meeting we know to be true: (1) Michael asked Boone for $175 to bond him out of jail, agreeing to pay him back $200. If Michael can't get the money, he will, instead, give Boone a dog – a Doberman – as payment; and (2) Boone contacted his girlfriend, Fawndretta, to pay Michael's bail.

A short while later Michael Fredrick is a free man. Boone remains in the cell a few days longer, deciding it best to serve out the rest of his time to avoid any future hassle.

Friday, February 26, 1982: Boone is released. He and Fawndretta drive to Michael's expecting to be repaid. Michael has neither the money nor the dog.

But he does give Boone a 12-guage shotgun, with the initials 'TB' carved into the stock end of the weapon.

And now, Man Three: Lesley James Lawhon, born November 2, 1951. Approximately 5'10" at 180 pounds, Les has been described as a 'good Christian boy'. Some have said he appeared a bit 'slow'. This may have been due to his epileptic condition. He takes a number of medications to keep his seizures in check but has not had an episode in almost 3 years.

Les held a job at Pigott's Cash & Carry, a hardware store in the small community of Medart, from June '73 to August '77. It is unclear if he was employed at the time his life intersected with those of Michael and Boone.

In one Wakulla Co. Sheriff's Office Incident/Narrative report, Les told local authorities that a red and white colored car appeared near his home. The car did not come to a complete stop, but drove directly into his driveway before turning around and leaving. Les also reported that another vehicle had parked in the bushes, toward the east side of his home, and that he could only make out the car's bumper portion. Even more peculiar, is the report of Les leaving worship service one Sunday afternoon to check for suspicious activity in and around his house.

In the end, when the deed was done, Michael Fredrick's release from jail would not be due to his family or friends, but to John Mills, Jr. (Boone). From this point forward their stories differ greatly, yet, it is fact that, in less than 3 months, Michael would accuse Boone of murder.

Les Lawhon, one of the tragic victims tangled within the web of this 'nightmare', would not live to tell his version of the story at all.

Chapter Five

'Saturday Night Live' actor, John Belushi, is pronounced dead in California at the tender age of 33, from a cocaine/heroin 'speedball' overdose. The date is Friday, March 5, 1982. The time, 12:45pm. On the other side of the nation, what began as a light drizzle, is now a stormy downpour drenching all of Wakulla County.

Belushi's death occurred late afternoon, by Eastern Standard (or, Wakulla) Time. In those same moments the home of Shirley and Les Lawhon is overcome by flames. Blackish smoke, with traces of grey, billows heavenward; looming across an already clouded sky, setting the tepid kettle of Wakulla emotions to simmering.

...

At approximately 4:15pm Wakulla resident Stella Mae Carter leaves home for a visit with relatives. It is raining, so she moves quickly through and around the drops. Once in the car she sees smoke rising in the distance.

Moments later, at the home of Verdelle and Calvin Carter, Stella Mae rushes in, alerting them that the house across the street – the Lawhon trailer – is on fire. Verdelle runs to phone for help as Mr. Carter rushes out into the dirt road.

Wakulla Deputy Sheriff, Larry Massa, is dispatched to the scene. By now the major flames – nearest the west end of the trailer – are leaping out of the heat-cracked windows.

Mr. Carter tries but cannot reach the front door – the heat is far too intense. He sprints to the back door – it's locked. Mr. Carter's body reminds him that he has a heart condition, which presently causes him to struggle. Others have arrived, moving Mr. Carter away from the trailer and back to his own home.

When volunteer firefighters enter, only a portion of the trailer's back-end remains; the raging inferno has finally been contained, leaving only charred metal and smoldering ash in its wake.

Deputy Messa checks what is left of the rubble, but finds no human remains.

Around 5pm Shirley Lawhon gets a call from the Wakulla Sheriff's office. Her home has burned to the ground. They can't find her husband.

What could have possibly filtered through the mind of Shirley Lawhon at that moment? She'd left for work that afternoon around 1:15pm. The last time she saw Les, he was lying on their living room couch.

It takes hours before the scene can be sealed off. Neighbors, friends, and concerned citizens who helped put out the fire gather wearily in the front yard.

Florida Department of Law Enforcement's (FDLE) crime lab analysts process the scene. They salvage a doorknob and pass it along to the firearms section of the department. No tire-prints. No shoeprints. No 'evidence'. Most likely the rain and constant foot-traffic have destroyed it all.

The State Fire Marshall's Office investigator finds that the fire began at the floor-level of the living-room. An accident, be it electrical or otherwise, is quickly eliminated. The expert conclusion is that an open flame was applied to a combustible product.

And thus the search for Les Lawhon began.

...

Les Lawhon evaporates completely from public view, but the mystery surrounding the fire, his disappearance and the possible motive, grows so bright that it blinds the third-eye of common sense. And, as is usual in small southern towns, the prophesying tongues begin to speak and, once they've exhausted their holy use, commence to wag.

Phone calls pour in from all corners of the county:

I saw an orange colored VW Beetle with a dented fender and a C.B. antenna on the roof by the Lawhon house on several occasions. Strange that I ain't seen it since the 'incident'...; There's buzzards flying all over Panacea. Maybe you'll find something there if you search hard enough...; My phone number was called by somebody at Les Lawhon's house on February 20. I don't know Les or Shirley Lawhon. I'm divorced and I live here with my daughter. She's only 18 years old...; I was fishing in Lake Ellen the day it happened til about 5:30, running trot lines. I saw a two-tone green van with 2 black men driving down to the public boat ramp. They stayed there for about 25, maybe 30 minutes then left. I heard an explosion and saw smoke over by Les Lawhon's house...; There's an awful lotta buzzards flying over here in the Sopchoppy area...

...

Among the more acerbic theories is that Les set the fire himself for the insurance money, and that his wife is in on the whole scheme. Some consider such comments blasphemous because, after all, Les' father is a pastor. This is quickly countered by the fact that his father is also an insurance salesman. One occupation brought souls into the fold; while the other put one in a position to buy almost anything.

Again, these are among the ruder theories. Others involve speculation about the Reverend Lawhon, drugs, and his son's abusive use of them. Some say that Shirley Lawhon may have known a possible suspect from the Wakulla Manor, her previous place of employment. Conjecture, like the pouring rain, touches everything, seeping deeper into the body of the county until it rests, eating at the bone.

The Rev. Lawhon writes a handwritten letter in response to the accusations:

REASONS WHY LES LAWHON COULD <u>NOT</u> HAVE BEEN THE PERSON WHO TOOK THE ITEMS FROM HIS HOME AND THEN BURNED HIS HOME - By Glenn Lawhon

1. The old worn out black and white RCA TV was taken. Les knew it was no good and would not have taken it.

2. The speakers to the Sony reel-to-reel tape recorder were left behind to be ruined by the fire. Les knew where the speakers were and would have taken them along because they were part of the tape recorder.

3. His medicine bottles were found in the ruins of the fire. Les would have taken his medicine with him.

4. Almost <u>ALL</u> of his clothing was accounted for, especially his favorite type of clothing like blue jeans. Undoubtedly the few items of clothing not accounted for were totally destroyed by the fire or taken by the robbers.

As a matter of fact, some of his wife's clothing was also unaccounted for. All suitcases were accounted for – therefore Les took no clothing with him.

5. Some very nice photographs of Les' favorite people were left behind to be destroyed by the fire. The frames of these photos were found in the ruins of the fire. Les would not have left these pictures behind.

6. None of the record albums were taken. Some of these were favorites of Les' and many would be difficult or impossible to replace.

7. As far as can be determined, all of the reel-to-reel tapes were destroyed by the fire. Some of these would be impossible to replace.

8. Les had hardly no money at all and no attempt has been made by him to withdraw any from the bank.

9. Les had no means of transportation nor driver's license.

10. This crime is totally out of character for Les. As Sheriff Harvey has said of some of the possible suspects, "It does not fit Les' profile."

11. Les was completely happy and was busy making plans for the future development of his home. He was in the process of planting a garden, was raising a brood sow for the production of pigs, and had just bought a hound dog to train for deer hunting.

12. Les was as happily married and as much in love with his wife, Shirley, and her with him as any couple I have ever known. Their relationship was one-in-a-million. He also loved his parents and all his other relatives as much as anyone I have ever known and was one of the most considerate persons I have ever known. He would

<u>NEVER</u> *do anything to cause this kind of heartache and worry to those he loved.*

MOST LIKELY CONCLUSION *(By Glenn Lawhon):*

The burglars had "cased" the house and knew that Shirley usually left for work at 2:00pm. They also knew that Les had been helping Tommy White do some work on my house that week and did not expect him home until around 5:00pm. They came to the mobile home at around 3:00pm expecting no one to be home. They were surprised to enter the home and find Les there. It is possible that Les "jumped" them or possibly even recognized them. They overpowered him and killed him in his home. Then they loaded all the missing items into their vehicle and also the body of Les. Then they set a slow fire to the mobile home to destroy fingerprints and bloodstains and other evidence of a murder and a struggle. They wanted the fire to be a slow fire to give them plenty of "get-away" time before the neighbors noticed the fire. They have disposed of the body of Les in some way to make it difficult or impossible to find for two reasons: (1) In case they are caught they would rather be charged with arson and robbery than to be charged with murder also. (2) By concealing the body of Les, they hope to cause law enforcement officials to suspect Les of doing this foul deed to himself for some unexplainable reason, and thereby cause the law enforcement officials to relax their vigil and give them (the culprits) more opportunity to escape justice and to commit more robberies (and possibly more murder and arson).

There are of course other possibilities, but the above is the most likely one.

...

Tuesday, March 9: Four days later, and Les Lawhon is still missing. On this day Michael Fredrick enters the Dust Collector's pawn shop in Tallahassee to sell a high school class ring, among other property. The salesperson writes down a detailed description of the ring on a store receipt. The description includes the initials inscribed on the ring's inner surface.

...

The Wakulla News, a weekly publication, is usually on the stands by late Wednesday afternoon, with a Thursday issue date. An article from the Thursday March 11, edition reads *"Lawhon Still Missing".*

A photo of firefighters struggling to contain the blaze appears above the headline. Other photos include that of Rev. Lawhon and Sheriff David Harvey perusing a map in order to begin the search.

Also is the snapshot of Jackie White and Shirley Lawhon. Mrs. Lawhon wears a light-colored raincoat, her left hand lifted to the side of her face. At first glance, one believes she is caught in the act of brushing back the long strands of her dark hair. On further inspection, one notices that her face, though youthful, is drawn and seemingly bewildered at what is taking place.

And then there's the photo of Les Lawhon himself. His smile is bright with a large dimple planted deep upon his cheek. It looks to be a family photo, for someone has been cropped out just below his shoulder. Les has thick, dark eyebrows and dark hair – parted on one side – that swoops down and across the forehead, its ends sweeping to the side in a feathered fashion.

**The Wakulla News
March 11, 1982:**

"The total possible reward for helping to safely find a 30-year-old Wakulla County man who disappeared Friday, March 5 has been increased to $15,000.

Wakulla Co. Sheriff David Harvey said Tuesday that a concerted air and ground search has failed to result in any information as to the whereabouts of Les Lawhon who is thought to have been the victim of a burglary – arson – kidnapping operation.

Harvey said a reward ... has been offered for information leading to the identification of the person or persons responsible and another reward ... has been offered for information leading to a safe return of Lawhon...

A ground search that involved nearly 40 volunteers also hasn't resulted in any positive information. The investigation has been spearheaded by a ten person special task force made up of five investigators from the local sheriff's department, three investigators from the FDLE and two investigators from the state attorney's office...

"Conceivably, everybody's a suspect. We haven't made any progress in that regard," Harvey said.

At this point, the most important thing is to find Lawhon, Harvey said, because Lawhon suffers from a serious epilepsy condition and must take several types of medication four times a day to control the disorder...

With medication, the epilepsy can be controlled, Harvey said, adding it was his understanding that Lawhon hadn't suffered a severe seizure for about three years...

"It's a very good possibility he's still alive," Harvey said...

Lawhon was discovered missing after a fire destroyed his mobile home in the Lake Ellen vicinity at about 3:30 PM Friday. The fire was apparently set to conceal a theft, Harvey said, because an investigation of the mobile home's remains showed that several guns, stereo components and other valuables had been removed.

"Everything is consistent with the burglary – arson – kidnapping theory," Harvey said. Lawhon lived at the mobile home with his 30-year-old wife, Shirley, a registered nurse at Tallahassee Community Hospital.

He is the son of Rev. Glenn Lawhon, pastor of the Wakulla First Baptist Church. A native of Winter Haven, Les Lawhon has lived in Wakulla County since 1970. His ancestors, though, were among the first pioneers to settle in the Wakulla–Leon County area...

His friends and relatives in Wakulla County are responsible for putting up most of the reward money, Harvey said..."

…

Fliers and handouts are posted all over the county with the photo of Les that appeared in the Wakulla News. The fliers advertise the reward and include the missing items from the scene:

A 19" Zenith color TV; 19" RCA black and white TV; .410-guage Galef shotgun; .12-guage Stevens shotgun; .30-30 caliber Marlin lever action rifle with Redfield scope and web fabric sling; .22 caliber Winchester rifle; Gibson guitar; Sony reel-to-reel tape recorder; ASP record player; Technics SA-400 FM receiver; 2 Profile 400 speakers; and an antique brass pendulum wall clock.

Friday, March 12: One week after Les' disappearance, Boone and Fawndretta are at the Wakulla Co. Courthouse. There are still issues to be settled regarding his father's estate, which is fairly large.

While there, Deputy Sheriff Victor Crook recognizes Boone and arrests him on the spot for a "violation of parole".

(Note: I am unable to understand what this exact 'violation' is. I could not find it in the records I've searched. From what I've gathered from my discussions with those close to Boone at the time, he may have left the county, or state, or may have missed an appointment with his parole officer. Either one could have easily been the 'violation'. But, again, I have failed in the attempt to find proof of what the actual violation was that led to the arrest.)

Boone asks to say goodbye to his girlfriend, which the deputy allows. As the lovers embrace, Boone tells Fawndretta to *"make sure you get everything out of the shed and in the back room and under the bed."*

Later, Boone is questioned in regard to his whereabouts since his February jail release. He states that he went to Tallahassee and spent the weekend at the home of his girlfriend and her parents. He also mentions that he worked around Buckhorn during the week, but couldn't recall the exact days.

When asked about his whereabouts on Friday, March 5 and the weekend that followed, Boone says he can't recall.

Victor Crook's notes read:

"At this point he (Boone) became uncooperative and would not give any more information."

Boone's mother, Blonzie, is now living in Tallahassee. She travels back and forth to the family house in Buckhorn, where Boone and Fawndretta stay occasionally.

It is to this house that Fawndretta returns after her conversation with Boone. She takes the property from the shed and inside the house, and moves it to her mother's home in Tallahassee.

Boone writes letters to Fawndretta from jail. One letter contains the following line:

"...for all they know, you could have a receipt for the stuff..."

The 'stuff', as Fawndretta understands it, are the items in both the shed and the house that he asked her to move.

Also contained within Boone's letter is his sage advice that she *"not be afraid"*, and that he had told her, time and again, about *"those Caucasians"*, and that *"they might just tell you, you could go to prison for 10 to 30 years just to see your reaction"*. He also mentions that she should read the letters he writes her *"with sense."*

Boone is questioned once again on March 17 about his whereabouts on the weekend of March 5. Victor Crook's notes read:

"Again he was uncooperative and would not give any information."

...

**Wakulla News
April 1, 1982:**

"April 5 will mark an entire month since Les Lawhon disappeared from his Medart home, but authorities still aren't any closer to solving the case than they were when they started.

Wakulla Co. Sheriff David Harvey said Tuesday, March 30, "Really, there's nothing to update."

Harvey said the task force composed of members of his department, the state attorney's office, and the Florida Department of Law Enforcement is still intact...

Asked what he thought the chances were that Lawhon is still alive, Harvey said, "I have no idea." ...

...

Later, Sheriff Harvey and a few Wakulla deputies attend a training session in nearby Quincy, Florida. They take with them the Les Lawhon case file. They present it to an FBI agent at the training session who specializes in the development of criminal psychological profiles. The Sheriff's Department requests the agent's assistance in its probe.

Chapter Six

May 1982. It's been almost two months. Residents of Wakulla's Shell Point community notice a terrible smell coming from somewhere in the area. The sickly sweet scent rides upon the wind, permeating the lightly-salted breeze of the Gulf Coast. No one, it seems, can pinpoint the source.

Tuesday, May 4: Tallahassee Police Department (TPD) investigator, Gary Lassiter, is checking the records of pawn shops in the area for items acquired through theft and later pawned for money.

He discovers a transaction involving Michael Fredrick. An arrest warrant has already been issued for Michael in connection with a burglary that occurred just two weeks earlier (April 19); approximately six weeks after the Lawhon incident; and five weeks after Boone Mills was arrested for his parole violation.

Inv. Lassiter learns that as Michael was filling out his portion of the receipt, he left his thumbprint behind.

A majority of items Michael pawned came from the April 19th burglary. The one item that catches Lassiter's attention is a 1969 high school class ring with the initials 'SED' inscribed on the inside band.

Lassiter places a call to an agent with the FDLE to help determine the ring's origin. The agent, in turn, learns that the ring may belong to Shirley Dunn. He informs Lassiter, who then calls the Wakulla Co. Sheriff's Office.

Lieutenant Charles Landrum, (WCSO), recalls the conversation with Lassiter went something like this:

INV. LASSITER: Charlie, I've been doing some checking on some property. Do you know a 'Shirley Dunn'?
LT. LANDRUM: Shirley Dunn...
INV. LASSITER: I've been checking class ring sales transactions... and checking around. It comes back and says 'Shirley E. Dunn'.
LT. LANDRUM: That's Shirley Lawhon.
INV. LASSITER: It appears that Michael Fredrick sold the ring to Dust Collectors in Tallahassee.

LT. LANDRUM: Well, that particular piece of property was not described to us as having been missing at the time that all these lists were compiled...

...

Approximately 11:30pm that same evening, Sergeant Charlie Ash (Leon Co. Sheriff's Office), receives a call from Sheriff David Harvey requesting assistance in finding Michael Fredrick on Grand Theft and Burglary warrants in Wakulla.

Thursday, May 6: Sgt. Ash contacts an 'informant' to help locate Michael in the "Frenchtown" area of Tallahassee. Predominately known as the "black" section of town, Frenchtown has a history that includes a nephew of Napoleon Bonaparte, musicians "Cannonball" Adderley, and Ray Charles.

That afternoon, Sgt. Ash is 'informed' that Michael is indeed in Frenchtown, at Crump's Tavern on Macomb Street. Ash and Detective John Franklin make haste to the location – and there he is.

Michael is taken into custody at 4pm, advised of his rights and questioned about a burglary. He is served his warrants from Wakulla and transported back to the county, where he is further questioned by Inv. Lassiter, and Sgt. Vause.

Their questions center on the April 19th burglary and how Michael came into possession of the class ring. From there, Lassiter and Vause simply wait; listening to find where Michael's defense will lead.

Friday, May 7: Sgt. Vause conducts interviews with the Wilson family who reside in the Hudson Trailer Park of Crawfordville.

Sgt. Vause's notes on this particular interview sets one quickly to wondering. Yes, a few of the things mentioned are shocking, some possibly revelatory. But the most curious aspect of the report is more visual than it is informational.

It seems that a person, integral to the truth of this story and these events, has been completely whited out. In other words, where this person's name should appear, there is only blank white space, as if applied by correction liquid or tape.

It is obvious who this person is, as well as their sex. Such glaring omissions automatically force the question of what happened – behind the scenes – that reports, directly from the Sheriff's office, should have been so carefully manipulated.

For the record: There is no "s" or second "e" in Michael's last name. Unfortunately, too many of the documents and court transcripts list his name with the extra "e" and "s". For the purpose of this writing they have been removed to avoid confusion:

"This officer (Vause) was advised that bond for (Michael) Fredrick had been posted in Leon & Wakulla Co by John Mills, Jr. (Boone) & (BLANK). (Fredrick) and Mills were reportedly incarcerated at the same time.

Upon release from jail Fredrick reportedly lived at Wilson's residence in Hudson Heights...

Fredrick...and Mills were described as "Close together"... Mike was reportedly "picked up" by Mills "almost every day"... Fredrick reportedly worked for Mills to repay money spent when Mills' (BLANK) paid for his release from jail.

...Fredrick reportedly was in possession of several rings and watches. Wilson described one of the rings as having a red stone, possibly a class ring. This was reportedly worn on Fredrick's "little finger".

Michael Fredrick was reportedly in possession of a .22 pistol which he carried in a holster. Fredrick also reportedly on occasion carried the weapon in his hand.

... Mike seemed nervous or upset when around Mills but left with him (Mills) almost every day. Mike was reportedly returned to Wilson's residence late at night by Mills.

... On one occasion (BLANK) had stated that she would "open up the devil" and he (the devil) would kill Fredrick. (BLANK) had reportedly been left at the Wilson residence by a subject who drove a "pink" Cadillac.

On another occasion (BLANK) reportedly stated that she had been told to "take him out" (Mike Fredrick). (BLANK) had stated that (BLANK) would use an ice pick to kill Fredrick. ...that these threats were made because Fredrick had not repaid money used to post his bond...

Wilson ... asked Mike to leave the trailer. This was because Wilson would go to work every day but Mike would not. Mike had then moved into a trailer with a girl called Mae who lived...in Hudson Heights ...

Mike had reportedly visited Wilson's trailer with "a guy from Georgia" in a maroon truck. The subject was reportedly accompanied by W/F & B/F (white female and black female) subjects. Mike had also been observed with a small black puppy around this time.

Wilson was reportedly told by Fredrick that Mills had stated he had a "contract deal" in Georgia to collect money from a guy. The subject was reportedly not at *home when Mills went to the residence. Mills had reportedly advised Fredrick that he had beat (the guy's) girl "to let him know he had been there."*

... Fredrick had "talked about doing Mr. Hudson"...

Wilson...had been contacted on 5-6-82 ("yesterday") by (BLANK)... had reportedly "asked where Mike was".

...

The icepick; the threats – all are enough to crush anyone's reputation on the street. However, during a follow-up interview on May 17, Mr. Wilson's view changes somewhat:

"...Mike had not brought property to the residence (Except on the one occasion with the subject from Georgia). Mike had, however been in possession of the ring mentioned by Wilson in a previous interview. A gold colored watch was also reportedly in Fredrick's possession on one occasion in "Frenchtown". The watch reportedly had diamonds instead of numbers on the face. Wilson stated that this was sometime in April.

...(BLANK) had occasionally accompanied Mills in the truck but had also come to Wilson's residence alone "looking for" Mills... (BLANK) was Mills' (BLANK) and at one time was in love with him... Wilson believed that (BLANK) "would have helped him".

...in reference to reported threats against Fredrick by (BLANK) that (BLANK) would not have harmed Mike. This officer was advised that Mike was not afraid of (BLANK) and stated that (BLANK) would not harm him."

...

Other than the alleged gold watches and rings, the relationship of Boone and 'BLANK' (obviously Fawndretta), is very telling.

Boone continues to write her from jail, but now she has pulled away – and Mr. Wilson knows this. But how? Is it a serious 'threat' when the icepick is spoken of, or is it a gentle, joking reminder – between friends – that the person who put their money out, now wants that money back?

Sgt. Vause's interview with Mrs. Wilson (the leading lady of the Wilson household) only adds to the confusion:

"... Ms. Wilson knew both "Boone" Mills and Michael Fredrick... Mills usually drove a truck described as "orange" and having a "white camper"... (BLANK) was a friend of Ms. Wilson's... (BLANK) had come to the trailer with Mills on two occasions on weekends in (BLANK's) car. Ms. Wilson stated that she had never seen (BLANK) in Mills truck but that (BLANK) could have visited the residence in the truck. This could have occurred while Ms. Wilson was at work at Metcalf's Crab Company... Mike had never brought any unusual property to the residence... Mike had been in possession of the ring which appeared to be a class ring with a stone which was possibly <u>blue</u> in color. Mike also reportedly had a gold colored watch which had "little diamonds in it".

...(BLANK) had never threatened Mike in Ms. Wilson's presence. On one occasion Mike was asked for money spent by (BLANK) to "get Mike out of jail". (BLANK) and Mike then entered a room at the trailer and held a conversation. When they came out of the room (BLANK) was reportedly "mad" & stated that Mike wouldn't pay (BLANK). Both subjects, however left the residence on foot, together. Mike was believed to be attempting to obtain transportation to Tallahassee for (BLANK). "

...

Was the friendship between Michael and Fawndretta close, or distant? Does it matter? It might, as far as Boone is concerned.

It is a tricky thing to be tangled in the web of the judicial system. Its reach extends far beyond the confines of any jail-cell. It spreads into the community and homes of regular folk. With the slightest, most unconscious effort of good will, these citizens can unknowingly pull the string that sends you, your freedom, and often your very life, tumbling into the abyss.

Many have seen their relatives and friends mangled by the southern prison system. It should come as no surprise that – when questioned by an officer of the law – they choose to keep their mouths shut. Some are all too aware that their words can be flipped in a manner that does not protect the innocent, but only condemns them.

Meanwhile, back at the station...

An onslaught of questioning continues: *Do you know anything about the disappearance of Les Lawhon? What's the connection between the robbery at Mr. Lawhon's home and the class ring?*

According to Sgt. Vause's 'Incident/Narrative Form', Michael states that:

"...the items sold had been obtained from subjects whose names were unknown."

Michael gives more than 7 different versions of where the ring came from: That he got it from someone in Frenchtown; or that he got it from someone named Miss Copeland; or that he stole it from Fawndretta's car; or that Boone came by with his truck – full of property – and took Michael with him to a lake, where Michael snatched the ring when Boone wasn't looking; or that Boone took him to an old airstrip and asked him to guard someone, but Mike said no; or that he went with Boone to check out the Lawhon's trailer and two other homes, but that he – Michael – had done nothing else; or that he and Boone both robbed the Lawhon trailer, but nobody was home.

Later, at trial, both the Defense and the Prosecution counsels agreed that Michael gave 10 conflicting scenarios concerning the ring's origin.

It's hard to know exactly what happened during the questioning of Friday, May 7th, but ultimately, Michael alludes to knowing where the body is, and what happened to Les.

Saturday, May 8: Two other men arrive to insert themselves into Michael's questioning.

One is FDLE agent, Ray Fredericks (this is why the name clarification is needed), and the other is state prosecutor's office investigator, Al Gandy.

Before Michael actually confesses his involvement in Les' disappearance, he leads both Inv. Gandy and Agent Fredericks to an abandoned airstrip in the coastal community of Shell Point.

It is here that the officials begin an extensive search. And it is here, in the tangled, wooded, almost desolate mass of an old airstrip, that Les, at last, is found.

...

And still Michael fluctuates. He won't confess to what it is that he, personally, may – or may not – have done; or who is responsible for how things played out; or who is actually a murderer.

Finally, on the night of May 8, Michael "confesses" to Agent Fredericks and Inv. Gandy that he and John Mills',Jr. murdered Les Lawhon.

The Wakulla Co. Sheriff contacts Blonzie Mills for her consent to have her family home in Buckhorn searched.

An account of how the search began and what transpired is given during the deposition of Lt. Landrum, on August 31, 1982. The following direct examination is done by Mr. Randolph, Boone's attorney:

MR. RANDOLPH: Had the name John Mills surfaced prior to the time that Michael Fredrick was arrested?
LT. LANDRUM: No.
MR. RANDOLPH: ...did you get involved in any way in the questioning of Michael Fredrick?
LT. LANDRUM: ...our contact with Michael Fredrick was through Sgt. Charlie Ash and Inv. John Franklin. That's when we got our hands on him.
MR. RANDOLPH: When you say 'ours', when he was brought to Wakulla County, were you in any way involved in the questioning of Michael Fredrick then?
LT. LANDRUM: No.

...

MR. RANDOLPH:...After you found out the name John Mills was involved in it, according to Michael Fredrick, was Mrs. Mills the first person that you talked to concerning this?
LT. LANDRUM: ...The Sheriff, I think, talked to her on a couple of occasions...

...

MR. RANDOLPH: Where did this conversation take place with Mrs. Mills?
LT. LANDRUM: In the Sheriff's office... The Sheriff summoned her.

MR. RANDOLPH: Who was present...?
LT. LANDRUM: Myself, Mrs. Mills, and the Sheriff.
MR. RANDOLPH: Did you tell her in any way what this was about, why you wanted to search the place?
LT. LANDRUM:... The Sheriff... advised her that we did have a burglary under investigation and arson, a missing person, and that John's name had come up in the matter... She agreed at the time to let us look... She unlocked the residence and let us go inside... It was probably a little before noon, maybe a little after noon.

...

MR. RANDOLPH: What information had you received, and from whom, as to what items may be in the house...?
LT. LANDRUM: ... Michael Fredrick apparently said that certain properties taken from this burglary were last seen at that location.
MR. RANDOLPH: Now, did you get this information directly from Michael Fredrick, or was it given to you by another law enforcement officer?
LT. LANDRUM: It was given to me by another agency... It was related to us by, I believe, Fredericks *(FDLE special agent)* and Al Gandy...

...

MR. RANDOLPH:...But the one item, this particular weapon, was found in the living room?
LT. LANDRUM: In the living room.
MR. RANDOLPH: Is this the first room you walk in when you go in the house?
LT. LANDRUM: It's through the front door.
MR. RANDOLPH: And it wasn't covered or anything?
LT. LANDRUM: No.
MR. RANDOLPH: Did Mrs. Mills tell you ... the last time anyone had lived in that residence?
LT. LANDRUM: I was just browsing around, as I say, just kind of making mental notes of things. The Sheriff was

having a conversation with her. I believe she told me or told him ... that nobody had lived there since Boone went back to prison... he was the last person to occupy the place.

...

MR. RANDOLPH: Now, so, you left there and you decided to come down at a later time?
LT. LANDRUM: ... once we came back to the office, I had an opportunity to think a little bit. I got ahold of the Lawhon's, you know, contacted them. I said something about a gun. I said, "Was that thing a Stevens double-barreled?" I think the information just said a Stevens model shotgun. I was informed at the time that it was a double-barreled and a model 311. That's what I had seen.
MR. RANDOLPH: Did you have the form that you showed me a few minutes ago in your possession at the time?
LT. LANDRUM: When I was at the house?
MR. RANDOLPH: Yes.
LT. LANDRUM: No, I did not.
MR. RANDOLPH: You subsequently got this form later on?
LT. LANDRUM: After I got back, I got an opportunity to look at the information.
MR. RANDOLPH: When you say 'look at the information', you mean the information that you had in your form that you had in your possession?
LT. LANDRUM: What was available to me. Whether it was the original of one of these things, I can't say... the Stevens double-barreled shotgun is – I believe what's on the list. There was no model 311, I don't believe, on the thing. There were no descriptive dates on the thing. But yet, the double-barreled aspect ... is what registered in my mind. All the time I was thinking 'single-barreled, single-barreled', because the other guns were single-barreled. Upon research and information, the

determination was made it was a double-barreled shotgun.

MR. RANDOLPH: After you researched the matter to contact the Lawhon's and got this information, you did call them, I assume, before you went back out there again?

LT. LANDRUM: Yes, I can't recall whether I talked to Shirley or to the father, Mr. Glenn Lawhon.

MR. RANDOLPH: You are not sure?

LT. LANDRUM: ... being perfectly frank with you, they were in and out of the office constantly... I just wanted a clarification in my mind as to what I was actually looking for specifically, the finest points that you could get... I had seen something that was described to me as being just about identical in nature. That was the reason for ... obtaining the search warrant. Also, some information was developed during that interim... the Mills's truck, the orange and white looking Dodge truck with a camper shell... Well, I had seen that camper shell in the back yard earlier.

...

"Upon research and information..."

It would've been helpful at this point to find out exactly who said what to the lieutenant and what information may have been handed to the Lawhon family, if any, that helped to make the "determination" as to what type of weapon it actually was that went missing from Les' home.

In such a case, details concerning who said what are highly important, especially when such information will be later testified to by authorities.

...

MR. RANDOLPH: At that time before you got the search warrant, you didn't have the truck or camper?

LT. LANDRUM: Yes, I believe we did have the truck.

MR. RANDOLPH: But you did not have the camper?

LT. LANDRUM: No.
MR. RANDOLPH: So, along with this information, you went to Judge Harper to get a search warrant?
LT. LANDRUM: Yes.

...

LT. LANDRUM: The search warrant was finally gotten together sometime before midnight on the eighth. It was in the early morning hours, probably around ... 1:15 AM
MR. RANDOLPH: When you went to Judge Harper for an application for a search warrant, you did not include the fact that you had seen the item or an item resembling that already in the Mills's residence, did you?
LT. LANDRUM: ... Yes, I did. It is about the second or third paragraph.
MR. RANDOLPH: ... Did you contact Mrs. Mills to let her know that you were coming with a search warrant to search the place again?
LT. LANDRUM: Mrs. Mills was not there. Maybe the Sheriff should answer this because he made the effort to contact her. She indicated to us that she was going out of town, but she didn't go out of town. I don't know whether she didn't want to be bothered or what, but during the interim period, we found that through whatever means – I really don't know – that (BLANK) as everybody called (BLANK) had been back and forth into the building. So, the necessity... to go to that location and retrieve whatever was there... we didn't know whether she had a key to the place or not.
MR. RANDOLPH: So, you had information about (BLANK's) involvement before Judge Harper signed the search warrant. Is that what you're saying?
LT. LANDRUM: Well, other than being Boone's (BLANK) supposedly, and possibly having knowledge from Fredrick that (BLANK) knew that (BLANK) had seen the property.
MR. RANDOLPH: When did you get Judge Harper to sign the search warrant, what time of day? ...

LT. LANDRUM: It was about 45 minutes, maybe an hour, before it was actually served.

MR. RANDOLPH: Was it the same day, I assume, that you had her sign the consent to search warrant?

LT. LANDRUM: Yes, it was... Information began to develop, and we deemed it necessary to go ahead and get a search warrant for what had been seen on the premises along with a camper shell.

...

MR. RANDOLPH: Are there any additional facts that Judge Harper may have gathered from his conversation with you and Sheriff Harvey before he signed the search warrant...?

LT. LANDRUM: ... We contacted Judge Harper and advised him that we were preparing a search warrant. Upon completion, we wished for him to be available to sign it. To my knowledge, when he came in, he was presented with this affidavit for a search warrant. He reviewed it and affixed his signature.

MR. RANDOLPH: There was no sworn statement? He didn't ask anybody to raise their hands, for you to give any additional information...?

LT. LANDRUM: No, he didn't.

MR. RANDOLPH: And to your knowledge, there was no other information given to him, whether it was sworn or not, before he signed the search warrant?

LT. LANDRUM: To my knowledge, I don't believe so.

MR. RANDOLPH: Now, once you went back to... Mrs. Mills' place, and you retrieved the firearm, did you get any other item there?...

LT. LANDRUM: ... On the return list, we retrieved the shotgun and... a white camper shell, that was sitting in the yard. That's the camper shell that I had personal knowledge of belonging on that rig. I've seen it many, many times. I knew that it had been removed.

MR. RANDOLPH: ... You mentioned this lady came down to make an identification of the truck. Did the

officers go back and place a camper on the truck that was in custody?
LT. LANDRUM: Yes.
MR. RANDOLPH: Why was that done?
LT. LANDRUM: Well, the information from the witness, whoever it was ... was that the truck that she had seen was equipped with a camper shell type topping on it. So, should you show her a vehicle without a top on it?
MR. RANDOLPH: Who was in charge of this procedure when she was showed this?
LT. LANDRUM: ... possibly Sgt. Vause may have been the one that showed it to her.

...

The vehicle believed to have been used in the crime was a '73 Dodge pick-up truck, brown/bronze in color, with a white camper on the back.

A "Ms. Turner" stated in a March 12, 1982 report to the FDLE and WCSO that a truck turned around in her front yard on March 5, not long before the fire at the Lawhon home.

She said the truck was rust colored and had a camper that was the same color, and that there were "2 or 3" people in it. She was unable to tell if they were males or females. She mentioned that she lived 2.6 miles from the Lawhon home.

On June 3, '82, Ms. Turner met with Sgt. Vause. This meeting was noted on an 'Incident/Narrative Form' bearing the same date. It reads:

"On this date this officer contacted M. Turner via PX. Ms. Turner was asked to come to WCSD to view a vehicle... Ms. Tuner pointed out a Bronze & White Dodge club cab pickup... This officer was advised that this was the same truck which had turned around in Ms. Turner's yard on the day of the Lawhon incident (3-5-82).

This reportedly occurred at approx.. 2:30-3pm. There had reportedly been no tag on the vehicle at that time.

Ms. Turner stated that there had been "2 or 3" subjects in the front seat of the vehicle at that time. These were believed to be B/M (Black Male) subjects by Ms. Turner. This officer was advised that it had been raining prior to that time but had "slacked off" & Ms. Turner had opened the door to her residence."

When she testified months later at trial, Ms. Turner said the truck was "pumpkin-like", with a white top, and that there were two people in it. When cross-examined, she admitted that, during an earlier deposition, she said there were three people in the truck, and that one of them could've been white. She also mentioned that she lived one half mile from the Lawhon residence, instead of the 2.6 miles she stated months earlier.

This is not consistent with the statements she made back in March, closer to the time of the actual event. The State, along with Boone's own defense counsel at the time, did nothing in response to the discrepancies in this witness's testimony.

...

MR. RANDOLPH: Now, (was) anything else gathered from the Mills' home...?
LT. LANDRUM: Well, we gathered up a body, (BLANK).
MR. RANDOLPH: From the Mills's home?
LT. LANDRUM: Yes. (BLANK) came into the house while we were serving the search warrant. (BLANK) came into the back door of the house.
MR. RANDOLPH: Did (BLANK) have a key to the house?

LT. LANDRUM: No, the house was open. We had already opened the house up.

MR. RANDOLPH: What did (BLANK) say when you first saw (BLANK)?

LT. LANDRUM: Well, I heard some conversation going on with a (BLANK). We hadn't brought a (BLANK) with us. Jesse Ransom, Mrs. Mills' son, was there and –

MR. RANDOLPH: He (came) up while you were –

LT. LANDRUM: Yes -

MR. RANDOLPH: -doing the search?

LT. LANDRUM: Yes.

MR. RANDOLPH: ... how did you get into the house?

LT. LANDRUM: We tripped the latch on the door. We didn't physically, per se, knock the door down. According to Mrs. Mills, nobody had a key to the place to her knowledge... we didn't want to go down and break in the house because we already knew there were some items there that had to be secured.

MR. RANDOLPH: Was the lock ever broken on the house?

LT. LANDRUM: No, there's a latch on the side door. I believe it is to the left of the front door. It was tripped up. You could make and move it off the line or something. That was the way the place was entered.

MR. RANDOLPH: Who did that?

LT. LANDRUM: I believe the Sheriff did.

MR. RANDOLPH: So, (BLANK) came in while you, the Sheriff and other officers and Jesse Ransom were there; is that correct?

LT. LANDRUM: That's correct.

MR. RANDOLPH: You heard a (BLANK) voice. What did you or the Sheriff do?

LT. LANDRUM: (BLANK) wanted to know what was going on. (BLANK) just kept saying, "What's going on?" Sgt. Vause was in there with us. He told (BLANK) that we were serving a search warrant. (BLANK) said, "Well, I want to know what's going on. This is a friend of mine's house." (BLANK) was informed that a search warrant was in the process of being served and to kindly have a

seat there. (BLANK) identified (BLANK) to Sgt. Vasue. I asked (BLANK) what (BLANK) name was. I didn't know it. I told Sgt. Vause, "Would you summon... someone to come pick (BLANK) up." I believe at that time we had already prepared arrest warrants for her.
MR. RANDOLPH: (BLANK) didn't say anything else at all other than "What's going on?"
LT. LANDRUM: We didn't give (BLANK) a chance. We just told (BLANK) to be quiet.
MR. RANDOLPH: So, (BLANK) was taken to the Wakulla Co. jail?
LT. LANDRUM: (BLANK) went to the Wakulla Co. jail with us.
MR. RANDOLPH: Did you do anything else out there –
LT. LANDRUM: After we completed the removal of the firearm in question and... getting the camper shell loaded... the house was re-secured, checked by Jesse Ransom, Mrs. Mills' son. We exited and came back.
MR. RANDOLPH: When you got back, you, I assume talked to (BLANK).
LT. LANDRUM: The Sheriff, apparently, had an extensive conversation with (BLANK).
MR. RANDOLPH: Were you present during this conversation?
LT. LANDRUM: In the initial stages, I don't believe I was.
MR. RANDOLPH: Well, just give me a synopsis of what you recall that (BLANK) said when you were in there. Did (BLANK) tell you she knew anything at all about what was going on?
LT. LANDRUM: Apparently, (BLANK) and the Sheriff's conversation generated some information about some property in question. Some of the items that we were talking about. The Sheriff had already had that information whenever I was made available to it.
MR. RANDOLPH: So, you were there at the beginning of the conversation with the Sheriff?
LT. LANDRUM: No, I wasn't.
MR. RANDOLPH: There was nobody else present in the room?

LT. LANDRUM: No, I don't think so.
MR. RANDOLPH: Do you know if they were recording that conversation or not?
LT. LANDRUM: I do not know. I know one thing. (BLANK) didn't act like(BLANK)cared for me too much.
MR. RANDOLPH: What do you mean by that?
LT. LANDRUM: Well, (BLANK) was distrustful because I had told (BLANK) to sit down and be quiet. We had a warrant for (BLANK) arrest down at the house. So, apparently, that offended (BLANK).

...

Sunday, May 9: Inv. Gandy and Agent Fredericks question Boone in regard to Michael's allegation that he, too, was involved in the murder of Les Lawhon.

Boone denies knowing Michael Fredrick; denies owning or driving an orange Dodge pickup truck; denies any knowledge of stolen property; and denies that he told Fawndretta to move anything from the family's home.

At this point, Inv. Gandy shows Boone photos of Les Lawhon. Gandy would later say that Boone was "visibly shaken" when he saw the photos. Boone loudly proclaimed to Inv. Gandy and Agent Fredericks: *"You all trying to hang something on me!"*

Also, Inv. Gandy testified later at Boone's trial that, when he interviewed Boone, he recorded none of it, even though he had a tape recorder present.

When Inv. Gandy was cross-examined, he said he only took half a page of notes. In short, there is no word-for-word accounting of what took place, or was said, for the entire interview. Mr. Gandy stated the conversation went on for over thirty minutes, yet he walked away with barely fifteen written lines. This, when dealing with the murder of one

Wakulla resident and, possibly, the impending death of another.

Chapter Seven

**Tallahassee Democrat
May 10, 1982
TWO LINKED TO DEATH OF CRAWFORDVILLE MAN
*(Janet Hinkle / Democrat staff writer)***

The two-month mystery disappearance of a 30-year-old Crawfordville man was solved by Wakulla Co. deputies late Saturday, when the man's body was found and two Crawfordville men were linked to the death.

...deputies were led to Lawhon's remains Saturday by Michael Fredrick, 21. Harvey said Fredrick confessed to the killing. Fredrick, who was arrested Thursday for an unrelated Wakulla County burglary... Harvey said Fredrick implicated two other individuals...

... John Mills Jr., 27, also of Crawfordville... Mills is currently being held in Baker Correctional Institution in Macclenny for violating parole. Mills was convicted of four counts of burglary in July 1978, Harvey said.

A search of Mills' home in Crawfordville's Buckhorn community early Sunday morning yielded a 12-gauge, double-barreled shotgun, also thought to have been taken from the Lawhon home.

Also arrested... was Mills' alleged girlfriend - Fawndretta Galimore, 22, of Tallahassee. During a 5 a.m. Sunday morning search of her...home, sheriff's deputies found two television sets, guns and stereo equipment thought to have been taken from Lawhon's trailer. Galimore was charged with accessory after the fact to burglary and grand theft...

Galimore was released Sunday on $1000 bond. According to someone close to the Galimore family, Mills had asked Galimore to store the items for him sometime during late March...

...

And later:

Wakulla News
May 13,1982
BODY IDENTIFIED AS LES LAWHON
Three Are Arrested

The skeleton of a man which was discovered near Shell Point last Saturday has been positively identified as that of Les Lawhon on the basis of dental records...

Those arrested included Michael Fredrick, 21, Crawfordville, who led investigators to the location of the body and confessed to being involved in the crimes, and John Mills, Jr., 27 of Buckhorn.

The woman... Fawndretta Galimore, 22, the daughter of former Chicago Bears professional football star...

The two Crawfordville men, however, are both considered prime suspects... Although Harvey would not go into the details of Fredrick's confession, he did say, "He admits his participation and led us to the body."...

"...it appears death was due to a shotgun blast to the head," Harvey said, but added until the autopsy is finished, it cannot be determined how many times Lawhon might have been shot or how long after the abduction that he was slain...

...

May 19, 1982: A Wakulla Co. Grand Jury indicts Michael Fredrick and John Mills, Jr., with one count each of first-degree murder; first-degree arson; kidnapping; burglary of a dwelling while armed; grand theft; and possession of a firearm by a convicted felon. The firearm possession charges are later severed.

October 4, 1982: Michael Fredrick enters into a plea agreement with the State of Florida. He pleads guilty to burglary, grand theft, and kidnapping, but pleads 'no contest' to second-degree murder and first-degree arson.

...

Some things would never see the light of day at Boone's trial.

Years later, in 1987, Boone's latest counsel were attorneys from the Office of the Capital Collateral Representative (CCR). This office was created in 1985, under the judicial branch of state government, with the sole duty of representing those convicted and sentenced to death by digging deeper into the legality and judgment of their sentences.

Representatives of this group, working with Boone on his case appeals, came to Wakulla in April 1987. Most all of the affidavits listed throughout this chronicle are due to their efforts. More than 50 different affidavits were compiled, written and signed by members – both black and white – of the Wakulla community.

Suspicions were heightened once the contents of the April 1987 affidavits became known, and they placed a great deal of Michael Fredrick's court testimony and personal statements under scrutiny.

Take, for instance, the sworn affidavit of Mr. Jesse Sampson:

"My name is Jesse Sampson. I live in Tallahassee, Florida...I was incarcerated at the Wakulla County Jail. While I was there, I shared a cell with Michael Fredrick for a while.

The police would take Mike out of his cell late at night when they thought everybody was asleep. Mike would be sleeping and they would wake him up to talk to him and question him.

When we were in the same cell together, he told me the state attorney, the prosecutor told him – Mike – they would go easy on him if he would testify against Boone (John Mills). Mike said they wanted Boone and they told Mike if they could get Boone, they would let Mike go. He kept saying 'they just want me to tell on Boone'.

Mike Fredrick told me the police and prosecutor threatened him that if he didn't say where he had got some ring from, they would put him in the electric chair. I told him you can't go to the electric chair for no ring. They also said if Mike would tell them about the ring, he would get off easy.

I know the police and them scared Mike Fredrick into talking. I remember one night he was sitting on his bed crying. He said, 'Jesse, I don't know what to do'.

Another night he came in all muddy like he had been through a hog pen or something.

I knew the police weren't happy with his story because they kept on pulling him out to question him more and would not let up until he said what they wanted him to say."

...

Again, this is where things become extremely delicate. Michael's own mother, Willie Mae Gavin, states in her April '87 affidavit:

"Mike was arrested in early May 1982, and questioned about the Lawhon case.

One afternoon, Al Gandy came by my house and told me that if Mike didn't tell the truth of what happened, Mike would be the one to get the chair instead of Boone Mills and Boone would go scot free. However, if Mike would tell them what they needed to know about Boone Mills' involvement, Mike would get off easy.

One time, maybe two to three weeks after Mike was arrested on this case, I went to visit him one afternoon, and Mike was very upset. A black deputy asked me to go in a room with Mike and see if I could get him to be what they called more honest. Mike told me he was telling everything he could tell but they still didn't accept what he was saying. I said, "Mike, tell them the truth, you have nothing to lose." He said, "I told them the truth and they won't believe me." I noticed there was a tape player going in the room when I was talking to Mike."

...

And then, there's the March 31 incident.

Only three weeks after Les' disappearance, Michael and another man, a mister 'A. Sharp', were questioned in connection with some stolen jewelry. Both men denied having anything to do with the stolen items, but later,

Michael told police that it was Mr. Sharp – not he – who stole them.

Or the April 19th burglary, approximately 6 weeks after Les' murder. Boone is in jail at this time, remember, having been arrested on a violation of his parole. Michael Fredrick is the only member of this unfortunate trio to roam free.

During Michael's October 4 change of plea, Mr. Kerwin, attorney for the State of Florida, states to the Court:

"...On the 19th day of April, 1982, the residence of P. Frizzel, located here in Wakulla County, was burglarized. Several items were taken out of the residence, including a stereo, master mixer with the serial number. The value of that stereo mixer would be in excess of $100.

On the 20th day, the next day then, of April, 1982, a Franklin County deputy sheriff arrested Michael Fredrick and a co-defendant in the case, 'D. Sparrow', in Franklin County.

At that time the subjects were in possession of the items stolen from the Frizzel house the day before. (Michael) Fredrick told Deputy Williams that he had met his co-defendant on April 17, some two days before the burglary, and that the items had been in the truck at that time. Those would be the facts."

...

Facts: Barely two months after Les' demise, Michael Fredrick pointed the finger of burglary at two different men, in two completely different incidents. In one of those incidents he claims to have met his accomplice for the first time just two days before the police arrested them; that the stolen items were already in the back of his newfound friend's truck when Michael met him. There seems to an awful amount of burglary *coincidences* surrounding this one person in a 6-week period.

And now, this same person, is expected to testify – for the State – in a robbery / murder case in which it appears he has a rather shady involvement.

But that's not unsettling.

The State held back a March 28, 1980 'Incident / Narrative Form', along with an 'Offense Report', and an 'Arrest Ticket', all filed by Sgt. R. Vause from two years earlier.

These items focused on Michael Fredrick's alleged burglary of someone's home. (Again, this was two years before the Les Lawhon incident.) Michael is clearly reported as stating to Sgt. Vause at the time that he had *"...ripped off a .357 to blow somebody away."*

Michael admitted that he also stole a checkbook from the residence and had cashed a few checks already.

These things were never brought up during Boone's trail.

Past incidents and threats; the desire to "blow somebody away" with a .357; the 10 different tales of how Shirley Lawhon's class ring came into his possession; his links to an ongoing rash of burglaries both before and immediately after Les Lawhon's disappearance, makes one wonder if a truthful version of any sort can arise from such a vigorously creative mind as that of Michael Fredrick.

Yet, Michael's October 4th plea agreement with the State of Florida, came with one glaring stipulation: That he testify 'truthfully' at the trial of John Mills, Jr.

Chapter Eight

**From the Journals of John Mills, Jr.
Date unknown:**

" I trust Allah to always be with me. He lives within me now as He always has. He's been right there during the time of my sins as well as when I did good. And it was Him who came with comfort and understanding that enabled me to stand up to my current position. Blind faith!

I live in blind faith now. I can't see the end. But I know that it's there, and to my liking. The only reason I know that it is to my liking is due to the fact that Allah is with me no matter where I am or where I might go. I might sin along the way, still. But I won't quit no matter how many times I have to get up after falling. My lesson in/on life is far from complete. But, I'm willing and determined to learn all it teaches.

Even before reading Mr. Frankl's 'Man's Search For Meaning', I wrote in one of my writings what I observed of people as they reacted to the accusations against me. I wrote that there are many ways to look at a situation. At any given location.

But for some reason it is not the onlooker's wish to look at all situations for what they really are. Maybe it is due to the fact that reality is feared by most of the human race. Where did it start? Who were the first to cast a problem to the side in hopes that it will better itself or simply go away? Or again, be dealt with by someone else? Why do many people speak their mind, only to be heard by themselves, as they are speaking into their bathroom mirror? Isn't it true that Allah gave each of us a mind, body, and soul in hope that we will begin a course in life that has Him as our destination?

Wouldn't it be fair to say that Allah put us here to love, help, and understand each other before making judgment on the Accused? Mistakes. Uncontrolled. Would it be to the point to say that it takes everybody to be everybody, since it takes everybody to make everybody, and maybe everybody needs everybody? Aren't we all from the same Allah that made us?"

Chapter Nine

His trial began on Monday, November 29, 1982. From the first bang of the gavel Wakulla had inkling that, although Lady Justice was blind, at her core, she was the true balance; the heart of American right and wrong. She would prevail. Some found great comfort in her sightlessness, for it made the scarcity of light in their own darkened consciences bearable.

A practicing Black Muslim was being tried for the murder of a young man whose father preached the gospel of Jesus Christ; a Reverend who pastored one of the largest, most overwhelmingly white-populated Christian churches in the area, and sold insurance to its residents countywide.

The jury of Boone's peers harnessed with the burden of deciding his ultimate fate, were all white. Of Wakulla's 11,000-plus residents of the time, not one black person – man, woman, business-owner, teacher, grandmother, stepfather, crab-picker, worm-grunter; dark residents whose families were generations old in the county – none, was deemed worthy enough to be on the jury. An icy indictment for any county in America and a revelatory indicator of fear's crushing ability to render a legion of 'good Christian folk' into an utterly impotent silence.

...

Michael Fredrick was the State's 'star witness' against a man who loaned him money to get out of jail. Fawndretta Galimore also testified on behalf of the State. It is said that she appeared voluntarily and that the State made no prior agreement with her in regard to her testimony.

What follows are the supposed events of that Friday afternoon in March of 1982. It is the story that most believe to be true. Gathered from an appeal to the Eleventh Circuit of the U.S. Court of Appeals (August 15, 1995), these statements have been recycled for over 30 years. They have appeared as 'factual' in court records, websites, newspapers, televised newscasts, and more. The source of this particular version is Michael Fredrick:

"On the morning of March 5, 1982, (John) Mills (Jr.,) picked up Michael Fredrick at Fredrick's residence in Wakulla County, Florida. Mills was driving an orange 1982 Dodge pickup truck that belonged to his mother.

Mills and Fredrick went to Mills' mother's house for a short while; after they stepped outside the house to leave, Mills went back inside and retrieved a single-barrel, single-shot, 12-gauge shotgun that Fredrick had given Mills earlier in the week and placed it behind the seat of the truck. Following a brief stop, the two set out to burglarize a house.

Mills and Fredrick then drove around Panacea, Florida in search of a target. After stopping at a trailer that appeared to be unoccupied but discovering that an elderly woman was at home, Mills and Fredrick left

Panacea and drove into the Lake Ellen area. At some point, Mills became disoriented in some heavy rain and turned the truck around in front of a house.

Sometime after turning around, Mills and Fredrick arrived at the trailer home of Les and Shirley Lawhon; because Shirley had gone to work in Tallahassee earlier that day in the Lawhon's only car, the trailer appeared unoccupied.

Mills parked the truck, went to the door, and knocked. Les Lawhon answered the door and let Mills in; shortly thereafter Mills reappeared at the door and motioned Fredrick inside.

When Fredrick entered the trailer, Mills was using the Lawhon's kitchen phone while Lawhon was rummaging through what appeared to Fredrick to be a phone book or a newspaper.

Soon after Fredrick entered, Mills dropped the phone, grabbed a kitchen knife, and held it to Lawhon's throat. Lawhon said, "Please don't hurt me. Ya'll take what you all want." Mills replied, "Shut up, cracker." Mills instructed Fredrick to check out the rest of the trailer; Fredrick looked into the trailer's bedrooms; no one was there.

Mills then told Fredrick to check outside. Lawhon, apparently realizing that he would be forced to leave with his assailants, asked if he could put on his shoes. Mills told him he would not need his shoes where he was going.

Fredrick left the trailer to check outside; Mills and Lawhon soon exited the trailer as well. Mills had taken a double-barreled, 12-gauge shotgun from the trailer and walked behind Lawhon with the shotgun to Lawhon's head. Mills threw the truck keys to Fredrick and asked him to drive.

Lawhon sat in the passenger's seat; Mills sat in the small space in the cab directly behind him, kept the shotgun trained on him, and gave Fredrick directions.

Lawhon was trembling. Near the end of the drive, Lawhon asked what Fredrick and Mills were going to do to him. Mills told him, "I'm going to do to you what your forefathers did to my forefathers."

After driving approximately seven miles, Mills, Fredrick, and Lawhon arrived at an abandoned airstrip. Mills forced Lawhon out of the truck, ordered him to his knees, and tied his hands behind his back with a belt.

Then, while Lawhon was on his knees, Mills struck him on the back of his head with a tire iron. Lawhon fell forward, bleeding from the back of his head. Mills watched Lawhon for a few moments and then turned to leave, saying, "Let's go."

When Mills spoke, Lawhon sprang up and ran. Mills, shotgun in hand, chased him. Mills caught up with Lawhon in a nearby canal and grabbed his arm; Lawhon butted Mills in the stomach with his head and fled up the far bank of the canal, disappearing into thick underbrush. Mills, still pursuing Lawhon, vanished into the underbrush as well.

Shortly after Fredrick lost sight of both men, he heard two gunshots. Mills returned to the truck; Lawhon did not.

Mills' shirt was bloodied in the stomach area. He warned Fredrick not to say "anything about this" and suggested that they "go back to the house and clean it out and get everything we can sell."

Fredrick and Mills got back into the truck; Mills drove. At some point, Mills took off the bloody shirt and threw it on the passenger side floorboard. Shortly thereafter, Mills stopped the truck and discarded the shirt in the bushes beside the road.

When Mills and Fredrick arrived at the Lawhon's trailer, they removed virtually everything of value, including Shirley Lawhon's jewelry and several guns. Mills exited the trailer last; he wiped the doorknob of the trailer as he left.

Although Fredrick was not aware of it at the time, Mills had set the trailer on fire. Mills and Fredrick stopped at a nearby lake to better secure a cover concealing the stolen property. At that time, Fredrick took Shirley Lawhon's high school class ring from her jewelry box.

After dropping Fredrick off near his house, Mills brought the stolen property to his mother's house, where he lived with his girlfriend, Fawndretta Galimore. He and Galimore put most of the property in a shed behind the house. Unbeknownst to Galimore, Mills put some of the property, including the firearms, in the house."

Chapter Ten

There were four motions made to move the trial from Wakulla to an area where a 'fair and impartial jury' could be empanelled. This was not to be.

Eighty Wakulla residents were summoned for jury selection. They were broken down into groups of three and interviewed about pre-trial publicity and exposure. Seventy-four had heard, or read about it. Of that number, 55 had read at least one article.

Nine were excused for preference, favoritism, or 'bias', and one because they highly preferred the death penalty. Eleven were excused because they opposed it.

The remaining fifty-nine venire group was placed in the courtroom to see who among them was competent enough to be on the jury.

The State Prosecution gave copies of this list to the Wakulla Co. Sheriff, a deputy sheriff, the bailiff assigned to the case, the Clerk of Court, and the Rev. Glenn Lawhon. They were asked for comments on those listed. The Clerk of Court later testified that he offered similar assistance to Mr. Randolph, Boone's attorney. Randolph reviewed the list with his investigator and one local black community leader.

It is unknown whether anyone from either group contacted those on the list before or during jury selection.

...

On the first day of trial, Mr. Randolph (the Defense) states:

MR. RANDOLPH: I think they have indicated they have some problems, obviously, with security and I want to make sure everybody is watched in that courtroom.

Mr. Randolph and the State Prosecutor agree that two officers – who happen to be minor witnesses in the case – should be excused from the 'witness sequestration' rule, and allowed to remain in the courtroom, for safety's sake.

The second day of trial:

MR. RANDOLPH: Judge, there is another matter I want to bring to your attention... Could we keep these first two rows (in the spectators' section of the courtroom) empty?

THE JUDGE: We have got them roped off already where there won't be anybody in them.

Later that day, the trial judge meets with counsel in chambers and states for the record:

TRIAL JUDGE: ...at the beginning of trial this morning, on 12-2-82, at the request of the Defense counsel and at the request of the bailiff, and also by the common sense of the Court, and looking at the courtroom, thought it in the best interest of the Defendant and all of the personnel of the courtroom, to block off the first two rows of seats behind the counsel for the Defense and the State, for their welfare or the possibility of any violence, and the same was done.

Day three: With the jury seated and two witnesses having already testified, Mr. Randolph asks for a brief sidebar where the following discussion takes place:

MR. RANDOLPH: Your Honor, I want the record to clearly reflect that what is going on, I think (we) need to keep the witnesses in the witness room. Rev. Lawhon just made a gesture, when the door was open right then, to the counsel table while he went to the water fountain. I don't know what he said or whatever, but I think we need to carefully watch him for security purposes. Because he made some gesture at that point.
MR. KERWIN (Prosecutor): Did he make it toward you?
MR. RANDOLPH: He made it toward the counsel table.
THE COURT: *(To one of the officers -)* Claxton, you make sure the witnesses stay in the witness room. They're already making gestures toward the counsel table.
MR. KERWIN (Prosecutor): For the record, Judge, I agree that needs to be stopped.

All agree that certain 'gestures' should be stopped. All agree that there need to be security measures, such as moving the crowd of spectators back from the main arena so no one will be hurt if "violence" should erupt.

No one 'agrees' to move the trial to a place where a 'fair and impartial' jury can be gathered.

Boone's Defense team files a motion to bring Professor Paul Alan Beck, director of the Research Center at Florida State University, onboard to conduct a public opinion survey of the county. The survey could possibly reveal the extent to which Wakulla residents may have been biased by media coverage, or influenced by Les' family at church, in social groups, or through phone calls made.

The State Attorney objects, saying the costs of such a survey would be a cost to the county, and the results may be found to be non-admissible, or inconclusive.

The Judge denies the Defense's Motion to Tax Cost, saying:

"And as far as the opinion poll being able to grant any Defendant to present a defense, I don't think it's going to help present in any defense. I'm sure it's strictly used for the purpose of venue motion only."

...

Wakulla's atmosphere, barely 31 years ago as of this writing, is best described by those who were there. Listed first, are portions of the affidavits from Boone's sister and brother-in-law.

Rachel Donaldson (Boone's sister):

"I went to the whole trial, every day, all day. There were always a lot of white people there, some days about 25 or 30, but some days up to 100. There were never more than six or eight black people there, including me... Rev. Glenn Lawhon and his wife and Shirley Lawhon were

there every day, too, right in the courtroom. All the white people sat near them. None of the white people would sit near or with me... There wasn't even one black person on the jury. They took the different people to another room to ask them about being on the jury so we wouldn't know what they said..."

Herbert Donaldson, Sr. (Brother-in-law):

"When Boone had the wreck that Jeff Lewis was killed in, he really changed. He got so moody and was really lonely and off by himself all the time after that. The Lewis family is real well-known and well-liked in Wakulla and Leon Counties, and even though it was an accident, I know a lot of people thought he should have served some time for that. That's where a lot of prejudice against Boone started... He never said anything about not liking white people... After John (Boone) was arrested on this murder, a white man named John Byrne said to me that John should be hanged for doing that. I told him that was my wife's brother, and not to talk like that around me. We exchanged words about it for several minutes. Later I told Roosevelt Randolph about it and I also told Mr. Randolph then I would be happy to come and testify about that in court. Mr. Randolph never mentioned it to me again..."

Alfred Bea (The Tallahassee Democrat):

"I live in Tallahassee, Florida. I covered the murder trial of John Mills, Jr. for the Tallahassee Democrat. I was in court every day...and observed most of the trial. I was surprised that Mills' trial was held in Wakulla Co. It seemed like he would not be able to get a fair trial there. I was also surprised that no black persons were seated on the jury and saw no reason why this should have been so... There was a great deal of hostility towards me as a newspaper reporter in the Wakulla Co. Courthouse. The judge conducted a portion of the jury selection in his chambers. When I tried to enter, I was stopped by the

bailiff and not allowed in. During a recess, I saw Judge Harper and told him I thought I should be allowed in chambers to observe the proceedings. He did allow me in, but reluctantly, it seemed to me... There were upwards of 75 people in the courtroom every day of the trial and the audience was overwhelmingly white. I received threats... Most notably, the victim's father, Rev. Glenn Lawhon, threatened me and threatened to burn down the Tallahassee Democrat office. I was told he called the paper and made the same threat. He accused me of trying to bring about a mistrial through my coverage. He was primarily worried about the trial being moved from Wakulla Co. because of too much publicity. Other people in the audience expressed the same concern and made negative comments to me... I have covered murder cases before but have never seen such a hostile trial atmosphere. It seemed like the outcome was a foregone conclusion and the proceedings were more a matter of going through the motions."

Fred Allen (Wakulla):

"I am 75 years old. I currently live in Crawfordville Florida. I am retired from my own business in scrap iron and metal in New Jersey. I left Florida in '42, but came back to Florida, to Wakulla Co., in 1979... I am not related to John Mills, Jr. I do not know John Mills, Jr. I am not a friend of his or his family... I watched the 1982 trial where he was convicted of murder and other crimes. I went every day and watched the whole trial. I didn't see the sentencing... They was about 40 people that really stayed day in and day out. Other folks just came and went all the time. I remember that around 100 people were there toward the end of the case. I don't believe it was a half a dozen blacks that were there on any day. Most of the white people sat behind the father, mother, and wife of Mr. Lawhon, the man who was killed. Some blacks appeared to be scared to sit near a white person. I'm not. I sat where I wanted to sit... I went to watch the trial because I wanted to see how the jury was selected. They had quite a few blacks to choose from. They had some blacks that I thought would qualify, but they turned all of them off. All of the blacks was excused. I don't think John Mills, Jr. got a fair trial. The odds was against him and his lawyer..."

Clyde Williams (Medart):

"I testified at a hearing on having John Mills' trial moved to somewhere else because I don't feel he could have gotten a fair trial in Wakulla Co. My testimony at that hearing is still the truth and my belief. I remember there was a petition that was signed by a lot of black people who believe that John couldn't get a fair trial in Wakulla Co. I don't know what happened to that petition. I went to as much of the trial as I could. There were never more than six black people there, but there were at least 30 white people there the day I was there. I remember seeing Sheriff Harvey, Glenn Lawhon, and his wife, and Shirley Lawhon all sitting in the courtroom. I remember when John Mills had the wreck where Jeff Lewis was killed. John was never tried for anything about that but I think a lot of prejudice started against John then and that it affected him bad. I believe that it's common knowledge in Wakulla Co. that Glenn Lawhon is very good friends with Judge Harper."

Clayton Lewis (Sopchoppy):

"When John was arrested for this murder case, I was really shocked. I just couldn't believe he'd ever do anything like that. I knew then and I know now that there was no way he could get a fair trial in Wakulla Co. Besides it just being a real racist county, where any black person accused of killing a white person is sure and certain going to be found guilty, I think a lot of people remember all about my cousin dying and were just real *prejudiced against John before they ever walked in the courtroom."*

Willie Mae Gavin (Mother of Michael Fredrick):

"...Sometime before Mills' trial, Mike was moved to the Leon Co. Jail for a week or so. I asked his lawyer to look into this and find out why, and he told me there had been threats that people in the county wanted to break into the jail and kill Mike and Boone Mills."

...

The testimony of several expert witnesses was presented, including that of Jim Skipper (FDLE), who was among the group that located the skeletal remains of Les Lawhon.

Wakulla dentist, Dr. Mooney, identified Les from his dental records dating back to 1978.

FSU anthropologist, Robert C. Dailey, a consultant for the FDLE, determined the cause of death was a gunshot wound to the head and neck. He found no evidence of a "blow to the head", as indicated by Michael Fredrick.

Firearms examiner, Don Champagne (FDLE), examined the doorknob from the trailer home. He found no evidence of forced entry. He spoke of the 'pellets' found in the mandible area of Les' skull, fired from a .410, or, a 12-guage shotgun. He could not tell the actual gauge of the weapon that did the damage.

Douglas Barrow, a crime lab analyst specializing in latent prints, examined the doorknob and stolen property. None of Boone's fingerprints were found. Mr. Barrow stated that the alleged murder weapon (a 12-guage shotgun, state exhibit #25) was never submitted to him by law enforcement for examination.

Crime lab analyst, Dorethea Munger, examined a .12-guage shotgun, tire iron, and the shirt that was found along the roadside. She found no blood on the shotgun, nor the tire-iron itself. She did find an indication of blood on the shirt that could have easily been "animal blood".

DNA testing, or profiling, would have been very helpful at this point. Unfortunately, at the time of Boone's trial, DNA was mainly used for paternity testing. It didn't make its way into criminal cases until around 1986-87.

Throughout the entire trial, .12-guage shotguns are mentioned. None of the guns found were used in the crime. As of this writing, no official 'murder weapon' has ever been found.

...

Shirley Lawhon and Rev. Glenn Lawhon were called to identify the recovered property. Both stated that the items belonged to Shirley and her late husband, Les.

During Rev. Lawhon's testimony, he was given opportunity to elaborate on Les' childhood, their father and son relationship, their hunting together, and how he was of help to his son during the purchase of a few State exhibit items.

With Rev. Lawhon being a Baptist minister, and Boone a practicing Muslim, faith plays a strong role in the trial. The State wastes no time in following up on Michael Fredrick's statement that Boone allegedly called white people 'crackers'; 'Caucasians'; and 'devils' (as stated by Fawndretta Galimore).

Apparently, in the Muslim branch of religion Boone followed, the male is referred to as a "King", and his wife, a "Queen".

This is not uncommon. Blacks, especially those who came of age during the 60's and 70's, often use these terms. Some feel their use links them to 'Mother Africa'.

Indicators such as these are as readily spoken as 'bruh' (brother), 'sista(h)' (sister), my man (good friend), or 'queen bee' (Number One girl).

Clothing often seen in some modern-day black-owned shops, or along the stroll of a street market, reflect this. The flourishing hats worn by black women in church on Sundays are referred to as 'crowns'.

Steven Spielberg, when directing the film version of Alice Walker's book, *'The Color Purple',* recognized this 'royalty' connection within the black culture, as did entertainers like Michael Jackson (*Remember the Time*, video), and Eddie Murphy (*Coming to America*, movie). In Alex Haley's book, *Roots*, when Kunta Kinte is born, his father holds him up to the skies and says to the infant, *"Behold: The only thing greater than yourself."* Only one thing is larger, more powerful than the child: The universe that created him. There is power in this motif, made all the more powerful by the black faces and lives that it represents.

It is the aspect of promised royalty that has inspired black gospel tunes such as *'Move On Up A Little Higher',* when Mahalia Jackson sings:

"One a-these mornings

Soon one morning

I'm gonna lay down my cross

Get me a crown..."

It is this sense of 'royalty' that stretches farther back than Shaka Zulu and the Zulu Kingdom (or, Zulu Empire); goes even further back to the Turin King List (or, Turin Royal Canon) of ancient Egypt – the list is endless.

Yet, when addressing Michael Fredrick about how Boone introduced his girlfriend Fawndretta, the State's questioning went like this:

STATE: ...And how did Boone Mills introduce you to Ms. Galimore?
MICHAEL FREDRICK: He said, "Fawndretta is my queen." He said, "this is my queen here, Mike."
STATE: What did he call her during the course of that introduction?
MICHAEL FREDRICK: His queen.

Fawndretta, during her testimony, said she called Boone by his Muslim name: "Ans Serene". For the rest of her questioning the State uses 'Ans Serene' as Boone's name to drive deeper the 'foreign' point:

STATE: Okay. Now let's go back to your relationship for just a second. Did Ans Serene refer to you in any special way?
FAWNDRETTA: As his queen.
STATE: And how would he refer to himself?
FAWNDRETTA: As a king.

...

STATE: What was his religious persuasion?
FAWNDRETTA GALIMORE: He was a Muslim.
STATE: Did he ever discuss his religion with you?
FAWNDRETTA GALIMORE: Yes, he did.
STATE: During the course of the discussion, did he ever mention white people?
FAWNDRETTA GALIMORE: Yes, he did.
STATE: What did he refer to them as?
FAWNDRETTA GALIMORE: Caucasians.

The State brings up the letter Boone wrote to Fawndretta, from jail, months earlier:

STATE: Okay. Did he tell you anything else?
FAWNDRETTA GALIMORE: Yes. He told me not to be afraid; that he has told me about those Caucasians time and time again.
STATE: All right. What had he told you about them?
FAWNDRETTA GALIMORE: That they were devils.

Later, during redirect, the State brings this up once more:

STATE: Ms. Galimore, what did he refer to white people in the letter as?
FAWNDRETTA GALIMORE: Caucasians.
STATE: And what did he tell you about those Caucasians in the letter?
FAWNDRETTA GALIMORE: That he had told me about them. Don't be afraid of them.

During the Prosecutor's argument, he said the following in reference to Fawndretta's testimony; a further attempt to turn Boone's faith into a mockery:

"And she is Ans Serene's girlfriend. She is his 'queen'; he is the 'king'... Boone Mills never discussed his business with his queen because he was the king... And what does she do? Just like the king ordered."

The State did not, however, tell the jurors that they were uncomfortable with Fawndretta's testimony before it ever began. During a brief recess, Mr. Kerwin (Prosecution) stated the following in chambers:

MR. KERWIN: Judge, about two or three witnesses down the road is Ms. Fawndretta Galimore...(she) was the Defendant's girlfriend at the time all this occurred... She was living with him down at his mom's house.

We want to...examine her about two things. I want to ask her... did she know John Mills; how did she know him; how long had she known him; where was she living.

And then I want to ask her about the day in March when John Mills, Jr. was arrested and told her to destroy the property. I specifically do not want to go into March 5th, the day Les Lawhon was killed.

I have several reasons for that... First of all, I don't feel that she is telling the truth about March 5, and I hate to call her and in some way vouch for her. Now if I can impeach her, then I wouldn't mind it all that much. Call her as a Court's witness or something. But I just don't feel like she is telling the truth about what happened on that day. I think she is telling part of the truth and part that ain't the truth."

Yet in the Prosecutor's closing arguments to the jury he states:

"...Fawndretta Galimore is not lying, did not lie under oath. She is mistaken about the day... I don't think she is lying. I think she is telling it as best she can remember."

After Fawndretta, came the testimony of Major Hines. Major is Boone's first cousin. His mother, Betty Jean, was Blonzie's sister. When younger, Major and his siblings would often stay at the Mills residence.

It is only natural to want more in life, and it is believed that Major's testimony harkens back to a story older than time: Those who have, and those who have not.

In December of '81, Major was kicked out of the Buckhorn Café, and another bar known as 'Buddy White's', for disorderly conduct when he caused a fight with another customer. He also, supposedly, at one point, threatened

Boone's brother, Jesse, Jr. with a knife. Major himself was 'stuck' during the altercation, and required stitches.

During testimony, the State asks Major about a conversation that he says took place between him and Boone:

MR. KERWIN: What was the nature of that conversation? What did he say?
MAJOR HINES: Asked me if I –
COURT REPORTER: I didn't understand you.
MR. KERWIN: You're going to have to speak up a little louder. He asked you to do what?
MAJOR HINES: Knock some Caucasians off. Do some burglaries.
MR. KERWIN: To knock some Caucasians off, do some burglaries?
MAJOR HINES: Yes.

Major said the conversation happened at Boone's mother's house in June or July of 1982. This would have been impossible. Boone was in jail at the time for his alleged 'violation of parole'.

It is unfortunate that even with Major Hines' testimony for the State against his cousin, he would, in essence, become a pawn for the Prosecution. The State said the following regarding Major's testimony:

"Major Hines is a terrible witness... He was put on the stand for a very specific reason. I wanted you to see another one of Boone Mills' friends... But the reason Major Hines was up there – you saw Major Hines. What did Boone Mills ask him about? He wanted to go do some burglaries, knock off some Caucasians...

You know, picture in your mind Major Hines. Did the word "Caucasian" belong out of that mouth? Does he look like the type of man that is literate enough to know that big a word? You heard the rest of his vocabulary. He could hardly string three words together in a row. That word "Caucasian" is what gives what he said the ring of truth.

Because you know where he got that word? Right there, the man that refers to white people as "Caucasians". Major Hines couldn't have fissured that word out in 20 years. Think about the rest of his vocabulary. It just wasn't there, ladies and gentlemen. He got that word from one source, Boone Mills... You shall know them by their friends."

One wonders: If Major Hines was a 'redneck', 'hillbilly', 'Florida cracker', or a back-woods countrified white male, would this American citizen have been spoken of so disdainfully in a court of law by a representative of the State? Especially when testifying on their behalf?

The pushing of Boone's Muslim beliefs among an all-white jury of southern bible-belted Christians; the odd back-and-forth of witness credibility with a man's life in mortal danger; and the berating of a Wakulla County citizen, in a court of law, in the attempt to put their perceived 'ignorance' on display, speaks volumes about American justice and those involved in bringing it about.

...

Crime scene analyst, Nayola Ruth Darby, testified that on May 8, she searched the scene where Les' remains were located. She found a wallet, wadding from a shotgun shell, and clothing.

From Blonzie's Dodge pick-up truck Ms. Darby collected vacuum sweepings, a red sweater, and a tire iron that were given over for examination. She also stated that a 'bandana' was found at the crime scene near Les' body.

FDLE micro-analyst, Linda Hinsely, examined the 'hair' found in the bandana. It was light-brown in color, and characteristic of a 'Caucasian' head of hair. Though she had only a strand to work with, she said it was possible that a detergent, such as a type of bleach, could've been present and not shown up in her test.

Possible 'animal blood'.

No murder weapon.

A bandana.

A strand of 'Caucasian' hair.

Tantalizing evidence for a case where the only white person involved, thus far, in this sordid episode of southern madness, is the victim, who was a dark-haired male.

Even more provocative is the FDLE micro-analyst who spoke the word 'Caucasian' during her testimony. How strange that she was neither insulted nor judged as to whether or not such a sacred word should be allowed to fall from her mouth.

Chapter Eleven

**From the Journals of John Mills, Jr.
July 25, 1992:**

In addition to all that's written within these writings, I also write other notes and opinions that represent the degree in which I have evolved; the ways I have endured – thank Allah! – and all that have led to my current disposition.

These different opinions and positions range from my so-called 'trials' down in Crawfordville, Florida, on and up to now. Therefore I will try to write them.

...as I sat in an all-white courtroom, in a so-called trial, defending myself on accusations of a crime against white people... What really sparked this writing is how much weight the judge, telling a white jury, how well the Constitution has worked for 200 years:

"Too Old of a Constitution to Include Me"

Prisoner: *If slavery truly ended in 1865, which was 126 years ago, as of 1991, what fairness can be in a constitution that's 200 years old? Unless, of course, it is designed in sole, and only, for the benefit of whites that live by the same constitution prior to 1865.*

For the court to say that the constitution has worked for 200 years, is only one way of saying that things are basically the same today, 1991, as they were prior to 1865.

So it seems that anyone being told this, as states have, will form an opinion that insinuates that most laws concerning blacks prior to 1865 is okay in today's court.

If that being the case 'fair trial for a black', is merely a five word joke among a courtroom filled with whites, except for the one black, him being the Defendant.

As a result of this 200-year old constitution, that's so often and proudly spoken of in our judicial court, the courtroom has become a place of deception to win, and not win, over this deception.

It is a place that I have come to see x-amount of tax paid servant breaks. Many of our laws are designed not to serve the public, but to meet an end. An end with a state that's fabricated to begin with.

It would seem, too, the key concern in a constitution is the truth.

But from what I have endured for the past 10 ½ years, (3-5-82 - 11-23-91) and in and out of the courtroom in Crawfordville, Florida, the jury might be the only persons in the courtrooms that are willing to be honest.

The only problem with that is if a judge is not impartial and looks the other way, or overlooks the true issues at hand. The jurors will only have the lies and deceptive productions presented during trail.

That, along with this 200 year old constitution is a JOKE. On the people who pay taxes and pretend that this system, as it is at present, is correct. Thank Allah for higher courts.

Until we also, as a people, learn to stop pretending that all is well and good between the both of us, there will be no sincere concern or understanding for what must be done if we are to truly let bygones be bygones and to strive together as a human nation instead of a divided one.

Even though there are indications that some unity is being sought from all sides, it's obvious that both sides are still dissatisfied with the explanations given by the opposition to justify their past behavior whether it be giving or receiving the conduct in question.

Being a proud black man I have all sorts of questions that I need answered from the black race. The most telling of these questions is: Why do so many blacks automatically believe whatever the white man is able to broadcast and publicize farther than a black man?

The white man told blacks that blacks were put into slavery, for the most part, because they (blacks) were only two-thirds human to them (whites) at the time.

But many blacks, being and feeling so rewarded because the white man had changed the term 'slavery' into 'share cropping', didn't bother to ask the white man to explain his position as to having sex/babies by the black women. The very race he said was one-third animal.

I ask those questions and many similar two-sided issues like it, and so far, I have no honest, or understandable answer, except 'Lies, lies, lies. Lies.'.

Chapter Twelve

In 1987, Boone's Defense attorney, Mr. Randolph spoke to the CCR about his overall experience in working on this particular case in Wakulla County:

"On May 24, 1982, the Hon. Judge Harper... appointed me to represent John Mills, Jr. ... As I began to prepare Mr. Mills' defense, it became apparent to me that it would be virtually impossible for Mr. Mills to receive a fair trial in Wakulla Co. My initial opinion was subsequently confirmed by events surrounding and occurring during the trial... Wakulla County is a sparsely populated, rural community... the educational, vocational, and political institutions are controlled by the white majority. Race discrimination plays an everyday role in the lives of almost 2000 black people in Wakulla Co....

Mr. Mills, a young black man from the small and almost exclusively black community of Buckhorn, was charged with the homicide of Les Lawhon, the son of a prominent white family whose members live throughout the county.

The victim's father, Glenn Lawhon, was the well-known minister of two Baptist churches in the area: First Baptist Church, and Sopchoppy First Baptist Church. Given the circumstances of the offense, the status of the victim's family, and the atmosphere in the community, Mr. Mills could have received a fair trial only if venue had been changed. There was a concerted effort by Wakulla County officials to maintain venue, despite the common knowledge that the dye was cast well before the trial...

From the beginning, my court appointed investigator, Paul Williams, reported to me that he believed State investigators were following him from one interview with potential defense witnesses to the next... one of our witnesses expressed to me her fear of retribution from authorities, and the community, if she testified for Mr. Mills. She had been warned by family and friends that she would face trouble... Another witness... who testified, was harassed and even arrested immediately after the trial. Ultimately, charges against him were dismissed...

Hostility in the courtroom was intense and reflected the racial dynamics of the offense and the community. White spectators, many of them members of the victim's family and friends... filled the first several rows of seats closest to the jury. I was extremely concerned about their influence not just on the jury but on the witnesses and trial court as well...

By the end of the trial, the trial judge also ordered armed guards to protect me on my way to and from the courthouse. It is the only time before or since that I have had to have an armed escort.

At one eerie point in the trial, the victim's father, Glenn Lawhon, while on the witness stand testifying for the State and identifying a rifle, pointed the rifle directly at me and John Mills. I interpreted the pointing of the gun in that direction as a threat to me and my client...

I was not aware that Carlton Tucker, the Clerk of the Circuit Court in Wakulla, was listed as a reference for the victim's father, Glenn Lawhon, on his application for filing for examination with the state office of insurance Commissioner. Had I known, I would've used this information during my cross-examination of Mr. Tucker...

The Prosecution never provided me copies of the State-written script of questions and answers for Michael Fredrick... nor was I aware that such a script existed. Had the State informed me of its existence, I would have requested a copy... I would have relied on it to help impeach Mr. Fredrick...

Mr. Fredrick, in my opinion, was an example of a classically coached witness, but I did not have proof of the extent to which he had been coached... I also did not know that the State was providing psychiatric treatment to Mr. Fredrick; that he was taking psychotropic drugs; that he was hallucinating, and that he was suicidal during his arrest and confinement...

The Prosecution never provided me with copies of Mr. Fredrick's psychiatric records. This information would help me further erode his credibility through cross examination, particularly since he denied receiving treatment."

...

Mr. Randolph brings up a lot. And all the things he didn't know call into question what the jury would have done if they knew.

Would they have felt any different knowing the _"Application for Filing for Examination as Ordinary-Combination Life Including Disability Agent"_ form – filed by Glenn F. Lawhon on March 13, 1978 – included not only Carlton Tucker, Wakulla's Clerk of Court as a personal 'reference', but the Honorable Judge Harper himself?

Would this have been seen as a 'conflict of interest'? Would this have been enough to warrant a change of venue, or, at the very least, a different judge?

Then again, Wakulla was very small at the time. Is it possible some members of the jury knew more about the personal relations of those involved than they would ever care to mention publicly? It is rumored that a few members of the jury were members from Rev. Lawhon's church.

...

During Michael Fredrick's testimony against Boone, he mentioned that before they (supposedly) went to Les' home, Boone took a .12-guage shotgun from the Buckhorn house and placed it in the truck. Later, when leaving the Lawhon's trailer, with Les in tow, Boone suddenly grabs a second shotgun from Les' bedroom.

Why would Boone use a second gun instead of the one that he (supposedly) brought with him for this specific – and deadly – purpose? Why not use the weapon that he's already familiar with?

Michael also testified that he had paid Boone a few dollars cash as down payment on the bail money debt he owed. This may be true. Michael's mother, Willie Mae Gavin, testified that Michael, Boone, and Fawndretta, came by her home one day to borrow money from her. Though she could not recall the exact date, it is likely that this is the money Michael is referring to.

On the day of Boone's release in February, he and Fawndretta visited Michael. Michael testified that he gave Boone a 12-guage shotgun with the initials 'TB' on the stock.

It is here that the long, sordid road of this case begins its sharp twist into the turn.

Michael says that his mother gave him the shotgun. But the 'Offense Report' from March 1980 (where Michael confesses to wanting to "blow someone away"), lists Michael as the prime suspect in the theft of a 12-guage single barrel shotgun, with the initials 'TB' carved into its stock. This prior offense is not mentioned during Boone's trial.

Michael admits on the stand that in February '82 (a month before Les went missing) he discussed 'making a hit' on another Wakulla resident by the name of Mr. Jewel Hudson. When he was recalled by the State, Michael said that 'making a hit' meant that he wanted to 'burglarize' Mr. Hudson. Michael also admitted he carried a firearm in his back-pocket during that time.

Apparently, both Michael and the State felt the need to clarify which criminal activities seemed more desirable at the time.

...

What about the shirt? How does it fit into all of this?

Michael first says the shirt was thrown on the floorboard of the truck. After giving the truck a complete comb-over, nothing is found by the FDLE's micro-analyst team to indicate or prove this.

Michael then says Boone threw the shirt into the woods after having committed the murder. Was there blood on his pants, or shorts? Blood on his shoes?

There was a great to-do about searching Boone's home, and later Fawndretta's, but what about searching the residence(s) of Michael Fredrick?

An 'Incident Report-Narrative Form', dated October 11, 1982, just over 5 months after Les' remains were found, stated the following:

"This Deputy along with Aux Deputies, R. Revell, M. Kemp, and D. DeFend began a search of the area along that grated dirt road on the east side while Deputy C. Welch drove along the roadway... a yellow shirt previously mentioned by Inmate Fredricks... Deputy C. Welch got out of the vehicle on the roadway in front of the residence of C. Miley and... proclaimed that he had discovered the shirt in question.

This Deputy observed a long sleeved yellow shirt balled up and partially hanging from the undergrowth. The shirt had started to become soiled by the weather and had soil on it that appeared to have been dried blood stain... took photographs of the garment then measured the distance from the shoulder of the ditch along the roadway and found it to be six feet.

This Deputy collected the garment in a plastic bag and marked the garment with this Deputy's initials and the date. The time of the discovery was 1740 hrs... sealed the garment in a brown paper bag and turned that over to Deputy Lt. C. Landrum for presentation to the State Lab for analysis."

...

Michael Fredrick testified that he mentioned the 'shirt' to authorities in May. With this, it becomes difficult to understand how such hard evidence in a murder case – found less than six feet from a highway ditch and within minutes of the deputies arriving – could sit in open abandon for almost six months, with no one making a move to find it. Again, the 'shirt' is located in mid-October, barely a month before Boone's trial.

Though it sounds suspicious, I, for one, am hesitant to say that the 'shirt' was manufactured and placed there by authorities. But, then again, I don't have to say it: Because someone else eventually did.

Still, Michael Fredrick identified the shirt in court as being worn by Boone the day of the murder.

...

It came out during Michael's testimony that he was "high on cocaine" when Les was murdered. Michael admitted that this was true. He did not, however, admit to other things:

MR. RANDOLPH (Defense): Mr. Fredrick, have you had any psychiatric treatment since January 1982?
MICHAEL FREDRICK: No, sir, I haven't.
MR. RANDOLPH: You have had no psychiatric treatment?
MICHAEL FREDRICK: No, sir, I haven't.

The State Prosecution team knew this was incorrect.

On May 26, 1982, approximately two and half months after Les was murdered, Michael tried to hang himself.

He was referred for evaluation by the WCSO and was seen around 2:30am. During his examination he spoke about having been incarcerated since May 7, and that he has "done nothing but think about what happened".

The intake forms state that he was "incorrigible/anti-social", "scared", having "flashbacks", and that he "needed drugs to help me sleep and settle my nerves." He says he is "innocent" and that "before they put me in the electric chair, I will do it myself".

Sleep disturbances have plagued him for the last 3 weeks. His mood is noted as "flat", and that there is "much denial of any wrongdoing". He admits his suicidal thoughts are persistent, and though his orientation appears good, "poor judgment" and "poor eye contact" are noted during the interview.

By June 7, '82, he states that he is not feeling "suicidal"; that the "medication" is helping, but he still has trouble sleeping. He is frightened about the case and being convicted of First Degree Murder. He doesn't feel his attorney is doing all he can.

June 14, '82: After taking 50mg of a prescribed medication, he feels some relief of the anxiety. After 2 weeks he refuses medication and no longer feels he needs it. After four sessions, he wants no more treatment, and is awaiting trial in October.

July 12, '82: There is no interview with Michael, but with the jailer who informs the counselor that Michael does not feel he needs to see anyone; is no longer taking his medication; and has not reported any suicidal ideas.

December 2, 1982: The day of Michael's trial testimony in John Mills' case. The notes read:

"20 y/o BM vomited stomach contents (x3) at 1:30pm felt sick all day. No/VN at this time. HEDA. Medical history: many c/o nervousness and trouble sleeping. Saw Dr. (BLANK), got prescription of (BLANK) 50mg. Has been out since Oct. c/o nervousness past 2 wks. State went to trial yesterday".

It appears the star witness had stage-fright to the tune of three vomitus trips to the bathroom.

Two medications that Michael was taking – combined - were prescribed for the treatment of: psychoneurotic patients with depression and/or anxiety; depression and/or anxiety associated with alcoholism; depression and/or anxiety associated with organic disease; psychotic depressive disorders with associated anxiety including involutional depression and manic-depressive disorders.

No one from the State Prosecutor's team mentioned this to the Defense. Michael was specifically asked if he received any psychiatric treatment since January of that year, and he was not truthful in his response. The State knew this.

In short, after striking a plea agreement with the one stipulation being that he "testify truthfully", Michael has failed to do so.

And still, when arguing to the jury, the State says the following:

"I'm not proud of Michael Fredrick, not proud of him at all. I'm not proud of what I was forced to do. Michael Fredrick was a liar. But, you know, he lied terribly, and I mean that in two ways: Number one, he lied a lot. As Mr. Randolph pointed out, he told you at least 10 different stories. And recall, if you would, the stories that he told.

He said he had gotten the ring from some lady named Corbett. The officers went to get Ms. Corbett and Ms. Corbett comes back and said, "Michael, what are you telling them?"

"No, no, it wasn't Ms. Corbett. I got it from Fawndretta Galimore's car." And they go up and they get Fawndretta Galimore. "No, no, it wasn't Fawndretta Galimore's car."

That is the second meaning of terrible. Michael Fredrick was a stupid liar. He is a bad liar. He can't lie convincingly. He can't do it. He tried for three days and he could never support one of his lies. He could never convince one of the officers. And they just kept asking him questions. And finally, finally, he got painted into a corner, and the only way out of that corner, ladies and gentlemen, was the truth. That's the only way...

Look to see if Michael Fredrick's testimony didn't have the ring of truth to it. You know, I think this is one of the things we need to use common sense on... One of the things I'm going to ask you to do, and ask you to do it right now, and I would ask you to do it when you get back there, is remember carefully Michael Fredrick's testimony, not just what he said, ladies and gentlemen, but how he said it. Was he sure of himself? I suggest he was. Was he strong? I suggest he was. Was he shaken by the cross-examination? I suggest he wasn't. And do you know why? Because Michael Fredrick is telling the truth this time...

There is only one way to be convincing. There is only one way to be strong. There is only one way to be sure. It is to tell the truth. Then you don't have to do anything but remember what happened. You don't have to fabricate, you don't have to plan ahead, you don't have to watch out for the pitfalls behind. You just tell what happened as you remember it. And that's the beauty of truth. And that's a lesson that most children learn early in life, and that is the lesson that Michael Fredrick didn't learn until after his arrest.

And I'm afraid it is a lesson that Boone Mills hasn't learned to this day. Compare Michael Fredrick's testimony right alongside with what Boone Mills tells you. Which one of those two had the ring of truth?"

...

The ring of truth. Great performances have little to do with talent, but study and development of craft are vital.

"The ring of truth" sprinkled delicately on the statements above, opens wide the door on the issue raised by Mr. Randolph (Defense), regarding whether or not Michael was "coached".

The State prepared a seventeen-page typed script with questions – along with answers that some feel to be crucial – typed directly on the page. This was given to Michael to study in his cell as he waited to testify. Portions of the alleged 'script' are as follows:

-Did you ever see the defendant again
-When (Saturday)
-Who drove the truck
-Was the camper on at this time
-How long did you stay in the Mill's house
-Why did you leave the house   (Boone said let's go)
-What happened as you left the house (Boone went back and got the shotgun)
...
-How do you know it was him if you've never seen him before in your life
-What happened (Boone went inside)
-How long was he inside
-What happened (Boone beckoned)
-What did you do
-Describe what you saw when you entered the house

- Boone on phone
- Lawhon at table
- Cake on table with knife

...

-What happened after you got in the house
-What did you do
-Did Boone Mills say anything to you
  -What
  -What did you do
  -Was there anyone else in the trailer
  -Had Mr. Lawhon been saying anything
    -Take what you want, don't hurt me!

...

-What was Boone Mills saying to him
-Who made the decision as to what happened next
  -What was the decision
  -What did you do (Go outside)
  -Why (Boone told you to)

...

-What happened at that point
  (Boone throws him keys, says drive)
  (Lawhon gets in passenger side into middle)
  (Defendant gets in passenger side, climbs into back)

...

-Was there much conversation in the truck up to this point
-Where did y'all go (Abandoned air strip)

...

-What did Mr. Lawhon do (Tremble and shake)

...

-What did Boone Mills do
  (Tied Lawhon)
  (Reached for tire iron)
  (Hit Lawhon in the <u>back</u> of the head)

...

-What happened then
-Which way did they run (To right)
-What happened (2 gun shots)

...

-Describe how Boone Mills looked as he came out of the woods
  (Bloody shirt)
  (Blood in the middle)

...

-What did he say (Go clean the house out)

...

-When was the first time you had seen that shirt (That day)

...

-Where was the shirt when you first saw it (Seat of the truck)

...

-When was the first time you realized that he had it on (When he came out of the woods)
-After he got rid of the shirt, where did y'all go
-Explain to the jury what happened when you got back in the Lawhon house
 -Both went in
 -Boone had the shotgun
 -Cleaned the house out

...

-What did y'all do with the items (Truck)

...

To rehearse with a witness makes perfect sense. To show the witness what their answers should actually be, as though they – the witness – were never at the scene of the crime, seems odd. The 'witness' is the one with a first-hand account. The answers Michael gave on the stand stayed very close to this "script". Fawndretta Galimore was also supplied with a similar "script".

In Michael's original statement to authorities, on May 8th, he said that it was he – not Boone – who went and got the gun from the bedroom inside Les Lawhon's home. This was not heard in court.

He also said it was he who helped drag the body into the woods. These statements were omitted from his tape-recorded confession. The revised version is the one that made it to court.

These are only a few crucial pieces of information that the State's Prosecution team chose not to share with the Defense, in their effort to single out the 'ring of truth'.

...

The affidavit of Gordon B. Scott:

"I reside and practice law in Quincy, Florida. I've been practicing law for 19 years and have been a member of the Florida Bar for 19 years. I've worked on over eighty (80) capital cases.

I represented Michael Tyrone Fredrick in Wakulla Co... Michael pled guilty to second-degree murder in return for his testimony against John Mills, Jr. ...

The atmosphere... was extremely intimidating and frightening to me. The case had a tremendous amount of notoriety. In my 19 years of practice, I have rarely, if ever, experienced a community as inflamed as that of Wakulla Co. concerning this case. Mr. Lawhon, the victim's father, was well known in the community and was talking to everyone in the area and it was my opinion his actions poisoned the community...

The atmosphere surrounding the case can best be described as a lynch mob mentality. For example, I was told by people in the Wakulla Co. Sheriff's Office that guns and ammunition had been bought to kill Michael Fredrick, John Mills, Jr., Fawndretta Galimore, and me.

Glenn Lawhon, father of the victim... submitted a letter that was included in Mr. Fredrick's pre-sentence investigation that scared me to death. I was extremely concerned about my physical safety and would not go into or out of the Wakulla Co. Courthouse without adequate security precautions...

In my opinion, there was absolutely no way a fair and impartial jury could have been impaneled in Wakulla Co. in this case. I cannot understand how or why the case was tried there given the pervasive prejudice in the community. This is particularly true in light of the fact that the victim was white and the defendants were black."

...

The letters.

The messages they convey are, indeed, frightening. But more than anger, there is the acute howl of a people in pain. Pain is no respecter of persons. It has touched our family, too.

These letters were submitted to the trial court, in October of 1982, as part of the pre-sentence investigation (PSI) reports for Michael Fredrick. The material was deemed prejudicial and inappropriate for consideration by the trial court or any sentencing body. Michael's attorney asked that the letters be stricken from Michael's PSI file.

One of the handwritten letters was titled "Father's Statement", dated October 14,'82. Here is a portion of that letter:

"Both of these murderers deserve to be put to death swiftly and in some horrible way. The word of God <u>commands</u> that such "creatures" be stoned to death publicly.

Even though there are many liberal (and crooked) federal judges who pretend to believe that capital punishment is unconstitutional, the Bible and the Constitution <u>both</u> make it clear that capital punishment is the law of God and of the United States of America. As a matter of fact, the Fifth Amendment makes <u>specific</u> mention of "capital – crimes."

The use of the Eighth Amendment which prohibits the use of "cruel and unusual punishment," to justify the state of executions is an insult to the intelligence of a moron and amounts to downright <u>treason</u> on the part of the federal judges who do it! They are <u>outlaws</u>!...

I feel it might also be in order at this point to write a few words for the benefit of any parole board or commission that should ever consider letting this murderer out on parole. This would be a very unwise and <u>unhealthy</u> thing for them to do. If Fredrick's (sic) is ever paroled during my lifetime, I promise those who do so that they will regret that stupid decision! ...

Fredrick's (sic) could have made an anonymous phone call to the family or to any other citizen of the County and revealed the location of the body before it was eaten by wild hogs, raccoons, and buzzards. Our pleas and even offers of reward for information leading to the location of the body of Les so we could recover it in time to give him a proper burial were in the newspapers and on television.

Yet Fredrick's (sic) was so uncaring and such a murderer at heart that he was not even moved to make an anonymous phone call. He is no better than a mad dog and should be shot down like one! ...

If it is not possible to give Fredrick's (sic) the death penalty because of our crooked criminal justice system, then he should <u>at least</u> be given the <u>maximum</u> possible years for each of the charges, and each of these sentences should run <u>consecutively</u> and with no possibility of parole. He should also be made to serve his time at hard labor to earn his keep instead of enjoying a lifetime of leisure in air-conditioned comfort with other sexual perverts (queers) like himself."

The emphasis placed on certain words is from the original.

An affidavit from Michael's mother reads:

Willie Mae Gavin:

" I tried to go to John Mills' trial. A white deputy stopped me at the door and told me I couldn't even go in the trial. He said, "You can't go in there while the trial is going on. Period." I had not been subpoenaed at that time. The deputy told me, "Mike wouldn't want you there" ...

I asked Mike's lawyer, Mr. Scott, what kind of sentence Mike would get. He said it was hard to say, being in Wakulla Co. and all. He said he didn't know – it could be 25 or 30 years or it could be as little as one year if Mike did good in prison...

The next morning of the day Mike was sentenced, I met Mr. Scott at the courthouse, and he said he was sorry, that the Judge had changed his mind and was going to give Mike a lot more time than we had thought. He said, "Mrs. Gavin, I'm so sorry. The Judge changed his mind this morning. I'm real sorry, and Mike is very upset about it." He told me that Rev. Glenn Lawhon had talked to Judge Harper in the judge's office that morning...

The Lawhon family was there in the courtroom when Mike was sentenced. Mike asked them to forgive him for the agony he put them through. I've heard on at least two occasions that Rev. Lawhon and Judge Harper are some kind of kin, but I don't know for sure...

Everybody around here is either a friend or some kind of relation to the Lawhons. A lot of people around here went to the church that Rev. Lawhon pastored. It would really be hard for any black person to get a fair trial in Wakulla Co. for killing a white person."

...

On January 7, 1983, the request from Michael's attorney to have these letters stricken from his PSI file, was granted. It was also the day Michael Fredrick was sentenced to 347 years, with no possibility of parole until the year 2097.

He was given "the maximum possible number of years for each of the (five) charges" against him. The sentences were to "run consecutively". With this, the prayers of the Rev. Lawhon may have been answered, directly in line with his request.

The Reverend's letter, along with those of his daughter, and Les' widow, Shirley Lawhon, had much to say. And Boone was mentioned in a few. Excerpts from those letters are as follows:

'Sister's Statement':

"A person wouldn't think anything of killing a jellyfish knowing of the possible sting it could bring and the useless purpose it serves. How much more should we think nothing of killing garbage like Michael Fredricks and John Mills... They are far more deadly than the jellyfish and far more useless...

They are dangerous, worthless people and keeping them alive at taxpayer's expense would make as much sense as bringing a jellyfish home and feeding and caring for it, or spending several thousand dollars a year to keep a mad dog alive. If Michael Fredricks and John Mills do not get capital punishment for killing my brother, there is no justice...

There is as much difference in my brother and the two who killed him as dark is from light. My brother had the characteristics of light and brought comfort to those who knew him. His murderers have the characteristics of the night... Michael Fredricks and John Mills have not only killed my brother... they have hurt us, Les' family, beyond words of description. A part of us is dead too.

And then, there are the things that are never to happen, the child that Les and Shirley wanted, never to be born. It is not only the things they have destroyed that was known, it is also the things they have prevented by murdering Les."

'Wife's Statement':

"I feel that Fredricks and Mills intentionally killed my husband and that both of them deserve the electric chair, which at times I feel is even too swift and painless. I think they should have to suffer the mental and physical anguish that they made Les suffer before they killed him...

You may think this is harsh of me to feel this way or think, I understand, after all it was her husband. Just let me say one thing. Put yourself in my shoes and in the shoes of the rest of his family. How would you feel if it were your husband, wife, son, or daughter? I'm sure once you have actually encountered this never ending nightmare your feelings would be the same."

'Father's Statement':

"The little finger of Les was worth more than all the mad dog murderers like these two "creatures" on earth...

According to the statement given to law officers at the time of her arrest, the accomplice Galimore was present in the home of mad dog Mills (John Mills, Jr.), and witnessed the unloading and concealment of all the items stolen from Les and Shirley... Ever since her arrest she has been very uncooperative with law officers. Indeed, it is my understanding that she and her lawyer have blackmailed the State into reducing the charges against *her in order to get her to give testimony in the Mills' trial... But in spite of her act of blackmail against the State, one way or another, she <u>will</u> pay for her crimes against Les and his family! This is a solemn promise!"*

...

Pain. It is from pain that the words above, and those throughout this chronicle of events, have been penned. From the pulpit to the poolroom: Pain is no respecter of persons.

It is in times of great peril and need that one reaches out to a higher power in prayer. It is in those times that we look to one another and ask wearily for others to 'pray for us' and 'keep us in their thoughts'.

But other people's prayers are not always good for you. Who can know the intent of a neighbor's intercession on behalf of someone else? Maybe a slight, or perceived wrongdoing – done by you – lingers in the heart of the one who prays. God's good medicine for some, when placed in the hands of a particular saint, may become poison for another.

"For I was an hungred, and ye gave me no meat; I was thirsty, and ye gave me no drink; I was a stranger, and ye took me not in; naked, and ye clothed me not; sick, and in prison, and ye visited me not.

Then shall they also answer him, saying, 'Lord, when saw we thee an hungred, or athirst, or a stranger, or naked, or sick, or in prison, and did not minister unto thee?'

Then shall he answer them..." (Matthew 25:42-45)

And still, one can only wonder: How would the spirit of all Wakulla citizens have been strengthened; what qualities of faith, hope, charity, and forgiveness would have been gained if the chosen had gone to the Wakulla jail – not as a mob, but as a miracle, and shown 'Mad Dog Mills' the mercy that God had shown upon them; if the believers had bent themselves low in prayer with the "creature" who – in the eyes of a God that made them all – was their brother?

"Agape", or the selfless love for human kind that can lead to such forgiveness, may prove to be impossible for the everyday sinner. But for those ordained to lead and instruct a flock of souls that number well into the hundreds, it is nothing less than a sworn duty.

...

In the Prosecutor's closing statements, during the guilt phase, the following is stated:

MR. KERWIN: Ladies and gentlemen, the Defendant, John Mills Jr., is consumed with hatred. He is consumed with hatred. And he hates the people who he thinks have been oppressing him. Listen to the testimony of Fawndretta Galimore. She said he called them devils. Major Hines –
MR. RANDOLPH (Defense): Your honor, I have to object. He has gone a long way in his closing argument. The closing statement he is making now is meant only for to show, to prejudice this jury against my client along those lines.
THE COURT: Just stay with the facts, Counselor.
MR. KERWIN: Judge, I am staying with the facts, and I have no intention of prejudicing this jury or any other jury. (To JURY-) He is consumed with hatred. He can't help but hate, and one man that he had no reason to hate, no reason to harm, the man that extended him a helping hand, the man that let him use the phone, the man that let him in his house, is dead at the hands of John Mills, Jr., the Defendant. Ladies and gentlemen, the evidence in this case, I think, is more than just beyond a

reasonable doubt. I think the evidence in this case is overwhelming. I suggest to you that each and every one of you can fulfill your solemn oath and return a verdict that speaks the truth. Find John Mills, Jr. guilty of murder in the first degree, premeditated murder, and I think you can do it with a clear conscience."

During this plea for the jury to administer eye-for-an-eye, death-seeking justice, the Prosecutor – literally – went down to the floor on both of his knees to make his point.

One day, as some in Wakulla are taught to believe, we will be asked to reveal all as we sit at the feet of a 'higher power'. We will have to answer for our actions.

Our pleas for prayer, along with the intentions that lie underneath, will – supposedly – be brought into question.

Will our explanations have the ring of truth?

Chapter Thirteen

From the Journals of John Mills, Jr.
11-26-92

Thanksgiving Day!!

Even as a kid, I've always regarded Man's Thanksgiving Day – the last Thursday of November each year – as a day to eat plenty of food. First of all, I've known for some time that Thanks must be given each and every day. Sometimes all through the day.

What I have come to realize since my arrest in '82 and having had to endure the sufferings of many disappointments and/or letdowns, is that all I took for granted prior to my arrest makes me feel shallow to not have given more value to all the little – thought to be – things in life that are actually so precious to me at this point in my life.

It's the small things that I now thank my Creator for 365 days a year. Not to be so shallow as to think one day out of the year can be any less or more in need of Thanks. For the days of my youth.

Chapter Fourteen

Relationships and love affairs often end. When they do, we come to the threshold of remaining good and trusted friends, or lifelong enemies. Some of us will have to take the terrifying risk of going it alone; breaking the chains that bind.

And then there are others who – once the jig is up – vanish into the great unknown; leaving a faint, barely discernible scent lingering in their wake. Their entire existence is nothing more than the vapor of memory.

Such is the case of Debra Mock.

Her name is mentioned at various points throughout the trial, yet she is never present. After numerous attempts by the Defense, she cannot be found. Her vanishing is similar to that of one spirited away by the Cinderella cleaning alumni, leaving only one thread of probable evidence behind, after the ball has ended.

Tina Partin, a young woman who, to some, was of dubious background, claims to have known Debra Mock. Ms. Partin chose to testify for the Defense. After a few preliminaries regarding her name, address, and the like, here is what she said:

MR. RANDOLPH (The Defense): Do you know Michael Fredrick?
TINA PARTIN: Yessir.
MR. RANDOLPH: Alright. When did you meet Michael Fredrick?
TINA PARTIN: Around the middle of January, first of January.
MR. RANDOLPH: 1982 ?
TINA PARTIN: Right.
MR. RANDOLPH: Did he give you any property?
TINA PARTIN: Yes sir.
MR. RANDOLPH: What did he give you?
TINA PARTIN: A ring.
MR. RANDOLPH: Did you turn that ring over to the sheriff's department?
TINA PARTIN: Yes sir.
MR. RANDOLPH: Do you know, or did you see, any other property, or any other rings, or jewelry, or other material in the possession of Mr. Michael Fredrick?
TINA PARTIN: No sir.
MR. RANDOLPH: Do you know a Ms. Debra Mock?
TINA PARTIN: Yessir.
MR. RANDOLPH: Do you know whether or not he gave her anything?
TINA PARTIN: She's got something, yeah, but it hasn't been turned in.
MR. RANDOLPH: Are those rings and other gold items that she has?
TINA PARTIN: Right.
MR. RANDOLPH: Have you seen those items?
TINA PARTIN: Right.
MR. RANDOLPH: But the police never recovered them. What is the relationship between Michael Fredrick and Debra Mock? Was she seeing him?
TINA PARTIN: He tried to.

MR. RANDOLPH: Okay. Now, would you describe this Ms. Debra Mock to us?
TINA PARTIN: She's about 5-foot, maybe, 5-foot-one; blonde, bleach blond hair, black roots, sharp nose, baby blue eyes.
MR. RANDOLPH: Is she a white female?
TINA PARTIN: Yessir.
MR. RANDOLPH: And how old is she?
TINA PARTIN: She's 16.
MR. RANDOLPH: Have you seen Mr. Fredrick and Ms. Mock together?
TINA PARTIN: Yes.
MR. RANDOLPH: Now, can you tell us what type of clothing Ms. Mock normally wears?
TINA PARTIN: Skirts, high heel shoes, blouses.
MR. RANDOLPH: Alright. I think you describe her hair as what color?
TINA PARTIN: Its bleach blonde. Her natural color is black, she dyes it blonde.
MR. RANDOLPH: Okay. What does she wear in her hair?
TINA PARTIN: What do you mean?
MR. RANDOLPH: Does she wear anything on her hair?
TINA PARTIN: She wore bandannas, you know?
MR. RANDOLPH: Alright. What color bandannas did she wear?
TINA PARTIN: Well, she owned a red one and she owned a blue one.
MR. RANDOLPH: Ms. Partin, I show you now, what has been marked as state exhibit No. 17, and ask you is the type of bandanna that she wore similar to this?
TINA PARTIN: She's got a red one just exactly like it.
MR. RANDOLPH: Alright, but you can't honestly say that's the same bandanna?
TINA PARTIN: No, I can't.
MR. RANDOLPH: But it looks similar to that?
TINA PARTIN: Yessir.
MR. RANDOLPH: And you say she has what color hair?
TINA PARTIN: Bleach blonde.

MR. RANDOLPH: Okay. Would that be kind of a light brown shade –

Here, Mr. Kerwin, from the State's prosecution team interjects:

MR. KERWIN (The Prosecution): Objection, Judge. He is suggesting an answer to her. She told him what color it was.

MR. RANDOLPH: (To Tina Partin -) What is bleach blonde to you?

TINA PARTIN: It's when somebody dyes their hair blonde.
 (As she glances around the courtroom -)
I can't see nobody in here that's got the same color.

MR. RANDOLPH: Okay, do you know whether or not this young lady, Debra Mock, has been in this area - in Tallahassee - since July of 1982?

TINA PARTIN: No.

Mr. Randolph ends his questioning, and Mr. Kerwin, for the State, begins:

MR. KERWIN: Ms. Partin, I'm not sure I understand what you said about this bandanna. Did Mr. Randolph say to you, "did she have a bandanna like this", and you said she had a red one exactly like it?

TINA PARTIN: She has a red one and she has a blue one. I don't know if this is hers or not. I can't say that.

MR. KERWIN: Okay. Is this in any way different from millions of blue bandannas?

TINA PARTIN: What do you mean by that?

MR. KERWIN: Well, is there anything special about this particular bandanna?

TINA PARTIN: No.

MR. KERWIN: Was there anything special about the bandannas that she wore?

TINA PARTIN: No.

MR. KERWIN: Did she wear the blue one more then she wore the red one?
TINA PARTIN: No.
MR. KERWIN: Now, you did describe her hair is bleach blonde, and it had black roots.
TINA PARTIN: Right.
MR. KERWIN: Was it fairly obvious to see the black roots?
TINA PARTIN: Yessir, you could see the black. These ladies know, when you dye your hair, if you don't keep it up it turns back.
MR. KERWIN: Okay. Did she have a problem keeping it up?
TINA PARTIN: No.
MR. KERWIN: Could you see her black roots?
TINA PARTIN: Yeah, but just a little bit.
MR. KERWIN: Okay. I don't have anything else.

Here, Mr. Randolph redirects:

MR.RANDOLPH (The Defense):But her hair, the last time you saw it, was in fact, blonde?
TINA PARTIN: Yessir.

In similar testimony, Greg Rosier also testified to having seen Debra Mock in the company of Michael Fredrick. Greg and Michael would hang out together on many occasions, and Mr. Rosier testified that he'd known Michael "practically, all my life."

He is in fact, a distant relative of Michael's mother. At one point, both Greg and Michael were dating two sisters, and would come in contact with one another on a daily basis.

It was during this period that the two men had a conversation beside Mr. Rosier's car. He testified that Michael mentioned that he wanted to make a 'hit' on Les Lawhon. There was also discussion about the gun Michael was known to have carried on his person, in his back pocket, at the time.

When asked about Debra Mock, Mr. Rosier testified that he had seen her with Michael once or twice at a small bar/dance club called 'Rock Bottom', in Shadeville, another community within Wakulla confines.

When asked to describe Debra Mock, Mr. Rosier said that she was about 5'4", looked to be between 160 to 170 pounds, with 'sorta dark' hair that was long. Their conversation continued regarding other details about Debra Mock's appearance:

MR. RANDOLPH *(To Mr. Rosier-)*: Did you notice at the time you saw her, did she have on any type of headdress?
GREG ROSIER: Yes she did.
MR. RANDOLPH: What type of headdress did she have on?
GREG ROSIER: She had what you call – at least what I call – a band; a band that goes around her head, something like a headscarf.
MR. RANDOLPH: And what color was this headscarf?
GREG ROSIER: It was blue.
MR. RANDOLPH: I show you what's been marked State Exhibit Number 17. I ask you, does this particular headband look similar to the one that you had seen?
GREG ROSIER: Yessir.
MR. RANDOLPH: Are you reasonably certain of that?
GREG ROSIER: Yessir.

...

Les Lawhon is described as a good neighbor, and a good Christian boy. During the Prosecutor's guilt phase closing argument, he spoke of Les in the following manner:

"Les Lawhon was a sickly man, disabled, young, early 30s. His wife was working full-time to help take care of him because he can't work. His family, all of these are

victims. All of these are the people that we all too often lose sight of. Let's not lose sight of them tonight...

(Michael Fredrick) told you Boone Mills was on the phone and that Mr. Lawhon was seated in the dining room. With Les Lawhon just a couple of feet from the phone, and he was looking through something. He said it might have been the directory, it might've been a newspaper.

I'm going to suggest to you that Boone Mills used that same ploy:
"Do you know where they live?"
"No but let me help you."
"Can I use your phone?"
"Sure."
It is the last good deed Les Lawhon did. The last time he helped a citizen or a neighbor, the last time he helped somebody that needed his help."

Throughout the entire trial, Michael Fredrick and others would say that John Mills, Jr. (Boone) was the great and powerful man behind the kidnapping, theft, and murder of Les Lawhon. For the entire case, only two things implicated him: The property he received as payback for the loan he made to Michael Fredrick; and the sworn words of Michael Fredrick.

During the trial, Michael testifies to the following questions:

Q: Had anybody promised you anything if you would tell them a particular set of facts?
MICHAEL FREDRICK: No, sir.
Q: Did anyone promise you anything if you would talk to them – I'm speaking about the law-enforcement officers now – if you would talk to them about John Mills, Jr.?
MICHAEL FREDRICK: No, sir.
Q: Mr. Fredrick, who brought up the name of John Mills, Jr.
MICHAEL FREDRICK: I did, sir.

Q: Did anyone suggest that name to you before you talked to them about it?
MICHAEL FREDRICK: No, sir.
Q: Has anyone promised you anything?
MICHAEL FREDRICK: No, sir.
Q: At any time?
MICHAEL FREDRICK: No, sir.

Upon cross-examination:

Q: Mr. Fredrick, you would say almost anything to keep you out of the electric chair, wouldn't you?
MICHAEL FREDRICK: No, sir.
Q: Are you saying then, that you have no problems with the electric chair?
MICHAEL FREDRICK: No, I'm not saying that, sir.
Q: But you don't want to go to the electric chair, do you?
MICHAEL FREDRICK: No, sir, I do not.
Q: And you are not going to the electric chair in this case, are you?
MICHAEL FREDRICK: From the way the charge is, no sir.
Q: Because you made a deal with the State of Florida, didn't you?
MICHAEL FREDRICK: I entered a plea, yes, sir.

Five years later, in 1987, Boone was granted an evidentiary hearing. In May of that year, Michael Fredrick signed an affidavit prepared by Boone's collateral counsel. The affidavit included the following passages:

MICHAEL FREDRICK: *(On May 8, 1982,) after the body was found in the woods, I made a taped statement with Gandy and Ray Fredericks. I was still telling different stories that didn't all add up.*

They would turn the tape recorder on and off. They also told me what they wanted me to say and made gestures with their hands to lead me on to say certain things.

For example, they would hold up a number on their fingers for the number of days they wanted me to say, or make a gesture of a camper top when they wanted me to describe a particular truck...

They made me say I had led them to the Lawhon trailer driving around but it was really them who took me there...

At the end of the statement when they asked me whether they have promised or threatened anything, they were shaking their heads "no" at me letting me know I should answer "no."

The truth is that they had promised me I would not be in any trouble and that I wouldn't do "nary a day of time" if I cooperated with them. Otherwise they said I would go to the electric chair."

...

However, when Michael arrived at the Rule 3.850 court's evidentiary hearing, the following took place on the stand:

Q: Do you swear that the contents of this affidavit are true?
MICHAEL FREDRICK: No, I do not.
Q: You do not?
MICHAEL FREDRICK: No, I do not.

...

Q: Did he (State Attorney Tim Harley) tell you that you would get in a whole lot of trouble if the contents of this affidavit are true or if you testified to this affidavit?
MICHAEL FREDRICK: No, he did not.
Q: He didn't?
MICHAEL FREDERICK: No, he did not.

...

Billy Nolas, an attorney, was employed by the office of Capital Collateral Rep. (CCR). He represented Boone after his January '88 evidentiary hearing, and worked with Boone during his preparation brief to the Eleventh Circuit Court of Appeals. Mr. Nolas stated the following in his affidavit:

BILLY NOLAS: ... *I was aware of Michael Fredrick's affidavit obtained by CCR in 1988 and the one obtained from him in 1987. At the John Mills hearing in federal court in January, 1988 the State represented to the Court and CCR that the information contained in Michael Fredrick's 1988 affidavit did not contain any Brady material or information relevant to an ineffective assistance of counsel claim. The judge agreed with the State and ruled the affidavit was not relevant...*

I did not have a basis for contesting the State's representation or the federal district's court's ruling. I had no additional information that Michael Fredrick had more to say than what he attested to in his 1988 affidavit. I was unaware that Michael Fredrick, in 1988, was still afraid of the State's actions and repercussions, and thus, was less than forthcoming.

I did not see a basis for pursuing this matter further. The State had accepted the 1988 affidavit as representing what Mr. Fredrick would say, and convinced the federal judge that even so, Mr. Fredrick's affidavit did not demonstrate State misconduct...

Had I known that Michael Fredrick had additional information to reveal, I would have done things differently and pursued this information. I would have really investigated the matter; contacted Mr. Fredrick and confronted him with the previously undisclosed information (including information about motive, bias, interest and motivation to distort, shade or withhold facts in order to assist the State)... It is very important evidence and raises important issues implicating the reliability and validity of Mr. Mills' conviction and death sentence."

It wasn't until November of 1996, almost 8 years after his previous statement, when Michael was confronted again – twice – by investigators of CCR, that he spoke the following under oath:

MICHAEL FREDRICK: *My name is Michael Fredrick. In 1982 I was arrested in Tallahassee. I was questioned in Tallahassee and taken to the Wakulla Co. jail. While in the Wakulla Co. jail I was coerced into making a statement. For three nights I was interrogated all night. I was physically assaulted. This was done by law enforcement and the State Attorney's office.*

I was shown an award poster with a photo of Les Lawhon. There was a reward of, I believe, $10,000 for information leading to his whereabouts. I was told that if I could lead the police to Mr. Lawhon's whereabouts I would be given the money.

The State brought up the name of John Mills. They said, something like, we know you have been hanging with John Mills, Jr. They also told me that they knew his girlfriend bonded me out of jail.

I was told that if I would testify for the State and help them convict John Mills, Jr., that I would serve "nary a day."

The State also contacted my mother. They told her that if I did not testify they would give me the electric chair. They told me that, too.

Because of all the pressure – the interrogations, physical abuse, threats – I made a statement that involved John Mills, Jr. I did not willingly make any statement about Les Lawhon or anything pertaining to Les Lawhon.

The State also promised me that if I testified for the State and helped them convict John Mills, Jr., they would take care of all my other charges.

Right after I was charged, the prosecutor began contacting me on how to testify. He told me to sit up straight in the chair and face the jury when I was testifying. He also typed up a script. The prosecutor did this so that I could remember what to say. I was coerced by the State to testify falsely. I was being coerced and coached prior to ever agreeing to change my plea.

In 1987 I signed an affidavit for CCR. That affidavit is true. But Tim Harley told me, in the Wakulla Co. Courthouse, that CCR was trying to put me in the electric chair. He also told me that if I testified to the sworn affidavit that I would go to trial for murder today. He told me that I would face the electric chair. Because of what Tim Harley said to me, I said the affidavit was not true."

...

While on the witness stand during Boone's original trial in 1982, Michael testified to the following about Les Lawhon's home:

Q: Had you ever been to that trailer before?
MICHAEL FREDRICK: No, sir.
Q: Do you know or did you know Les Lawhon?
MICHAEL FREDRICK: No, sir.
Q: Did you know his wife, Shirley Lawhon?
MICHAEL FREDRICK: Yes, sir.
Q: How did you know her?
MICHAEL FREDRICK: I used to work at the Wakulla Manor.
Q: Did you know where she lived?
MICHAEL FREDRICK: No, sir.
Q: Were you ever at her house?
MICHAEL FREDRICK: No, sir.

Q: Your mother works there at the Wakulla Manor, too, doesn't she?
MICHAEL FREDRICK: Yes, sir.
Q: Has your mother ever told you where Shirley Lawhon lives?
MICHAEL FREDRICK: No, sir.
Q: And had your mother taken you by where Shirley Lawhon lived?
MICHAEL FREDRICK: No, sir.
Q: Had you ever been to that trailer before in your life?
MICHAEL FREDRICK: No, sir.
Q: Had you ever seen Les Lawhon before March 5, 1982.
MICHAEL FREDRICK: No, sir.

On further examination, Michael was also asked about the elusive Debra Mock:

Q: Now, isn't it a fact, Mr. Fredrick, that on March 5, 1982, that Ms. Debra Mock, the day that you went over and murdered Les Lawhon, that she was in that truck?
MICHAEL FREDRICK: No, sir, I didn't even know Debra Mock during March 5, 1982.
Q: You're saying you started dating her after that?
MICHAEL FREDRICK: It wasn't a dating.
Q: You had a relationship with her, didn't you?
MICHAEL FREDRICK: One night affair.
Q: That is the only time you have seen her?
MICHAEL FREDRICK: No, it's not the only time I've seen her.
Q: But it is your testimony that she was not with you on March 5, 1982, the day that you went out there and killed Les Lawhon?
MICHAEL FREDRICK: I did not kill Mr. Les Lawhorn and Debbie Mock, I did not know of her at that time.

...

The State's Prosecution team may have known a lot more than was revealed before the trial even began.

In the State's fifth motion in limine, the State asked that Boone's Defense team not mention certain things about Michael Fredrick at trial:

MR.KERWIN: During the course of the deposition, Michael Fredrick was asked did he procure white women to work as prostitutes. Was he paid to burn down the Barwick Crab House. And there was allegations that he was a drug dealer. Now, he admitted selling drugs. So let me go to the first two first: Judge, we're not talking about allowing the Defense attorney to develop his case. I don't see what saying Michael Fredrick – asking him, "Isn't it true, Mr. Fredrick, that you procured white women to work as prostitutes," has got to do with this case at all, except if Mr. Randolph wants to show bad character or propensity. And Judge, the courts in Florida have said you cannot use specific instances of conduct to show bad character or propensity to commit a crime. And, you know, just the allegation that, "Isn't it a fact that you procured white women to work as prostitutes," I mean, that is just – it's got nothing to do with this case.
MR. RANDOLPH: Your Honor, maybe we could save some time. That was not a question that I was going to ask, in the first place, that he procured white women to work as prostitutes. That question phrased in that manner is not one which I think would be appropriate or has probative value. I'm not saying that there won't be other matters that will come out related to white women, because I think I will be able to show that it is in fact relevant.
THE COURT: Number one as written –
MR.KERWIN: Are you talking about sale of property? I mean, I'm just saying, if there is anything to do with him procuring, pimping, dealing with prostitutes in a sex trade or something like that, I don't see how that is relevant.
THE COURT: Number one as written then, is granted.
MR.RANDOLPH: Right.
THE COURT: You say you're not going to use it anyway.
MR.RANDOLPH: No, I'm not going to use that.

THE COURT: How about number two?

MR. KERWIN: Number two is the same thing, Judge. I mean, it's just a bare allegation.

MR. RANDOLPH: Judge, I don't have anything to back it up, I mean anything that I can admit to back it up.

THE COURT: Number two?

MR. RANDOLPH: Right. I don't have anything that I can really -

THE COURT: Okay. If you can't, it is granted them.

MR. RANDOLPH: I'm not going to ask that question. I can't.

THE COURT: Number three?

MR. KERWIN: Number three, Judge, he said that he sold drugs but I don't see how the fact -

THE COURT: I think he's got a right to ask him if he sold drugs or anything then to show his character to a degree. I'm going allow number three not as a drug dealer but that he sold drugs.

MR. RANDOLPH: Judge, I think the testimony would come out that on the day of this incident he said that he was on cocaine at that time, or that morning.

MR. KERWIN: Fine. The use of drugs, I'm not talking about.

MR. RANDOLPH: Well, some of the other witnesses – we'll just have to wait and see how it develops – but as written -

MR. KERWIN: You're not going to ask him about drug dealing-

MR. RANDOLPH: I just say I'm going to ask him about drug dealings, but I didn't say as written, the way it is now, no.

...

Maybe Boone's Defense team should have worked harder for the right to ask Michael Fredrick a great deal more than they did. But then again, they may not have known, or were not made privy to the information that would come out close to 15 years later.

During the time of trial in 1982, the State knew about a woman named Marsha Porter. During the period when Les Lawhon had disappeared and the search for him began, Ms. Porter spoke with Detective Charlie Ash of the Leon County Sheriff's Dept.; the same Mr. Ash who received a phone call from Sheriff David Harvey in Wakulla, requesting help in finding Michael Fredrick; the same Mr. Ash who arrested Michael at Crumps Tavern, in Frenchtown.

Again, the State knew of Marsha Porter during the trial of 1982. Her official affidavit – from CCR – came years later:

MARSHA PORTER: *"My name is Marsha Porter. In the early 1980s I was living in the Frenchtown area of Tallahassee. I was a prostitute and a drug addict. While working the streets I met a white girl by the name of Debra Mock. Debra's nickname was 'Dee'. She told me she needed money and asked me about turning "tricks." We soon became friends and Dee would stay at my place in Frenchtown.*

A black man by the name of Michael Fredrick hung out in Frenchtown. He would claim that he could provide some of the girls working the street a better life…he won their trust and became their pimp. Michael Fredrick became Dee's pimp.

Michael Fredrick set up many of Dee's "dates." Michael Fredrick was a very violent man. I saw him beat his girls.

A white man by the name of Les Lawhon started hanging out in Frenchtown with Michael Fredrick. Everyone called Les "pumpkin head." His picture is attached to this statement. I would see Les and Michael together. Les Lawhon was one of Dee's regular customers.

Les often invited Dee and Fredrick's to his trailer for alcohol and drugs. He lived in Wakulla County. Les said that everyone would have to leave before his wife got home from work. I once gave Les, Dee, Michael Fredrick, and a woman named Twana Byrd a ride over to Les' trailer.

I remember one time I picked up Dee at the El Camino after one of her "dates" with Les Lawhon. Michael Fredricks was beating Dee in the parking lot. Les locked himself in the room and would not come out. I saw him looking out the window and watching Fredrick's beat Dee.

In 1982 I noticed that Les was not coming to Frenchtown anymore. I asked Dee about Les and if she had seen him. Dee said, "You don't have to worry about that goofy motherfucker anymore." That was the last time Dee and I talked about Les.

I did, however, talk about Les Lawhon with a police officer named Charlie Ash. I knew Charlie because he would eat at a restaurant in Frenchtown where my mother was a cook. Charlie knew my whole family. I always called him "Uncle Charlie."

After Les Lawhon stopped coming to Frenchtown, Charlie Ash asked me a lot of questions about Les, Dee Mock, and Michael Fredrick. He showed me some pictures, too. I told Charlie that the three of them would get together in Frenchtown, and about how Fredrick's would hook up Les and Dee at the El Camino Motel so they could have sex. I also told Charlie about driving to Les' trailer and the drugs. Charlie told me that he already knew what I was telling him. Sometime after I talked to Charlie Ash, Dee Mock moved to Alaska.

I have never known a black man named John Mills, Boone, or Ans Serene. I do not remember anyone using those names hanging out in Frenchtown back in the time when Dee Mock, Les Lawhon, and Michael Fredrick were doing their thing.

Up until about one year ago, I was living in the streets and moving around a lot. Part of the time I was living in Tampa and South Florida. I was known as "Sporty Red". Because I used that nickname, most people did not know my real name. About a year ago I got treatment for my drug addiction. I am now clean, use my real name and have a place to live."

...

Marsha Porter gave the investigators with the CCR other names of people who knew of the connection to Michael Fredrick, Debra Mock, and Les Lawhon. People such as Bertha Earl:

BERTHA EARL: *"My name is Bertha Earl. Around 1981 and 1982 I was a prostitute in the part of Tallahassee known as Frenchtown. My pimp was a black man named Michael Fredrick.*

At that time there was a white man who came to Frenchtown looking for girls to have sex with him. I always called him "goofy pumpkin head". His picture is attached to this statement. This white man hung out with Michael Fredrick. He would ask Michael to hook him up with a girl. This man asked Michael for a girl many times.

Michael Fredrick was also the pimp for a white girl named Dee Mock. Dee had blonde hair and wore a blue bandanna. Michael would usually hook up Dee and this white man for sex.

This white man would ask us to go to his trailer to do drugs. Michael Fredrick, Dee Mock, and me would go to his trailer in Wakulla and cook up cocaine. We did this several times.

This is the first time anyone has asked me about going to the white man's trailer with Michael Fredrick and Dee Mock and the white man being in Frenchtown..."

...

Monica Hall was arrested in 1982 in Franklin County with Michael Fredrick. She saw something very peculiar that Michael and Debra Mock were doing once; she talks about it in her affidavit:

MONICA HALL: *"My name is Monica Hall. In the early 1980s I knew a white girl in Frenchtown named Dee Mock. Dee had blonde hair and always wore a blue bandanna. She was a small woman.*

Dee was a prostitute in Frenchtown. Dee was going with a black guy named Michael Fredrick. Michael Fredrick was also Dee's pimp. They were always together. I knew them for about six months or so.

Sometimes Michael Fredrick, Dee, and me would hang out at the El Camino Motel. Dee turned a lot of tricks at the El Camino Motel. One time, Michael Fredrick, and Dee Mock were selling guitars, amplifiers, and stereo equipment.

A couple of months after they were selling all of that stuff the three of us were arrested in Franklin County. A black guy named 'Sunshine' was with us. Michael Fredrick was throwing handfuls of pills out the window as the cops followed us. One of the cops that pulled us over told Dee and I, "Don't you know that you are riding around with murderers and ex-cons?" The cop then took us to a friend's house in Wakulla.

After the arrest in Franklin County I never saw Dee again. I heard she left town."

...

And then there's Tonya Lockhart. Her information is the most chilling of all the confessions:

TONYA LOCKHART: *"In the early 1980s I was living in the Frenchtown area of Tallahassee... I met a white girl by the name of Debra Mock. I knew Debra as 'Dee'.*

Dee was a prostitute in Frenchtown and was doing a lot of drugs. I would hang out in or around Crumps Tavern. Dee and I would smoke pot and drink beer together.

Dee would always wear a blue bandanna tied around her head. I could always recognize her on the streets by her blue bandanna and dyed blonde hair.

In early 1982 I was hanging out in Crumps Tavern in Frenchtown when Dee came in the bar. Dee sat down and started bragging about someone being killed. Dee said, "I left my bandanna where he was killed, but no one can link it to me."

Dee was not wearing her bandanna that night. I never saw Dee wear the blue bandanna again. Later she left town and I never saw her again..."

...

Due to the State failing to disclose the identity of these witnesses, Boone's counsel would have no way of knowing the connection of these people to Michael, Debra 'Dee' Mock, or Les Lawhon.

Such information would have crumbled the entire testimony of the State's 'star witness'. No evidence linked Boone to Les' death other than the word of Michael Fredrick, and the property Boone claimed Michael gave him as payment for a debt.

If Monica Hall is being truthful (almost 15 years later, why exactly would she lie?) then even the property that was stolen comes into question. Michael said he took only the class ring when Boone wasn't looking. Yet, someone is swearing to the fact that he and 'Dee' Mock were selling – on the street – items strikingly similar to those taken from the Lawhon home.

Michael's testimony of not knowing Les Lawhon and having never been to Les' house, all falls apart. The premise that he drove around with Boone and suddenly – in the middle of a rainstorm – wound up at Les' front door, doesn't necessarily have the 'ring of truth'.

It was a Friday afternoon, when most everyone would've been at work, with the kids at school. Why roam such great lengths; from Sopchoppy, to Panacea, to Medart; from one house to the other, when there are numerous houses in between to choose from?

Michael stated in his original confession that it was he who went into Les' bedroom and took the shotgun. Again, this confession was later changed, when it was taped.

Did Les, simply, tell Michael where the shotgun was? Or could it be that someone who, having been in Les' home before, knew exactly where the weapons were placed?

If the company being kept were that of a, shall we say, 'intimate' nature, making use of the bedroom necessary, could that person know something more about the layout, the bedroom, the secrets of the house itself?

Even more fascinating is the note from Rev. Lawhon stating why Les could not have burned down his own home or abandoned his loved ones.

The Reverend's note says that almost every stitch of Les' clothing was accounted for. It is Shirley's clothing – female items – that are missing. It is doubtful that Michael would've needed these clothes. But maybe someone else, like a young woman, or 16-year old teenage girl, did.

There was no forced entry into Les' home, as proven by FDLE analysts. The knob was turned, the door was opened. Someone was let in.

Maybe the Reverend Lawhon was onto something when he wrote in his letter:

"It is possible that Les "jumped" them, or possibly even recognized them..."

Could it be, that someone who knew Les, along with a second person who knew Les' desires, arrived at his door one dark, stormy afternoon and said, "Come, take a ride with us"?

Or: A person(s) arrived simply to pass the time with Les, doing who knows what?

A toxicology test would have been helpful being that Michael Fredrick testified in court that he was high "on cocaine". Two of the previous sworn affidavits speak of drug use – both the practice and witnessing of it – between Michael, 'Dee' Mock, and Les. Sadly, Les' remains would've been too decomposed after months in the wilderness, battling nature's elements, for anyone to find out.

Knowing the person(s) as he may have – from what the testimonies above lead us to believe – Les opened not only his door, but his heart as well, answering "Yes" to a situation presented him, possibly believing he was in the company of friends, never to be heard from again.

Warning: The race card will now be pulled.

The question: Why must a black person's love, or respect for black history, black culture, black people, and the black experience overall, be equated with a hatred of white people?

I can hear the sighs of exasperation; can feel the tingling on the back of my neck as the burning eyes of Wakulla's angered begin to roll, saying to themselves, "this issue is unimportant".

Yet, when revving up their internet, flipping their television channels, turning their radio dial, or thumbing through their magazines and newspapers, they see daily exactly how important it is, and how living in blindness has caused painful, treacherous – and often deadly – accidents, well into the new millennium, on our watch. If this were not so, the election of a black president would not have come as such an American shock – complete with heartfelt tears and jeers – in such an enlightened, colorblind age as our own.

All that to ask: Is it possible that after being raised in a predominately white county of 11,000; where most businesses were owned by whites; where the judicial, educational, and financial systems were run, populated and owned by whites; where the majority of social events, and media outlets were dominated by whites, that – triggered by the death of his best friend (also white), and an initial stint in jail for his refusal to 'snitch' on others, Boone was finally beginning to embrace the Black American male he actually was?

Is it possible that he finally accepted the self-evident truth that 'all men are created equal'? And that all men are brothers? And that he shared this newfound knowledge with others like himself in Wakulla, only to encounter opposition from the bible-belted saints while doing so?

Is it possible that in a Christian county, where prayers are given not only from the pulpit, but before official business meetings, that Boone, a practicing Muslim, repudiated – by his very presence and beliefs – those holy passages that spoke of certain people forever destined to be slaves?

Then again, what sane Wakulla juror, or judge, would ever believe the statements of a convicted felon, and a handful of modern-day Mary Magdalenes, against the good Christian son of a preacher-man?

...

A Motion to Compel the Disclosure of Documents was filed November 5, and 14, of 1996. The Office of the State Attorney, The Wakulla Co. Sheriff's Office, and the Leon Co. Sheriff's Dept. were among the three State agencies asked to disclose any and all documents regarding the case and those involved.

Counsel was informed by State Attorney Tim Harley that the Wakulla Co. Sheriff's Office had been contacted and were in full compliance with their request. Yet, the wrong documents were received. Counsel was told Leon Co. Sheriff's Dept. had no documents that met their requests. Without these records, the Defendant is unable to fully plead any claims for relief, or stay of execution, and therefore, the Defendants motions will be denied or dismissed.

All attorneys working on the John Mills, Jr. case knew the importance of this information. Others knew it too. And of the utmost importance, was locating Debra Mock.

How does a 16-year-old (allegedly) drug-addled prostitute from Wakulla County disappear to Alaska, or to places unknown, with no way for the law, lawyers, or national databases to reach her? We often hear of feats like this being accomplished by seasoned criminals who manage to elude the law for years; or by authorities who take action to protect a victim. Ms. Mock, in this instance, was not a victim, but possibly an accomplice to a crime.

If nothing more, she may have had information important to this case that could have saved a (possibly) innocent man's life. Again: She was someone's teenage child. Where is she?

A trip to Alaska – on her part – would require some serious preparation and cash. No one can speak about her ability to plan for her future, but the likelihood of that much cash being located in Tallahassee's Frenchtown section in 1982 – and even today – by an (allegedly) drug stimulated 16-year-old prostitute, is sincerely doubtful.

'Crowd sourcing', as outreach for public funding is currently known, may not have been considered the most legal route for a young woman of her (alleged) talents. But, a guiding hand that could touch – and make speedily available – certain resources, would've been. And if this were the case, who, one must ask, could've extended her this sorely needed assistance?

Even more frightening, is the 'reason' why this young child had to ever encounter such a brutal life-situation that led to her disappearance to begin with.

Why was a teenage girl, from our county, left to roam aimlessly in this way? Then again, given the world and the ways we've not only inherited, but have created, the inability to pull our young ones closer, as opposed to the impulse to drive them away, is all too common.

Her face appears in the local 1982 high school yearbook during her freshman year, for that year only. Then, as the saying goes, the lady vanishes. A dark, menacing hand reaches down from the clouds, plucking her away as easily as the dandelion crouched among the roses. To this day, her whereabouts are not known.

Until she arrives to answer for her alleged role in this affair, there is reasonable doubt.

Wakulla: A county built on the un-godliest of mysteries, where the churches roll on.

PART FOUR
Did you hear what he said...?

Chapter Fifteen

It is best that John Mills, Jr. speak for himself. To represent who he was at the time his hometown – his family – stood in the shadow of the nightmare. The testimony that follows begins when he is first examined by his own lawyer, Mr. Randolph:

RANDOLPH: Would you state your complete name for the record?
Mills: John Mills, Jr.
RANDOLPH: Mr. Mills, have you ever been convicted of a felony?
Mills: Yessir.
RANDOLPH: How many times?
Mills: Four.
RANDOLPH: Are you currently incarcerated in the Wakulla County Jail?
Mills: Yessir.
RANDOLPH: Mr. Mills, are you referred to as Ans Serene?
Mills: Yessir.
RANDOLPH: What type of name is Ans Serene?
Mills: Islamic.
RANDOLPH: Is there difference between an Islamic Muslim and a so-called, or, Black Muslim?
Mills: Is there a difference?
RANDOLPH: Yes.
Mills: No sir.
RANDOLPH: Are you afraid of the Islamic faith?
Mills: No sir.
RANDOLPH: Are there any white people in the Islamic faith?
Mills: Yes sir.
RANDOLPH: Are there all nationalities in the Islamic faith?
Mills: Yes sir.
RANDOLPH: How are white people referred to in the Islamic faith?
Mills: Caucasian.
RANDOLPH: Is that how you refer to white people?
Mills: Yes sir.
RANDOLPH: How long have you been studying this religion?

Mills: Six years.
RANDOLPH: Mr. Mills, where have you lived most of your life?
Mills: Sopchoppy, in a place called Buckhorn.
RANDOLPH: Prior to your incarceration, back in I think it is '81, were any of your associates – I think you use the term – Caucasians?
Mills: Sir?
RANDOLPH: Were any of your associates then, Caucasians?
Mills: Yes sir.
RANDOLPH: Who were some of those?
Mills: Mr. Joe Morgan Cruise, Johnny Cruise, Gilbert Sanders, Brett Craig, Sam Dunlap, Sam Sanders…
RANDOLPH: Are those people that you just named, people that live in the Buckhorn community?
Mills: Yes sir.
RANDOLPH: Have any of those persons that you just named ever stayed overnight at your house?
Mills: Yes sir.
RANDOLPH: At that time were you also living in the same house?
Mills: Yes sir.
RANDOLPH: Since you have been incarcerated since the later part of '81 or '82, have you any chance to come in contact with any – what you refer to as – 'Caucasians', along with Fawndretta Galimore?
Mills: Yes sir.
RANDOLPH: And who were they?
Mills: Joe Morgan Cruise, in Panacea.
RANDOLPH: Alright. When was that, by the way?
Mills: It was around… in February, if I'm not mistaken.
RANDOLPH: Alright. Where did this take place?
Mills: I went by his house. I used to work for him on a shrimp-boat, and I went by his house. I hadn't seen him in some time. He was a friend of mine, he was an elderly dude, you know, and I went by to see him.
RANDOLPH: What was your father's name?
Mills: John Mills, Sr.
RANDOLPH: And is Mr. Mills – John Mills, Sr. – still alive?
Mills: No sir.
RANDOLPH: What is your mother's name?
Mills: Blonzie Mae Mills.

RANDOLPH: And the area that you said – that you did live in down in Buckhorn – does your family own a great deal of property, down that way?
Mills: Yes sir.
RANDOLPH: And is that why you were living down in the family home?
Mills: Yes sir.
RANDOLPH: When did you meet Fawndretta Galimore?
Mills: In November.
RANDOLPH: November of what year?
Mills: '81.
RANDOLPH: And where did you meet her?
Mills: At a friend's house in Tallahassee.
RANDOLPH: Okay. How would you characterize your relationship with Ms. Gallimore?
Mills: Boyfriend / Girlfriend.
RANDOLPH: Mr. Mills, under your religion – the Islamic religion that you've embraced – what did you refer to her as?
Mills: Queen.
RANDOLPH: And what did you refer to yourself as?
Mills: King.
RANDOLPH: As you talked to her on a day to day basis, what did you normally call her?
Mills: Fawn.
RANDOLPH: Fawn? Is that her nickname?
Mills: Short for Fawndretta.
RANDOLPH: When did she move to Buckhorn with you?
Mills: It was in December.
RANDOLPH: December of what year?
Mills: '82, if I'm not mistaken.
RANDOLPH: You mean '81. This is '82.
Mills: '81.
RANDOLPH: Did she stay with you there, in your mother's home?
Mills: Yes sir.
RANDOLPH: Could you describe the house there in Buckhorn that the two of you lived in?
Mills: It is a 4-bedroom house, on the left-hand side, and it's got a carport on it. And it has a café, not too far from it.
RANDOLPH: Was that your father's café?
Mills: Yes sir.
RANDOLPH: Were there any weapons kept inside the house?

Mills: Yes sir.
RANDOLPH: What kind of weapons?
Mills: All different types of guns. Antiques, mostly.
RANDOLPH: Alright. And whose firearms were they?
Mills: My father's.
RANDOLPH: Where were they kept?
Mills: In various parts of the house; under the bed, and places of this nature.
RANDOLPH: What kind of work, Mr. Mills, were you doing during this period of time?
Mills: Carpentry.
RANDOLPH: Carpentry for whom?
Mills: Myself.
RANDOLPH: You say carpentry for yourself. Is that in conjunction with anyone else in your family?
Mills: My mother.
RANDOLPH: Alright. And what would you do for your mother and yourself in the carpentry line?
Mills: Repairing houses.
RANDOLPH: Does your family own several houses down there in that area?
Mills: Yes sir.
RANDOLPH: Have you had those houses down there for a long time?
Mills: Yes sir.
RANDOLPH: And those were the ones that you were repairing?
Mills: Yes sir.
RANDOLPH: When did you meet Michael Fredrick?
Mills: In February.
RANDOLPH: And where did you meet Michael Fredrick?
Mills: In the Wakulla Jail.
RANDOLPH: Okay. Were you in the same cell with him?
Mills: Yes sir.
RANDOLPH: How would you characterize your relationship with Michael Fredrick?
Mills: Friend.
RANDOLPH: Did you stay in there for the period of time with Michael Fredrick.
Mills: Yes sir.
RANDOLPH: In the later part of February, did you, in any way, arrange to get Michael Fredrick out of jail?
Mills: Yes sir.

RANDOLPH: How did you do that?
Mills: I called Fawndretta and told her I wanted him to bond out.
RANDOLPH: Okay. And this is the same Fawndretta that we have discussed already?
Mills: Yes sir.
RANDOLPH: And how was the money to be given for the bond?
Mills: He told me if I would get him out of jail, he would give me $200 the day that I got him out. The bond that I got him out on was $175, which would be $25 difference, on that day that he got out.
RANDOLPH: That is, if he could get out on the same day you asked Fawndretta to get him out on?
Mills: Yes sir.
RANDOLPH: Was that the agreement between you and he?
Mills: Yes sir.
RANDOLPH: When was he to pay you back?
Mills: The day that he got out.
RANDOLPH: Were you still incarcerated at that time?
Mills: Yes sir.
RANDOLPH: When was the first time you checked on the money that had been paid for the bond?
Mills: When Fawndretta came back to visit me, I asked her had Michael paid her. She said no. So I got out about 3 days after that, if I'm not mistaken, and I went by to see him. I asked him did he have my money. He looked as though he was surprised to see me. He said no.
RANDOLPH: Alright. So you went by his house. And where was he staying at that time?
Mills: In Crawfordville.
RANDOLPH: Did he indicate to you in any way when he would be able to come up with the money?
Mills: No, he didn't. He said he would get it.
RANDOLPH: Alright, but he did not have it on the first occasion that you went by?
Mills: No sir.
RANDOLPH: Now, after that day in which you have described to the jury as talking to Michael Fredrick about your money, did you start going around with him. When I say 'going around', going from place to place with him.
Mills: Yes sir.
RANDOLPH: Did you go to his trailer?
Mills: Yes sir.

RANDOLPH: Did he, in turn, come to your house?
Mills: Yes sir.
RANDOLPH: On these occasions in which the two of you were riding around, or going from place to place, who would be driving?
Mills: I was.
RANDOLPH: Okay. And why were you doing the driving?
Mills: He said he didn't have no transportation, and knowed some people he might be able to get my money from. So I took him to these places that he wanted to go.
RANDOLPH: Alright. Did you take him to other places, other than on a search for money?
Mills: No sir.
RANDOLPH: Okay. Were there any discussions at all at that time about when the money was going to be paid, when you were going around with him?
Mills: Yes sir.
RANDOLPH: Was there ever an understanding about any other items of property that could be given in return for the money? – the $200, I think, that you said was owed?
Mills: Yes sir.
RANDOLPH: And what kind of understanding was that?
Mills: He said he was going to give me some Dobermans; that he had some Dobermans that his mother was keeping for him. And he also said that he had some guns and stuff that he was going to give to me. So we went by his mother's house for some Dobermans. There wasn't no Dobermans, he was lying to me there. And I got tired of him lying to me so I told him that each day that he didn't pay my money now, would be a dollar on a dollar, for each day he didn't pay me my money.
RANDOLPH: You're referring to the $200?
Mills: Yes sir.
RANDOLPH: Alright. Did he indicate to you at that time that he would get the money?
Mills: Yes sir.
RANDOLPH: To your knowledge, was any money ever given to Fawndretta during that same period of time by Michael Fredrick?
Mills: No sir.
RANDOLPH: Now, a few minutes ago you indicated that as you rode around together that you would be doing the driving. What kind of vehicle would you normally ride in?
Mills: Mostly the truck.
RANDOLPH: Would you describe that truck for the jury?

Mills: It's a Dodge '72 truck, got a camper.
RANDOLPH: Is that the same truck that a photograph has been introduced on?
Mills: Yes sir.
RANDOLPH: I show you some exhibits which I think are marked 4-C, and I ask you to take a look at those and tell me whether or not that looks like the truck that you and Michael Fredrick rode around in.
Mills: Yes sir.
RANDOLPH: Alright, and is that the truck that was owned by your mother?
Mills: Yes sir.
RANDOLPH: Were there ever any occasions during this time, when you were riding around from place to place, that Michael had the truck himself?
Mills: Yes sir.
RANDOLPH: Was it on more than one occasion?
Mills: Yes sir.
RANDOLPH: If you would, let us move to March 5, 1982, the day that he gave you the property. When is the first time that you saw Michael Fredrick on that day?
Mills: Someone dropped him off at my house. I was surprised to see him. He came in and knocked on the door, and I asked him did he have my money from the beginning, and he said no. And he suggested to me that he would like to use my truck.
RANDOLPH: Alright. Now who was at home during that time?
Mills: Me and Fawndretta.
RANDOLPH: What time of day was this?
Mills: It was around 1:30 or two, something like that.
RANDOLPH: And where was Fawndretta at that time?
Mills: She was in the room, on the bed.
RANDOLPH: What were you wearing on that occasion?
Mills: I don't exactly know.
RANDOLPH: Alright, I want to show you something, Mr. Mills. I show you what has been marked as State Exhibit #5 – which is a shirt – and I ask you if you have seen – if that is your shirt?
Mills: No sir.
RANDOLPH: Have you ever worn a shirt of this nature?
Mills: No sir.
RANDOLPH: Do you know whether or not this particular shirt was in the truck or not?
Mills: No sir.

RANDOLPH: But you have never had that shirt on?
Mills: No sir.
RANDOLPH: Do you know what Michael Fredrick was wearing that day?
Mills: No sir.
RANDOLPH: Now how long did the three of you stay in the house before anyone left that premises? – there in Buckhorn, the house itself?
Mills: About 30 minutes or so, something like that.
RANDOLPH: Alright. And the first time that you left, would you tell the jury about that?
Mills: The first time that I left, I told him that I needed to go to Sopchoppy if he wanted to use my truck. So I went to Sopchoppy and picked up some honey in the Jr. Food Store. I must've stayed gone about 10 or 15 minutes.
RANDOLPH: Let me ask you this: The first time you left the house, was anyone in the truck with you?
Mills: Yes sir.
RANDOLPH: And who was that?
Mills: Michael Fredrick.
RANDOLPH: Alright, and you stayed gone about 30 minutes?
Mills: 10 or 15 minutes, something like that.
RANDOLPH: And you said it is the Jr. Food Store that you went to?
Mills: Yes sir.
RANDOLPH: Alright. Did you come back to the house?
Mills: Yes sir.
RANDOLPH: Was Mr. Fredrick still in the truck with you?
Mills: Yes sir.
RANDOLPH: Once you arrived back at the house, where is the first place that you went?
Mills: In the kitchen.
RANDOLPH: What was the purpose of going in the kitchen?
Mills: To put some honey on the table.
RANDOLPH: Alright. Where in the house did Mr. Fredrick go?
Mills: He was in the truck.
RANDOLPH: He did not get out?
Mills: No sir.
RANDOLPH: Did you go back of the house?
Mills: Yes sir.
RANDOLPH: And before you left the house, did you retrieve anything at all from the house?

Mills: No sir.
RANDOLPH: Now, you say Mr. Fredrick was still sitting in the truck?
Mills: Yes sir.
RANDOLPH: Why was he still sitting in the truck?
Mills: Him and Fawndretta didn't get along too good. And he didn't like being around her. She was giving him bad vibes, he said.
RANDOLPH: So when you came back out and got in the truck, did you get under the steering-wheel, or did you get on the passenger's side?
Mills: I got up under the steering-wheel.
RANDOLPH: Okay, now, where did the two of you go at that time?
Mills: Kilgore Road.
RANDOLPH: Alright, now, I'm not familiar with –
Mills: That's about a mile away from my house; we have 40 acres of land over there.
RANDOLPH: Let me make sure that everybody understands where you are – where exactly – what road is your house on; the Mills residence?
Mills: It's on 98.
RANDOLPH: Okay, and is that right there in the middle of the Buckhorn community?
Mills: Yes sir.
RANDOLPH: How far is this Kilgore Road from your house?
Mills: About a mile
RANDOLPH: In which direction?
Mills: The right.
RANDOLPH: You turn right?
Mills: Which is west.
RANDOLPH: You turn right, as you were doing, out of your yard; is that what you're saying?
Mills: Turn left if I was going out of my yard.
RANDOLPH: Is there anything down there – any type of fixture, or building – or anything down there near Kilgore Road for identification?
Mills: No sir.
RANDOLPH: Alright, but it is called the Kilgore Road?
Mills: Yes sir.
RANDOLPH: Now, you indicated that you went to the Kilgore Road; was Mr. Fredrick still in the truck?

Mills: Yes sir.
RANDOLPH: What happened when you got to the Kilgore Road?
Mills: The purpose of me going to the Kilgore Road – he suggested to me, did I have anywhere that I could go 'til he got back, in the truck. I told him yes, I needed to go over there and check out some timber we planted years ago.
RANDOLPH: Alright now, does your father own land on Kilgore Road?
Mills: Yes sir.
RANDOLPH: Where is that property in relation – how much land are you talking about?
Mills: 40 acres.
RANDOLPH: And how much land – where is that land in relationship to the road?
Mills: It's about, maybe, 100 yards from the road
RANDOLPH: Okay, and that is his entire spread back there?
Mills: Yes sir.
RANDOLPH: Now your father is no longer living. Do you now partially own that property?
Mills: Yes sir.
RANDOLPH: In regard to – you said you partially own that property; do you partially own everything else in Buckhorn?
Mills: Yes sir.
RANDOLPH: As far as your father is concerned?
Mills: Yes sir.
RANDOLPH: Alright. Do you stand to become a wealthy man when the estate is settled?
Mills: Yes sir.
RANDOLPH: And how much do you think that is valued at?
Mills: $250,000.
RANDOLPH: As your share of it?
Mills: Yes sir.
RANDOLPH: Is there a lawyer working on that case at this time?
Mills: Yes sir.
RANDOLPH: Who is that? Who is the attorney?
Mills: In the case now? – Judge Porter.
RANDOLPH: Alright, now when you got out to Kilgore Road, what happened? Was there any discussion at all between yourself and Mike?
Mills: No sir.
RANDOLPH: What happened at that point?
Mills: I got out of the truck, he said he would be back in a little bit.

RANDOLPH: Okay, was there anyone there at the place near those acres that your father left at that time; any other person down there?
Mills: No sir.
RANDOLPH: And why were you going there again?
Mills: We had planted some pines some years ago; I was going there to check the pines we had planted, to see how big they had gotten.
RANDOLPH: Could you tell us what kind of day it was?
Mills: It was a misty day.
RANDOLPH: How long did you think – how long did you stay there at that time?
Mills: Approximately 2 or 3 hours.
RANDOLPH: Okay. And what were you doing during that 2 or 3 hour period?
Mills: I was observing the trees.
RANDOLPH: And did it take you the entire time to walk through those 40 acres?
Mills: No sir.
RANDOLPH: What happened?
Mills: I was waiting for Fredrick to get back, but he never showed, so I just stayed there looking.
RANDOLPH: Where were you when Fredrick returned?
Mills: Side of the road.
RANDOLPH: Okay. Could you tell the jury whether or not he had (something) on the truck when he returned?
Mills: Yes sir.
RANDOLPH: What did he have on the truck?
Mills: All types of property; stuff in the truck.
RANDOLPH: Now, you see the documents which have been marked as evidence in this case by the State, right beside you?
Mills: Yes sir.
RANDOLPH: Are those the same items, basically, that were on the truck?
Mills: Yes sir.
RANDOLPH: Did Mr. Fredrick give you all of that property?
Mills: Yes sir
RANDOLPH: Now you said – I think you told the jury – that it was about $200 that he owed you?
Mills: Yes sir.
RANDOLPH: Why did he give you all of this property?

Mills: After the debt he didn't pay me I told him that it would be a dollar on the dollar each day he didn't pay me, because he had been lying to me. And he said the property was just to show how much he appreciated me getting him out jail. He said I didn't have to get him out, but it was just to show appreciation that I did.

RANDOLPH: You took all the property?

Mills: Yes sir.

RANDOLPH: Alright, where was that property taken?

Mills: At my house.

RANDOLPH: Did you then, in turn, drive the truck back to your house?

Mills: Yes sir.

RANDOLPH: What happened to this property once you got it back to the house?

Mills: Me and Fawndretta unloaded it off the truck.

RANDOLPH: Okay. Where did you put it?

Mills: Put it in the shed.

RANDOLPH: And where is the shed in relationship to your house?

Mills: Right out of the backdoor.

RANDOLPH: Now you said – I think earlier – that you have lived in the Buckhorn community all you life. Did you know Mr. Les Lawhon?

Mills: No sir.

RANDOLPH: Alright. Did you go down to Pigott's and Langston's?

Mills: Yes sir.

RANDOLPH: Is it a possibility that you could have come in contact with him?

Mills: Yes sir.

RANDOLPH: To your recollection, have you had a conversation with Mr. Lawhon?

Mills: No sir.

RANDOLPH: Now on the day – let's get back to the property – on the day that Mr. Fredrick came back with the property, did he tell you where the property came from?

Mills: No sir.

RANDOLPH: Did you ask him where the property came from?

Mills: No sir.

RANDOLPH: Were you eventually arrested, Mr. Mills – at this courthouse – in connection to another matter, unrelated to the Les Lawhon case?

Mills: Yes sir.
RANDOLPH: Who was with you at that time?
Mills: Fawndretta.
RANDOLPH: And why were you down there at the courthouse?
Mills: It was concerning – discussing – my father's estate.
RANDOLPH: Is that with the Judge?
Mills: Yes sir.
RANDOLPH: Judge Harper?
Mills: Yes sir.
RANDOLPH: Alright. Where were you arrested?
Mills: Out back of the courthouse.
RANDOLPH: Okay. And, at the time, was Fawndretta with you?
Mills: Yes sir.
RANDOLPH: Alright. Did you make any statement to her at that time that you were arrested?
Mills: Yes sir.
RANDOLPH: What did you tell her?
Mills: I told her to get the stuff out of the shed.
RANDOLPH: Okay. This is the statement you made to her right at the back of the courthouse?
Mills: Yes sir.
RANDOLPH: Why did you tell Fawndretta to take the stuff out – to remove the stuff?
Mills: My mother's house had gotten broken-in once before and a lot of valuable stuff was stolen out of there.
RANDOLPH: Do you keep a lot of antiques and things in your own house, other than the guns that you described?
Mills: Yes sir.
RANDOLPH: I mean, talking about the house in Buckhorn?
Mills: Yes sir.
RANDOLPH: Now you were taken into custody and taken to the jail by the Sheriff's Department at that time. Is that correct?
Mills: Yes sir.
RANDOLPH: Did you later see Fawndretta Galimore again?
Mills: Yes sir.
RANDOLPH: While you were in jail?
Mills: Yes sir.
RANDOLPH: And did she come over to the jail to see you?
Mills: Yes sir.
RANDOLPH: Alright. Did you have any conversation with Fawndretta at that time?
Mills: After I got arrested?

RANDOLPH: Yes, at the jail.
Mills: That day?
RANDOLPH: No, not the same day, once you got in jail.
Mills: Yes sir.
RANDOLPH: Did you ask her anything at that time?
Mills: I asked her had she moved the property out of the house.
RANDOLPH: Okay. And what was her response?
Mills: She had.
RANDOLPH: What was your understanding again as to what this property was that you had at your house as relationship to Mr. Fredrick? – what was your understanding as to why he had given you the property?
Mills: In payment of a debt.
RANDOLPH: Now you have heard testimony from Officer Gandy; that he talked to you. Is that correct?
Mills: Yes sir.
RANDOLPH: Was there another gentleman with him when he came to talk to you?
Mills: Yes sir.
RANDOLPH: And how many people were in the room at the time Mr. Gandy talked to you?
Mills: Two of us. Mr. Gandy's associate and myself.
RANDOLPH: Now, did you tell Mr. Gandy the truth that day?
Mills: No sir.
RANDOLPH: Alright. You told him that you did not have any knowledge of this property, and that you did not know Michael Fredrick. You said that was not the truth?
Mills: No sir, that was not the truth.
RANDOLPH: Alright. Why did you not tell Mr. Gandy about this deal that you had with Michael Fredrick?
Mills: Me and Mr. Gandy had had some quarrels before. We had some misunderstanding.
RANDOLPH: Was that when you were first arrested in another separate matter?
Mills: Yes sir.
RANDOLPH: Alright, so he was involved in that arrest – the last time?
Mills: Yes sir.
RANDOLPH: So you did not disclose to him anything?
Mills: No sir.
RANDOLPH: Have you heard testimony from Ms. Galimore concerning a letter that was written?

Mills: Yes sir.
RANDOLPH: Did you write Ms. Galimore a letter?
Mills: Yes sir.
RANDOLPH: In that letter did you make a statement about 'tell them you had a receipt for the stuff' ?
Mills: Yes sir.
RANDOLPH: What receipt were you talking about?
Mills: Receipt for bonding Michael Fredrick out of jail concerning the property, if anything would come up.
RANDOLPH: Alright. Did you any time refer to Caucasians as 'devils' in that letter?
Mills: No sir.
RANDOLPH: What reference – or what do you call – again one more time, I think we may have touched upon this – but your reference to white people, again, in your religion is what?
Mills: Caucasian.
RANDOLPH: And the reference to black is?
Mills: Balatians.
RANDOLPH: You call black people 'Balatians'?
Mills: Yes sir.
RANDOLPH: Mr. Mills, I want you to look at this jury, and I want to ask you this: Did you go to Les Lawhon's trailer on March 5th, 1982 to burglarize his trailer?
Mills: No sir.
RANDOLPH: Did you – at any time on March 5th, 1982 – go to the trailer of Mr. Les Lawhon and commit arson?
Mills: No sir, I did not.
RANDOLPH: Did you at any time on March 5th '82 go to the trailer of Mr. Les Lawhon and kidnap him?
Mills: No sir, I did not.
RANDOLPH: And finally, Mr. Mills, did you in any way pick up and take Mr. Les Lawhon to the area where his body was found, and shoot and kill Mr. Les Lawhon?
Mills: No sir. I did not.
RANDOLPH: I've no further questions, Your Honor.

The cross examination of John Mills, Jr., by Mr. Harley, prosecution for the State of Florida:

MR. HARLEY: Mr. Mills these convictions you refer to, were they for felonies?
Mills: Yes sir

MR. HARLEY: How many
Mills: Four.

It is here that Boone's lawyer, Mr. Randolph, interjects:

MR. RANDOLPH: Your honor, may I approach the bench on that?

The following conversation was held at the bench, outside the hearing of the jury:

MR. RANDOLPH: I want to strenuously object and protest the State asking that question again when he knows very well the rules are clear that once that question is asked and answered properly that he cannot go back in and ask that question again.
MR. HARLEY: Judge, I don't know that that's the rule, I think that is a proper impeach
MR. RANDOLPH: You cannot impeach a witness – and I ask for a mistrial on that point – because you cannot impeach a witness after he has admitted that he has been convicted of a felony and told the truth a number of times. The only purpose for doing that is to bring that to the jury's attention again, and you cannot do that.
MR. HARLEY: He did exactly the same thing on Michael Fredrick. It is a proper question.
THE COURT: Objection overruled. Mistrial at this time is denied.

The following was held in open court -

MR. HARLEY: Mr. Mills, you sat here and heard all these people testify about how you were together with Michael Fredrick during the period of time after you got out of jail, haven't you?
Mills: Yes, sir.
MR. HARLEY: All those witnesses were telling the truth, weren't they?
Mills: Yes sir
MR. HARLEY: Every one of them you heard testify –
Mills: No sir –
MR. HARLEY: -about you being with Michael Fredrick on many occasions after you and Michael Fredrick got out of jail –
Mills: Repeat the question.

MR. HARLEY: Weren't they telling the truth when they said that you and Michael Fredrick were together on several occasions during the short period of time between when you got out of jail and Les Lawhon was killed?
Mills: Yes, sir.
MR. HARLEY: It is true, isn't it, that the person you spent the most time with other than your girlfriend, Fawndretta Galimore, was Michael Fredrick, from the time you got out of jail in February until when Les Lawhon was killed. Isn't that true?
Mills: No sir
MR. HARLEY: Who did you spend more time with?
Mills: Fawndretta.
MR. HARLEY: Other than her, there is no other person you spent more time with, is there?
Mills: No sir
MR. HARLEY: Now, let's go back to the period of time before you got out of jail. You heard Sheriff Harvey testify about the jail records?
Mills: Yes sir.
MR. HARLEY: You're not going to dispute that those were true, aren't you?
Mills: No sir.
MR. HARLEY: Those records are true, aren't they?
Mills: Yes, sir.
MR. HARLEY: You were in jail with Mr. Fredrick, in the same cell for 12 days, isn't that correct?
Mills: I don't know exactly how many days it was.
MR. HARLEY: Does that sound about right?
Mills: It sounds about right.
MR. HARLEY: The jail cells are very small?
Mills: Yes sir.
MR. HARLEY: You heard some of these witnesses also testify that you are the leader between you and Mr. Fredrick. You wouldn't dispute that would you?
Mills: As far as my face is concerned, you know, I speak with wisdom.
MR. HARLEY: You're a little bit older than Mr. Fredrick, aren't you?
Mills: Yes sir.
MR. HARLEY: How old are you?
Mills: 26
MR. HARLEY: How old is Mr. Fredrick?

Mills: I don't know.
MR. HARLEY: A direct answer: Are you the leader between you and Mr. Fredrick?

Again, Boone's lawyer, Mr. Randolph interjects –

MR. RANDOLPH: Your Honor, I have to object: He's answered that question one time before.
MR. HARLEY: I would like a yes or a no answer, Judge.
THE COURT: Let him answer it.
Mills: I am the leader between – I can't say that I have this mind to tell him what to do, or not to do. I can suggest.
MR. HARLEY: I would still like an answer to my question which is: Were there witnesses who testified that between the two of you, that you were the leader – did you hear those people say that?
Mills: Yes sir, but they don't have my mind, sir.
MR. HARLEY: Would you agree or disagree with their statements?
Mills: I would agree. I would agree.
MR. HARLEY: Mr. Mills, lets go through some of your testimony. You testified that you refer to white people as 'Caucasians'
Mills: Yes sir.
MR. HARLEY: But you also refer to Caucasians, in some of your letters to Fawndretta, as 'devils'.
Mills: No sir.
MR. HARLEY: Never did?
Mills: No sir.
MR. HARLEY: You wrote letters to Fawndretta after Les Lawhon was killed. Do you admit that?
Mills: I wrote her a letter after Al Gandy came questioning me.
MR. HARLEY: You wrote her many letters, didn't you?
Mills: Yes sir.
MR. HARLEY: Did you ever refer to Caucasians as 'devils' in those letters?
Mills: No sir.
MR. HARLEY: You also testified about white people staying at your house.
Mills: Yes sir.
MR. HARLEY: And you listed all the names of these people?
Mills: Yes sir.
MR. HARLEY: When was that?

Mills: Previous occasions.
MR. HARLEY: Not recently?
Mills: After I got out. But back when I was home.
MR. HARLEY: That was a long time ago, wasn't it?
Mills: No, it wasn't.
MR. HARLEY: How long ago was it?
Mills: Two to three years, four years, something like that.
MR. HARLEY: What was your name then?
Mills: John Mills.
MR. HARLEY: Your name was John Mills, Jr., right?
Mills: Yes sir.
MR. HARLEY: How long has it been An Serene?
Mills: Three years. You have to stay in the faith for at least 2 years before you can accept an Islamic name.
MR. HARLEY: This money that was used to bond Michael Fredrick out, whose money was that?
Mills: Fawndretta's.
MR. HARLEY: It wasn't your money at all, was it?
Mills: Sir?
MR. HARLEY: It was not your money at all, was it?
Mills: The money was, in purpose, for me.
MR. HARLEY: Did she tell you where that money came from?
Mills: Yes sir.
MR. HARLEY: Where did she tell you it came from?
Mills: From her mother.
MR. HARLEY: It wasn't even from Fawndretta, was it?
Mills: No, it was from her mother to get me out of jail.
MR. HARLEY: It certainly wasn't from you, was it?
Mills: No sir, but I had some money in the bank at the time.
MR. HARLEY: This 200 dollars that you say you wanted a 'dollar for a dollar' for, you weren't entitled to a cent of it, were you?
Mills: Yes sir.
MR. HARLEY: How?
Mills: It was my money.
MR. HARLEY: It was Fawndretta's grandmother's money, wasn't it?
Mills: No sir.
MR. HARLEY: Well, whose money was it that was used to bond Michael Fredrick out of jail?
Mills: It was my money. Fawndretta's mother had given me the money to get out of jail, so it was my money.
MR. HARLEY: It came from Fawndretta.

Mills: It was a debt from her mother to get me out of jail.
MR. HARLEY: She loaned the money to Fawndretta so that Michael Fredrick could get out of jail. Is that where the money came from?
Mills: She loaned it to me, to Fawndretta.
MR. HARLEY: Say that again.
Mills: She loaned it to me through Fawndretta.
MR. HARLEY: Did you talk to her grandmother?
Mills: No sir.
MR. HARLEY: Of course you didn't, you talked to Fawndretta, didn't you?
Mills: I did not talk to Fawndretta's grandmother. I talked to Fawndretta's mother.
MR. HARLEY: And Fawndretta got the money?
Mills: Sir?
MR. HARLEY: Didn't Fawndretta want the money back?
Mills: Yes sir.
MR. HARLEY: It was Fawndretta's money that was used. It was not your money that was used to bail Michael Fredrick out.
Mills: It was my money.
MR. HARLEY: Well, let's go on to another area: You said that Michael Fredrick drove this truck by himself on other occasions.
Mills: Yes sir.
MR. HARLEY: How many times did he drive the truck on other occasions?
Mills: Several times.
MR. HARLEY: Who saw him drive the truck on those earlier occasions?
Mills: I can't say.
MR. HARLEY: Nobody saw him drive the truck on any other occasion, did they?
Mills: I can't say.
MR. HARLEY: You can say – right now. If you have anything to support that, you can say it –

Again, Boone's lawyer, Mr. Randolph interjects –

MR. RANDOLPH: Your Honor, I have to object to this –
THE COURT: (To Harley) Don't argue with the witness now, Council, just ask questions.

MR. HARLEY: (To Mills -) Do you know the name of any single person who has seen Michael Fredrick drive that truck, by himself, on these occasions that you're talking about?
Mills: Do I know any witnesses?
MR. HARLEY: Yes sir.
Mills: No sir, I can't recall.
MR. HARLEY: Anybody see him drive the truck on that day you talked about; the day that Les Lawhon was killed?
Mills: Not to my knowledge.
MR. HARLEY: Let's talk about that day. I want you to start in the morning and tell the jury what you did that entire day; the morning that Les Lawhon was killed.
Mills: I don't even know the exact day he was killed.
MR. HARLEY: Let's assume it was the day you got all this property –
 (Mr. Harley gestures toward evidence -)
 -right here.
Mills: Alright sir.
MR. HARLEY: What did you do, the first thing that morning?
Mills: I was at home that morning, working, I guess; painting my father's place down there. And I came home for a little short break, and Michael Fredrick came up to my house, and knocked on the door. I confronted him about my money, and he said he didn't have it. I asked him why he didn't have it, so he suggested to me that he wanted to use my truck.
MR. HARLEY: And you were painting down there?
Mills: Yes sir.
MR. HARLEY: Do you remember what you were wearing?
Mills: No sir.
MR. HARLEY: Don't you have any idea?
Mills: No sir.
MR. HARLEY: What color were you painting with?
Mills: Red, trimming.
MR. HARLEY: Now, what time did you start painting?
Mills: It was in the morning.
MR. HARLEY: What time?
Mills: I can't give you an exact time. Maybe 8, 9, somewhere 'long in there, I don't know exactly.
MR. HARLEY: What did you paint?
Mills: The café.
MR. HARLEY: Where in the café did you paint?
Mills: Outside the café.

MR. HARLEY: What color did you paint it?
Mills: Red.
MR. HARLEY: Had it already been painted?
Mills: Has it already been painted?
MR. HARLEY: Yes sir.
Mills: It was being painted over.
MR. HARLEY: Had it been recently painted?
Mills: No sir.
MR. HARLEY: This is the first time it had been painted with red – the trim – of that house?
Mills: Yes sir.
MR. HARLEY: Recently. And you were doing that this morning?
Mills: No. I had been coming down on occasion to help my mother paint the place, down there, inside and outside, because she was remodeling it.
MR. HARLEY: Did you say that this was the first time it had been painted this day? Didn't you just testify that the day you got this property was the first time you painted the trim of this house?
Mills: It was the first time I trimmed it. It wasn't the first time I had painted it though.
MR. HARLEY: When else had you painted it?
Mills: On several other occasions.
MR. HARLEY: Now, what time, about, did you start painting the trim?
Mills: Like I said, around 8am or 9, I don't exactly know.
MR. HARLEY: Who else was with you?
Mills: Me and my brother. I guess that was about all.
MR. HARLEY: Where was Fawndretta?
Mills: She was at the house.
MR. HARLEY: Was she helping you paint?
Mills: Sometimes.
MR. HARLEY: Was she out there that morning helping you paint?
Mills: No, she wasn't.
MR. HARLEY: Well, when – you said that she was sometimes, or did you say that she was not painting?
Mills: Right.
MR. HARLEY: That morning, did she help you paint?
Mills: No, she didn't.
MR. HARLEY: What was she doing?
Mills: She was at the house.
MR. HARLEY: Did you all go anywhere?

Mills: No.
MR. HARLEY: You stayed at the house that entire morning, or you stayed at the café that entire morning?
Mills: No.
MR. HARLEY: Tell me what else you did.
Mills: I went back at the house, and I came back at the café and stayed over there another little short while, painting again. I don't know what time Michael Fredrick came to the house, but it was at the time that I was at the house coming back from the brick; from the café.
MR. HARLEY: Did you ever go over to Michael Fredrick's that morning? Go to Michael Fredrick's trailer at Hudson Heights?
Mills: No sir.
MR. HARLEY: Do you know where that is?
Mills: Yes sir.
MR. HARLEY: You have been there on several occasions, haven't you?
Mills: Yes sir.
MR. HARLEY: Did you ever go into town that day?
Mills: No sir.
MR. HARLEY: So you were only at the café, and at your house in Buckhorn on that morning?
Mills: Yes sir.
MR. HARLEY: Anybody else come by?
Mills: No sir. Just Michael Fredrick.
MR. HARLEY: What else did you paint that day?
Mills: That was all.
MR. HARLEY: Just the trim of the café?
Mills: Right.
MR. HARLEY: Red?
Mills: As far as I know.
MR. HARLEY: Who was painting with you?
Mills: Jesse, he was there. He wasn't doing too much work, but he was there.
MR. HARLEY: How did Michael come up?
Mills: I don't exactly know. I was at the house at this particular time.
MR. HARLEY: Michael doesn't have a vehicle does he?
Mills: Not that I know of.
MR. HARLEY: You have never seen him with one, have you?
Mills: No sir.

MR. HARLEY: Isn't it a long way from where he was staying at that time to get to your house?
Mills: Yes sir.
MR. HARLEY: Had he ever walked that before?
Mills: No sir, not that I know of.
MR. HARLEY: Isn't it true that the way he got together with you was that you went over and picked him up?
Mills: No sir.
MR. HARLEY: You can't remember how he got to your house – he just showed up?
Mills: Yes sir.
MR. HARLEY: Did it rain any that morning?
Mills: It was misty.
MR. HARLEY: But you were painting outside?
Mills: Yes sir.
MR. HARLEY: Did it bother you, the fact that it was raining, 'misting', outside, but you were painting outside?
Mills: Did it bother me? – no.
MR. HARLEY: It was okay to paint under those conditions?
Mills: Yes sir.
MR. HARLEY: Would it affect the paint at all?
Mills: No.
MR. HARLEY: It was raining pretty good, wasn't it?
Mills: No sir.
MR. HARLEY: Just 'misting'. Now, when Mr. Fredrick got there, you left and went to the food store and got some honey and came back. Is that right?
Mills: Yes sir.
MR. HARLEY: Now – and then, you left with Mr. Fredrick. The two of you left, and who was driving?
Mills: I was.
MR. HARLEY: And he all of a sudden said 'do you have some place you want to go'?
Mills: Yes sir.
MR. HARLEY: What else did he say?
Mills: That's all I can recall right now. He asked me did I have anyplace I wanted to go; to wait until he got back.
MR. HARLEY: What is the weather condition now?
Mills: Misty.
MR. HARLEY: So did you ask to be let off at a house or anything?
Mills: No. I asked him to take me over to Kilgore Road.

MR. HARLEY: Are there structures, shelters there?
Mills: No sir.
MR. HARLEY: It's pinewoods, isn't it?
Mills: Yes sir.
MR. HARLEY: Were you worried about being out in the rain?
Mills: No sir.
MR. HARLEY: That's okay with you?
Mills: Yes sir.
MR. HARLEY: You didn't ask Mr. Fredrick where he was going, of course?
Mills: No sir.
MR. HARLEY: You just let him go?
Mills: Yes sir.
MR. HARLEY: And it just happened you just wanted to be out in the pinewoods this rainy day?
Mills: No sir, well – I wanted to go to check out the land – the pine on the land.
MR. HARLEY: Have you been wanting to do that for a long time?
Mills: Yes sir.
MR. HARLEY: Well, why didn't you do it on a day when it was sunshiny? Was there anything keeping you from doing it on a better day?
Mills: Yes sir.
MR. HARLEY: What was that?
Mills: Work. I didn't have the time. This one particular time, it was something I wanted to do.
MR. HARLEY: You were spending a lot of time going over to Michael Fredrick's trailer, weren't you?
Mills: Anything was popping up those days, I don't know.
MR. HARLEY: But your work prevented you from going on a better day and looking at these pine trees? Is that what kept you from going on a better day to look at the pine trees, all the work you were doing?
Mills: Possibly.
MR. HARLEY: Well, what was it if it wasn't that?
Mills: I don't know.
MR. HARLEY: Now, were there people around when you got out on Kilgore Road?
Mills: No sir.
MR. HARLEY: And you walked around there for 2 or 3 hours?
Mills: Yes sir.
MR. HARLEY: It started raining pretty good, didn't it?

Mills: Yes sir, it did rain.
MR. HARLEY: Did you go anywhere?
Mills: No sir.
MR. HARLEY: How far is this from where you live?
Mills: About a mile.
MR. HARLEY: Did you decide to stay out in the rain there?
Mills: Wasn't nowhere for me to go.
MR. HARLEY: What did you find out about these pine trees?
Mills: They was tall, they grow'd.
MR. HARLEY: Did you do any other work with them?
Mills: Did I do any other work with them?
MR. HARLEY: Yes sir. Did you do anything other than observe that they were tall?
Mills: No sir.
MR. HARLEY: Can't you ride by there and see what the conditions of the pine trees are at any time?
Mills: No sir.
MR. HARLEY: You needed to do it that day –
Mills: No. From the road, you can't just ride by and see the pines. It is a thicket. You have to go down the road.
MR. HARLEY: You didn't do anything else other than stay in those woods all day?
Mills: Yes sir.
MR. HARLEY: You don't know the name of any persons that could have seen you out there that day?
Mills: No sir.
MR. HARLEY: Now, you also testified about a conversation that you had with Fawndretta Galimore when you were arrested. Do you remember about when you were arrested?
Mills: It was in March, if I'm not mistaken.
MR. HARLEY: And officers came up and arrested you, and you all of a sudden became concerned about the security of your house.
Mills: Yes sir.
MR. HARLEY: The shed. Did officers say anything to you to indicate you'd better take care of the property you got because there may be some criminal activity, or something?
Mills: No sir.
MR. HARLEY: What happened at that time to indicate to you that you'd better have the property removed? You decided at that time that the property needed to be moved, didn't you?
Mills: Yes sir.

MR. HARLEY: This is the time when the deputies were coming up to arrest you, isn't that right?

Mills: They issued me a warrant – saying they had a warrant for my arrest, so I didn't know how long I was going to be in jail.

MR. HARLEY: Had you had burglaries that day, or something? Had you had burglaries at your mother's house that day?

Mills: No sir.

MR. HARLEY: Had you had any the day before?

Mills: No sir.

MR. HARLEY: But all of a sudden when the officers have a warrant for your arrest, and you were afraid you were going to be in jail for a while, you decide that's a good time to move the property?

Mills: I knew that Fawndretta wasn't going to be staying at the house by herself, so I assumed that she was going to leave, you know, to get the stuff out of the house.

MR. HARLEY: It couldn't be that you were afraid that if somebody found this property, you could be linked to the death and disappearance of Les Lawhon was it?

Mills: No sir.

MR. HARLEY: It was because of the security risk at Blonzie Mills' house – your house?

Mills: Yes sir.

MR. HARLEY: Had anybody tried to break-in and try to get this property while it was there, in the shed you have talked about?

Mills: No sir, not that I know of.

MR. HARLEY: And I think you said you later saw her – and you were still so concerned about the property being safe – that you specifically asked her if she had taken care of the property, didn't you?

Mills: Yes sir.

MR. HARLEY: Isn't it true, that you asked her because you were very concerned about this property – right here – because you knew that if anybody found that property, that John Mills, Jr. would be linked to this murder?

Mills: No sir.

MR. HARLEY: I want you to go down to the occasion when you were interviewed by Mr. Gandy. You remember when he came down? Did he advise you of your rights?

Mills: Yes sir.

MR. HARLEY: Did he tell you, you had the right to remain silent?

Mills: Yes sir.

MR. HARLEY: What did you tell him when he told you you had a right to remain silent? What did you tell him?
Mills: I didn't tell him anything.
MR. HARLEY: Did you tell him you understood your rights?
Mills: At the particular time he came down he advised me of my rights, and he came on firing questions at me. He had read me my rights, so I assumed that something wasn't – just right, you know?
MR. HARLEY: Alright. Did he have his tape-recorder with him?
Mills: He had a lot of stuff with him, books and stuff, I don't know –

MR. HARLEY: He specifically asked you about the tape-recorder, though, didn't he?
Mills: No sir.
MR. HARLEY: Do you deny that he specifically asked you do you want the conversation recorded?
Mills: Yes sir.
MR. HARLEY: Did you want it recorded?
Mills: It wouldn't have mattered to me.
MR. HARLEY: How long did this conversation last?
Mills: 10 or 15 minutes.
MR. HARLEY: What kind of misunderstanding had you had with Mr. Gandy?
Mills: He tried to set me up.
MR. HARLEY: How is that, sir?
Mills: Some burglaries that occurred some years ago, and I'd knew of them, and I agreed to take him and Sheriff David Harvey to the burglaries. And he said if I take him to where the stuff was located he would give me a deal in the courtroom.
MR. HARLEY: How did you know about these burglaries?
Mills: I know the person that committed them. And when it came down for me to go to court, you know, they turned their back on me, you know, saying that I did this, so I was in the middle of it.
MR. HARLEY: And what did you do?
Mills: I did time.
MR. HARLEY: Now, Mr. Gandy said that he asked you some questions about a burglary in Wakulla County. Did he ask you that question?
Mills: Yes sir.
MR. HARLEY: What did you say?
Mills: I told him I didn't know anything about any burglary.

MR. HARLEY: Did he ask you if you owned, or knew, anything about a 12-guage shotgun?
Mills: Yes, I told him. He asked me did I know anything about any guns. I told him no, I didn't know anything about any guns.
MR. HARLEY: He specifically described a shotgun, didn't he?
Mills: I can't exactly recall.
MR. HARLEY: Didn't he describe it as a double-barreled Stevens shotgun – 12-guage shotgun?
Mills: I can't recall
MR. HARLEY: Didn't he give an exact description of the gun that you had in your shed –

Boone's lawyer, Mr. Randolph, interjects -

MR. RANDOLPH: Your Honor, he's asked the question 3 times. He said he 'didn't recall'.
THE COURT: Ask the question.
MR. HARLEY: (To Mills -): Describe the gun that you had in your shed
Mills: I can't recall.
MR. HARLEY: Did he ask you if you knew anything about any other property, for instance did he ask you knew about a 19-inch Zenith color TV?
Mills: I can't recall.
MR. HARLEY: Well, think about it.
Mills: It is so much –

Mr. Randolph jumps in again -

MR. RANDOLPH: Your Honor, he's already answered the question, he said he couldn't recall –
THE COURT: Answer the question.
MR. HARLEY: Did he ask you about a 19-inch black and white TV?
Mills: I can't recall.
MR. HARLEY: Did he ask you about a .410-guage shotgun?
Mills: I can't recall.
MR. HARLEY: Did he ask you about a 30-30 caliber Marlin lever action rifle?
Mills: No sir. He just told me that he had found some stuff in Fawndretta Galimore's house that she said was contained (pertaining) to me. I remember that.

MR. HARLEY: Okay, but you don't remember him going through any list of property then?
Mills: No sir. He just told me that they had found some stuff in her house.
MR. HARLEY: Did he ask you anything about a Gibson guitar?
Mills: No sir, not as I can recall.
MR. HARLEY: What about a Sony reel-to-reel tape recorder?
Mills: I can't recall.
MR. HARLEY: What about a record player?
Mills: I can't recall.
MR. HARLEY: What about a Technics receiver?
Mills: I can't recall.
MR. HARLEY: What about stereo speakers?
Mills: I can't recall.
MR. HARLEY: What about an antique glass pendulum wall-clock?
Mills: I can't recall.
MR. HARLEY: But he did ask you about property? If you knew anything about property, right?
Mills: He said they was down there doing some investigation on some burglaries, and asked me did I know anything about them. I told him no, I did not. Then he came down and said they had found some stuff in Fawndretta Galimore's house. This is how the letter came about. I wrote her a letter telling her not to be afraid of anything of this nature.
MR. HARLEY: Before you get to that, I want to stick to the conversation that you had with Mr. Gandy.
Mills: Alright, sir.
MR. HARLEY: He did ask you about a shotgun, but you're not sure, that he asked you about any of this other property, is that what you said?
Mills: I can't recall.
MR. HARLEY: Alright, did he ask you if you owned or ever drove a Dodge pick-up truck?
Mills: Yes sir.
MR. HARLEY: What did you tell him?
Mills: I told him I didn't own a truck.
MR. HARLEY: Did he ask you if you had ever driven an orange Dodge pick-up truck?
Mills: Yes sir.
MR. HARLEY: What did you tell him?
Mills: Yes sir.

MR. HARLEY: You admitted that?
Mills: Yes sir.
MR. HARLEY: So he is lying?
Mills: Yes sir. He lied about a lot of things.
MR. HARLEY: I see. Did he ask you if you knew Mike Fredrick?
Mills: Yes sir.
MR. HARLEY: Do you remember that? – you remember when he asked you if you knew Mike Fredrick?
Mills: Yes sir.
MR. HARLEY: What did you tell him?
Mills: No sir, I didn't.
MR. HARLEY: And why did you tell him that? You told him that you did not know Mike Fredrick?
Mills: Yes sir.
MR. HARLEY: You knew Michael Fredrick very well, didn't you?
Mills: No sir. I know Mike Mitchell. He didn't tell me his name was Mike Fredrick. He told me his name was Mike Mitchell. So I knew Mike Mitchell. I didn't know a Michael Fredrick. I know Mike as a person that he was referring to.
MR. HARLEY: Mr. Gandy use the name Mike Mitchell?
Mills: He used the name Mike Fredrick. Did I know a Michael Fredrick.
MR. HARLEY: What did Mr. Gandy ask you?
Mills: He asked me did I know a Michael Fredrick.
MR. HARLEY: What's this about Mitchell?
Mills: I didn't know a Michael Fredrick. I said I know a Michael Mitchell. I did not know a Michael Fredrick. I do not know a Michael Fredrick.
MR. HARLEY: Who was the man that was in jail with you?
Mills: He told me his name was Michael Mitchell in the jail, at that time I was in there with him. I did not know him. He had seen me and said that he knowed me.
MR. HARLEY: This is what you called him – Michael Mitchell?
Mills: In jail.
MR. HARLEY: Do you know Richard Gavin?
Mills: Yes sir.
MR. HARLEY: Do you know that Michael is his stepson?
Mills: No sir.
MR. HARLEY: Did you have a flier – like this – with Mr. Gandy, when he interviewed you?
Mills: Yes sir.
MR. HARLEY: Did he show you this flier?

Mills: Yes sir.
MR. HARLEY: Did he show you the picture of Les Lawhon?
Mills: Yes sir.
MR. HARLEY: What was your reaction?
Mills: Never seen him before.
MR. HARLEY: Did you have any physical reaction – ?

Mr. Randolph jumps up -

MR. RANDOLPH: Your Honor, I don't know what kind of question that is – I object to it.
THE COURT: Objection sustained.
MR. HARLEY: (To Mr. Mills -) Did you remain calm?
Mills: Yes sir.
MR. HARLEY: No change in expression?
Mills: No sir.
MR. HARLEY: Mr. Mills, did you know at that time that Les Lawhon's body had been found?
Mills: No sir.
MR. HARLEY: You had no way of knowing, did you?
Mills: No sir.
MR. HARLEY: Did Mr. Gandy tell you that the body of Les Lawhon – this man – had been found between the Spring Creek?
Mills: Yes sir.
MR. HARLEY: What did you do?
Mills: He told me that, he showed me this picture of Mr. Lawhon, saying that I killed Mr. Lawhon, and stuff of this nature, started prying me. I told him I didn't know anything about it. I said "What are you Caucasians trying to do? Trying to frame me with some charges?" He said – he just came out and said – 'You killed this man', you know? I said no, man, I didn't kill no one.
MR. HARLEY: Didn't he just tell you where the body had been found?
Mills: No sir. Mr. Fredericks – Mr. Gandy's associate – told me that. He said 'You killed Mr. Les Lawhon, didn't you Mr. Mills?' I said, 'No sir, I did not kill Mr. Lawhon."
MR. HARLEY: Alright, Mr. Mills, these letters, after that conversation with Mr. Gandy, did you have occasion to write Fawndretta Galimore letters?
Mills: No sir. I hadn't heard anything from her in some time, so I didn't know what the deal was with our relationship. So I wrote her a letter asking her had she turned her back on me, and stuff of this

nature. Had she forgotten me because some life problems had occurred.

MR. HARLEY: Didn't you tell her – you had gone over with her time and time again – about those 'Caucasians', and they don't have anything. As far as they know you have a receipt for the stuff.

Mills: Yes sir.

MR. HARLEY: Did you write her that letter? Did you write a letter with those things in it?

Mills: Yessir, similar to that.

Mr. Randolph jumps in –

MR. RANDOLPH: Your Honor, may we approach the bench upon this matter?

A conference is held at the bench between council and the court. Once it is over, the questioning continues:

MR. HARLEY: You testified you remembered saying those things in that letter?

Mills: Repeat the question again.

MR. HARLEY: Did you say something about "those Caucasians don't have anything on you. For all they know you have a receipt for that stuff"?

Mills: Yessir, I did. Mr. Gandy questioned me, saying that they had questioned Ms. Galimore, saying that she said this, and said that concerning me, you know, and I replied in a letter, and I wrote her – and told her – that I have told her over and over again, you know, about people trying to tell lies, and especially Caucasian people. That's what I was referring to as Mr. Gandy –

MR. HARLEY: What lie were you thinking they were telling?

Mills: Like they come down there lying on me saying that they had something, and they didn't.

MR. HARLEY: Did she have a receipt for this property?

Mills: Yessir.

MR. HARLEY: She had a receipt for all these items here?

Mills: She had a receipt for bonding Mr. Fredrick out of jail concerning that.

MR. HARLEY: And the Caucasian people were lying about that?

Mills: Yessir, as Mr. Gandy came at me.

MR. HARLEY: Why didn't you say 'show them the bond receipt'?
Mills: If they asked her about any property, where it came from, I told her to show them the receipt for it.
MR. HARLEY: You didn't say that, did you? Did you say – in that letter for her – to show them the bond receipt?
Mills: I said show them the receipt for the stuff.
MR. HARLEY: 'The stuff'. If you were talking about a bond receipt, was there any reason to be mysterious about it? Was there any reason to try to hide anything? Why couldn't you just come out and say 'show them the bond receipt'?
Mills: People –... Before we send mail out in the institution, your mail is read before you send it out, so I couldn't write exactly what I wanted to say in the letter.
MR. HARLEY: How in the world could this possibly get you in trouble while you were incarcerated, if you mentioned something about (quote) 'Show them a bond receipt'?
Mills: I don't know.
MR. HARLEY: It couldn't, could it?
Mills: I don't know.
MR. HARLEY: What could get you in trouble is if you indicated that you knew something about some stolen property that was connected with a murder.
Mills: I was leery of it.
MR. HARLEY: You were more than leery of it, weren't you, Mr. Mills?
Mills: Yessir, I was leery of the stuff, but I didn't think nothing of it.
MR. HARLEY: Why were you leery of it?
Mills: Well, a debt like that, for the amount of money, you know, and just come out and say 'well, this is just to show my appreciation for stuff', I have to get a little leery.
MR. HARLEY: You knew good and well – never mind. Isn't it true that you were not talking about a bond receipt? There is no question to be leery of one receipt.
Mills: No sir.
MR. HARLEY: You were worried about putting that in a jail letter.
Mills: Well, sir, I put it in the letter, I told her to read the letter with sense.
MR. HARLEY: Read it with 'sense' – did you tell her that?
Mills: Yessir.
MR. HARLEY: You also told her to read between the lines, didn't you?
Mills: That's what I mean: With sense.

MR. HARLEY: Did you tell her that right after you said, quote "For all they know you have a receipt for that property – that stuff"?
Mills: Yessir.
MR. HARLEY: So if they confronted her about any stuff of this nature, as far as they know, she had a receipt for it.
Mills: That's what I replied on the letter.
MR. HARLEY: Let's talk about the letter a little bit more, Mr. Mills. Did you express your feelings for Fawndretta in those letters?
Mills: Yessir.
MR. HARLEY: You really loved her, didn't you?
Mills: Yessir.
MR. HARLEY: And you express yourself completely, didn't you, in these letters?
Mills: No sir.
MR. HARLEY: Did you tell her how much you loved her?
Mills: Yessir.
MR. HARLEY: Did you tell her that she was your 'other half'? That she was your 'queen' and you were the 'king'?
Mills: Yessir.
MR. HARLEY: Now, is there anything about jail regulations that would have prevented you from saying, quote: "I would like to get married. Why don't we get married?" – end quote.
Mills: No sir. In Islamic, you phrase yourself in different terms when you express yourself toward your other half, and stuff of this nature, because it is a completely different faith from the people they meet here, in the United States.
MR. HARLEY: My point is, when you were saying, quote: "Read between the lines", end quote, did that have anything to do with the fact that you might want to marry her?
Mills: No sir. When I mean 'read between the lines', I was referring symbolically.
MR. HARLEY: 'Symbolically', right after you said, quote: "For all they know, you have a receipt for that stuff", end quote.
Mills: Yessir.
MR. HARLEY: Speaking in symbols. Mr. Mills, lets go back to the day this happened. You say Mr. Fredrick came to pick you up in the woods there?
Mills: Yessir.
MR. HARLEY: And you were standing out by the road?
Mills: Yessir.
MR. HARLEY: Where, exactly, were you?
Mills: Kilgore Road.

MR. HARLEY: Where on Kilgore Road?
Mills: In the woods.
MR. HARLEY: How far down the road?
Mills: Maybe 200 yards.
MR. HARLEY: Same spot he had left you at?
Mills: Yessir.
MR. HARLEY: You just happened to be back there when he came back?
Mills: Yessir.
MR. HARLEY: Standing out in the rain. What happened after that? You got in the truck?
Mills: Yessir. I asked him – I suggested – did he want to come back to my house and have a cup of tea, because I had just left Sopchoppy to get me some honey and stuff, and he suggested no, he had someone coming to pick him up.
MR. HARLEY: I'm sorry, I missed a part of that, you went where? – where did you go?
Mills: I suggested to him, did he want to go back to my house for a cup of tea.
MR. HARLEY: And what did he do?
Mills: He said no. He had someone coming; picking him up.
MR. HARLEY: Where did you take him?
Mills: I didn't take him anywhere. I left him there.
MR. HARLEY: You left him in the piney woods, on Kilgore Road?
Mills: Yes.
MR. HARLEY: Is that real close to his house?
Mills: No sir.
MR. HARLEY: It's a long ways, isn't it?
Mills: No sir, it's about 200 yards from the road from where he took off at from 98.
MR. HARLEY: From that point, where you left Michael Fredrick, to the point where he was staying, is a pretty good ways, isn't it?
Mills: Yessir, maybe 12 miles, or something like that.
MR. HARLEY: But now you're saying that he wasn't going to walk home; that someone was going to pick him up?
Mills: That's what he told me.
MR. HARLEY: Do you have any idea who that was?
Mills: No sir.
MR. HARLEY: You never found out who it was?
Mills: No sir.
MR. HARLEY: Was there a house there to stand, or anything; a structure that he could stand under?

Mills: No sir.
MR. HARLEY: Any kind of marker to indicate where he was?
Mills: No sir.
MR. HARLEY: And did he just get out in the rain, too?
Mills: Yessir.
MR. HARLEY: He'd rather do that than go to your house?
Mills: Yessir.
MR. HARLEY: You would have taken him to your house, wouldn't you?
Mills: I suggested it.
MR. HARLEY: You would have taken him to his house, wouldn't you?
Mills: Yessir.
MR. HARLEY: Taken him anywhere he wanted to go?
Mills: Yessir.
MR. HARLEY: But he wanted to stay out in the rain?
Mills: Yessir.
MR. HARLEY: Mr. Mills, did you see Major Hines testify?
Mills: Yessir.
MR. HARLEY: He was telling the truth, wasn't he, when he said he had known you all of his life?
Mills: Yessir.
MR. HARLEY: Are you all cousins?
Mills: Yessir.
MR. HARLEY: Mr. Hines testified about a conversation that you had with him in Buckhorn. Do you remember that?
Mills: Yessir.
MR. HARLEY: Do you remember that conversation?
Mills: No sir.
MR. HARLEY: Never had it?
Mills: No sir.
MR. HARLEY: Now, could you have had that conversation in Buckhorn last month, November? Could you have had a conversation with Major Hines in November?
Mills: No sir.
MR. HARLEY: Could you have had one in October of this year?
Mills: No sir. I talked with Major Hines on previous occasions.
MR. HARLEY: When would those have been?
Mills: It was a land – a person – living in one of our houses, a tenant – this is the name I'm looking for – he was a tenant in one of our homes out there and he got behind with his rent a couple of times. He and some girl was fighting and busting up some stuff in

the house. And so my mother told me to go and tell him he had to get out, and –

MR. HARLEY: I want to direct you to when you could have had a conversation with him in Buckhorn. Could you have had a conversation with him or anybody else in that house in June or July of this year?

Mills: No sir.

MR. HARLEY: Could you have had one in May of this year?

Mills: No sir.

MR. HARLEY: In April of this year?

Mills: No sir.

MR. HARLEY: You were not in Buckhorn at all were you?

Mills: No sir.

MR. HARLEY: Now, you were in Buckhorn and you were living in the house in the first part of this year, weren't you?

Mills: Yessir.

MR. HARLEY: You were there in January and February weren't you.

Mills: Yessir.

MR. HARLEY: Mr. Mills, you were suspicious of this property that he all of a sudden drove up with and walked away from, right?

Mills: I was leery of it.

MR. HARLEY: Did you have any idea how much it was worth – these 2 color tv's?

Mills: Maybe 2 or 3 thousand, I assumed.

MR. HARLEY: This is for a 175-dollar bond?

Mills: A 175-dollar bond. For each day that he didn't pay a bond it was one dollar on a dollar. Which, I guess, got it up to about 1500.

MR. HARLEY: Isn't it true that the reason you have several thousand dollars-worth of property, and he got a high school ring, is because you did the dirty work in this case?

Mills: No sir.

MR. HARLEY: Why didn't you go ahead and put this property in your house?

Mills: I didn't want to. Fawndretta didn't want me to.

MR. HARLEY: I see. Isn't it true that you had a conversation with Major Hines, in the first part of this year, that you said you wanted to knock off a few Caucasian people?

Mills: No sir.

MR. HARLEY: Isn't it true that that's exactly what you did on March 5 of this year?

Mills: No sir.
MR. HARLEY: Isn't it true that you have told your own mother that you knew Les Lawhon from Pigotts?
Mills: No sir.
MR. HARLEY: Didn't you tell her that on the telephone? Didn't you tell her that after you had been arrested; that you knew Les Lawhon?
Mills: No sir.
MR. HARLEY: Thank you.
MR. RANDOLPH: I don't have any further questions.

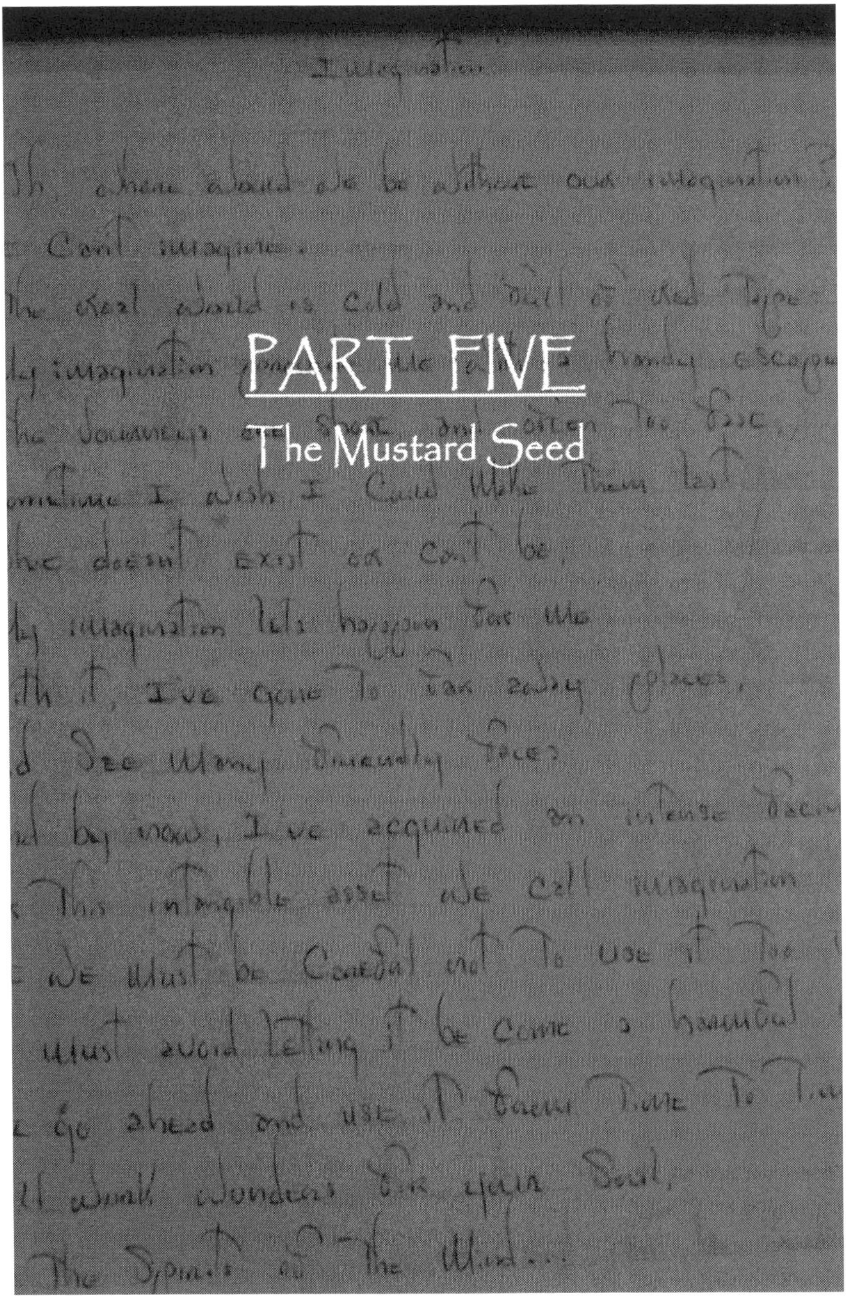

PART FIVE

The Mustard Seed

Chapter Sixteen

SPRING 2011

"YES – he did it", cried a voice cutting through the meeting room of the Wakulla Co. Public Library. There was an undertone of cold righteousness curled beneath its delivery, causing the entire room to go silent. Like the chill that accompanies a straight-edged razor after smooth and deadly use, the words slit deep, numbed us.

As I watched the audience sway and bob to seek out the 'voice', the word 'upstaged' flitted through my mind. A white woman, from Sopchoppy, bearing that legendary southern drawl, repeated herself as if speaking the gospel:

"Yes he did it – my Pastor said so!"

I had been approached by a member of Wakulla's Historical Society to plan and act as moderator of an event that I titled, 'Buckhorn: A Ghost Town Revisited'. It was a good faith effort on their part to bridge the gap between Wakulla's history, and the black Wakulla citizenry that were often omitted from it. My mother, grandmother, cousins, former residents of Buckhorn and others from the Wakulla community were in attendance.

I had managed to pull together a panel of both blacks and whites from the county to share their memories about the historically black area that was now all but extinct. The panel spoke about Buckhorn's beginnings from as far back as they could remember, along with events that took place like the annual May 20th celebrations, the old Buckhorn School

Christmas pageants, and political rallies during the election seasons.

One would expect the eyes of the fifty-odd persons to be glued on the panel and myself, which is how it was, for a while.

Towards the end of the program we came to the demise of the Buckhorn community. We spoke of the death of my grandfather, John Mills, Sr. I asked the panel if they felt the conviction and incarceration of his son, Boone, played a part in the eventual decline of the area; did they feel that the overall morale of Buckhorn residents began to falter because of this.

It was this question that prompted the outburst. And now, we simply sat there behind plastic folding tables trying to adjust our senses to what was, only seconds before, a pleasant remembrance.

Out of the corner of my eye I saw Grandma Blonzie move as swiftly as her 70-plus years would allow, gripping the sides of her walker for balance.

The 'voice' sat directly behind her. Grandma swiveled around to face the woman, then – her mouth tightened, her eyes narrowed – realizing that, once again, she'd be forced to suffer fate's cruelty in life.

The Sopchoppy woman, as Grandma was quick to divine, was blind. From the uncontrollable blinking and twitching of her eyelids, it was all too plain to see.

The audience was becoming disgruntled. The blacks merely glanced around, as if the 'voice' had confirmed a long held suspicion. The whites, a few who had spoken earlier about how comforting it was to see a diverse panel and audience together in positive discussion, seemed embarrassed that such a thing would crawl from their kitchen with guests sitting at the table.

I said something to the effect of "Okay, let's discuss that", when I was quickly cut short by the vice-president of the Society.

The 'voice' was a board member of the Society and, at the time, so was I. It became apparent that someone feared where an honest conversation could lead. 'Honest' because we were experiencing something real about our county's history instead of the sugar-coated fables we'd been brought up to believe.

Practically everyone in the room was old enough to remember or, at least, recall the nightmare of 1982. Before us lay the chance to hear reactions from both sides; the opportunity to learn something about the perceived 'other' that may not have been taken into consideration before. As it stood, we would not be allowed to find out.

It was quickly decided – against my objections – that we should at once abandon this unique opportunity (unique for the Wakulla community) and go our separate ways.

And so, bereft of sight once more, we penetrated the sultry, humid Florida night; feeling our way into those intensely private corners, which are the dark rooms of the southern world.

The woman's voice, ringing through the library like a wounded Scarlett O'Hara, stirred something within me. She would not have said such a thing unless she felt deep within that she was right.

Was she?

Thirty years ago she and others had the system, courts, media – almost an entire community – stepping forth as one unit to kill Wakulla's version of Frankenstein's monster. This is exactly what they and the State of Florida did. The all-American lust for revenge – heightened by the common fear of retribution from those in the community (black) who were frequently misunderstood and denied – created a sinister camaraderie among the people. Their tacit agreement was to hide in God's shadow and use His name as the weapon that allowed them to commit murder. 'Vengeance is ours', cried The People. And it was so.

And I was among them. I stood with them in silence knowing that my silence alone was a conscious action. For years, I believed that the American system of Justice was always right. In a similar way I was taught to believe war was right. Having lived through 9/11 in New York; seeing the havoc madmen – on both sides of the globe – could wreak, as we sat there, powerless, waiting for madmen to work their madness out, was itself – quite maddening.

It's been often quoted that "the definition of insanity, is doing the same thing over and over again, and expecting different results." After countless wars, casualties, and death, there are still wars. Have we forgotten that wars were fought by brave soldiers in the hopes that their children – their descendants – would never have to walk into battle? After numerous executions, murder remains. Like war, its history is repeated by those who've learned nothing from it. Injustice remains.

The outside taught me to believe my Uncle was a murderer, a liar, and unrepentant thief. Why else (many have asked) would he be in prison unless he was absolutely guilty?

It has taken me a while to learn, and learn the hard way – by experience – that nothing under the stars is absolute when man has a hand in it. Like so many, I expected to know the meanings and mysteries of life when I reached a certain age, only to find that people, well into their nineties and beyond, go into their final sleep wondering – still – if they lived their lives right.

Unjust. I must face the fact that that is what I have been. For me to look with anger upon the woman who yelled out such a horrible statement that night at the library, is to assume that she knew all the things surrounding this case.

If it took me years of digging and researching (as it has) to unravel these mysteries around my Uncle's execution, who am I to blame her for what it is that she – literally – did not know? That is what makes the writing of this family chronicle – a Wakulla family chronicle – all the more crucial: All the things we did not know.

...

Upon my return to Florida I began to look more thoroughly into the information my Uncle left behind. And though it is a lot, and highlights so many things that were not made public, it won't bring him back.

It won't bring Les Lawhon back.

I've never met Les Lawhon in this life, but his face has become so familiar to me. On days when the traffic in

Wakulla is low and few people are milling about, I visit his grave, asking him to point me in the direction of truth.

Not long ago I began a small radio program that centered on Wakulla's history and culture. The theme of one episode was 'Faith and Social Work'; how the work of the church spreads beyond its doors and into the community.

I spoke with a Pastor, only a few years younger than I, who ran a Christian-based home for men in recovery. I realized later, that the Pastor and I went to school together and, oddly enough, were in a play at the Wakulla Co. Courthouse many years ago; the same courtroom where my Uncle's trial was held.

I asked the Pastor why he chose to preach the Word and start a home for men in need. He mentioned that both of his grandfathers were pastors. He, in a way, simply followed in their footsteps.

It was then that he mentioned his grandfather's name; a name that I knew all too well: Reverend Glenn Lawhon.

We stopped the interview and stared at one another for a moment. He knew what I knew.

Who could have guessed that the young man I performed in a play with all those years ago; who – under deadline – I would conduct a last minute interview with, almost 30 years later, was a nephew just like me.

He was the nephew of Les Lawhon. And I, the nephew of the man tried and convicted for killing him.

The Pastor and I speak every now and then, having developed a mutual respect for one another. We even laugh. I'm thankful to know someone who uses their faith as a means to uplift others who've stumbled, or have fallen on the rocky road of life. I can't explain what it means to me that he and I can talk about the past without hurting one another. We are aware that it is a thing that certain people in both our families will never, ever do in this life. Before I wrote one word of this chronicle, I sat down with this unlikely friend, and told him my intentions so that no one would be caught unaware.

...

Not long after his son's trial, the Rev. Lawhon ran for public office, only to pull out soon after. He would later succeed in his campaign to all but abolish the office of Capital Collateral Representative (CCR). Whether the third man that signed as a 'personal reference' on Rev. Lawhon's insurance application, Mr. James Thompson, former Speaker of the House of Representatives, had anything to do with the push that broke up CCR, is unknown.

I reached out to the Rev. Lawhon. Throughout our phone conversation, I had to state who I was four times. I had the sense that he was not mentally well.

When I asked if he thought John Mills, Jr. received the proper justice for the murder of his son, his response went like this:

Lawhon: Yes.

Me: Why?

Lawhon: He was – what they call – one of them Muslims. That means he don't believe in Jesus Christ, and he'll burn in hell for it.

Nothing about the case, or the facts; only the faith. When I say that religion played an important role in the trial, this is what I mean.

Again, I had the sense that the Reverend was not well. Therefore, I can't, in good conscience, state the rest of his comments.

...

I decided the time had come for me to write a letter to Michael Fredrick. This was his reply:

"November 4, 2010

Dear Herb,

I received your letter the other day and was somewhat confused with what it was that you were in search of concerning mine and your uncle's convictions. To be totally honest with you, Mr. Donaldson, at first, I was a little heated at you for such brave approach knowing so little about me, but then I realized that I had to respect your efforts in hope of knowing the truth.

Yes, three families were torn and there has been nothing so great to come of this mishap.

I was a teenager myself (19 yrs) when this all took place, and I looked up to your uncle, as if he were my big brother, for I had not one.

I admired your uncle, because he opened my eyes to many things about life. He had big dreams of becoming a very successful person, but in those dreams, there was something much darker... something I've yet to understand. I really don't know if it were because of his embracing Islam when he was incarcerated before, or was it something that had happened in his life long before we ever got to know each other. But regardless of when, he had a very deep hatred for white people.

Personally, my mom didn't raise me to hate the other color. She just always told me to be wise.

Now, in regards to the events that took place on that rainy day.

I would be lying to you if I told you that I saw your uncle shoot the man, because I really didn't, but I did hear (2)shots from the wooded area they were tussling around in. But to say that I saw the shooting wouldn't be the truth.

In your letter you said that you and your family just wanted closure.

Well, let me just say this: The state presented a lot of evidence that had nothing to do with the events that took place, but does it really matter now?

They put me on the stand, and made me LIE about the shirt they said Les Lawhon's blood was on. FDLE LIED and said that they found Les Lawhon's blood on that particular shirt, which was a bold face lie. But what was I supposed to do in a no-win situation, having my ass beat day after day and night after night?

They made me take polygraph examination over 17 times, hoping to catch me in a LIE, but each time I pass, because I told <u>the truth</u>.

I don't know what you believe or what you believe in, but <u>GOD</u> knows that I didn't kill Mr. Lawhon, nor ever had any intentions of doing such a thing!

For many years, I've asked...Why? What was the real motive? Did your uncle know this man? Here I am after serving over 28 years of my life incarcerated trying to figure this out, yet I'm still without the answer.

Mr. Donaldson, I have absolutely nothing to lose by lying to you, and to be straight up with you, it really doesn't matter if you believe what I told you or not, but the truth is, I've never killed anyone in my life... I don't have the heart. This doesn't mean that I am a coward of some sort, but I would rather run away a coward than to take someone's life!

I'm truly sorry if this isn't what you would have wanted to hear, but I didn't kill Mr. Lawhon.

Even after they convicted and sentenced your uncle to death row, I tried to help, by somehow having his life spared. I wrote CCR and explained to (BLANK), about the same shirt, before your uncle was put to death, but nothing ever came of that, and that was the summer of '96 (July 2, 1996).

The fact that they lied about the blood on the shirt, was enough evidence to get your uncle's conviction overturned, and he would've had a fair trial somewhere else other than Wakulla County. Perhaps they still would have gotten a conviction, but at least he would've still been alive, and in a position to at least fight for a further freedom.

If for some reason or another, I die today or tomorrow, everything I've shared with you in this letter is the truth.

As for visiting me... That's your choice, I welcome you!

May God continue to bless you and yours. - Michael"

…

Not long after receiving this letter, I was at the local Flea Market with my mother when Michael's mom, Mrs. Gavin, approached. We said our hello's.

As is always the case in such moments, something in our eyes said more than our mouths could speak. She asked if I felt better about things now. Obviously, I thought, Michael has told her about my letter.

To make it easy, I lied, for all of us. I said things were fine. My mother smiled, and was kind as well, but we both knew that we were in a place that Mrs. Gavin could not understand. Her son is alive. She need only get in her car and go to him. And even if she is limited, unable to touch or sit alone with him without guards – unable to bring him home for a hearty meal – the fact remains: He's still here. He's alive.

Les Lawhon is dead – for no reason. My Uncle is dead – for no reason that can be proven. Not even the possible 'animal blood' on the shirt has been proven. Michael, in his letter above, even says this. How can one claim to have told the truth, the whole truth, and nothing but the truth, while simultaneously admitting they were forced to lie?

In short, Michael Fredrick's letter to me, I cannot be sure of. He mentions in his letter that he was 19 when all of this took place. Newspaper reports, as well as his prison report sheets that list the date of his birth, shows that he was not 19, but 21. It is public knowledge that almost anything that leaves prison walls is inspected and read. I wonder still about all the things he couldn't – wouldn't – say. And I wonder, too, why he would become "a little heated" about my wanting to know more.

I've no desire to further distress Michael or his family, but am seeking the truth to one murder and a possible second. Statements in his letter such as: *"...and to be straight up with you, it really doesn't matter if you believe what I told you or not...,"* move me, but not in ways that are positive. Maybe it does matter. Because, if I believed you, I and others may be willing to stand as advocates in your corner and give support to the innocent where and when it is due.

...

A friend that I'd known since elementary school, passed away during our high school year. Many years later, upon my return to Wakulla, I met her older sister for the first time. She, like my friend, is very kind and easy to talk to. Recently, we saw one another in passing and decided to sit and catch up.

When asked what I'd been up to lately, I told her that I was working on a book. When further pressed, I mentioned that it was about my Uncle and his execution on Florida's death row. She wanted to know more, and so, I told her.

When I mentioned his name, this look came over her face that is not easy to describe. She stopped all that she was doing and told me she was sorry. I told her there was no need to apologize and was ready to move onto another subject, until she mentioned that she knew of the case, because she was a member of the jury.

This, of course, captured my attention. She told me that she couldn't understand why she was chosen; after all, she was barely a 20-year-old at the time with no idea of the judicial process, or her particular role in it.

Though I did not say so, it seemed very obvious – to me - why she was selected.

...

It is often difficult, walking through the Wakulla minefield of personal relations. To have heard, but to not know as fact, who was heavily coerced, threatened, or paid to keep their silence, when two men are dead. But still, we strive, our family, to be okay. We have to be. What else can we do? I have no idea how to go about clearing my Uncle's name other than writing this book, hoping that it brings awareness to what I feel was a serious injustice.

The Innocence Project cannot help because my Uncle is not alive. The local NAACP chapter has not responded to our outreach. Most everyone tells my family and I to move on, or that the past is the past; forgetting that each of us is a part of 'living' history.

If the shoe were on the other foot and they were left to visit the grave of their son, daughter, parent, or spouse, on birthdays, holidays, and death anniversaries, could they shake off – so easily – the residue of aching pain, as they've so nonchalantly advised us? What we will – or won't – do now, sets the tone; provides the example for what the world will – or will not – become later.

Happy, mindless American fantasy seems preferable for those who choose to remain in the bliss of blind innocence; who chose to forget that 'happiness' – like the sun and its moon, the night and its day – has an opposing side, possessing equal force, each making our living all the more important.

In the journey of discovering my Uncle, I've met many who have been forced to see through and beyond the illusion of happiness. I met 'Mary' at a play reading. The play's premise was forgiveness. Afterwards, I learned that Mary's teenage daughter was sexually assaulted by a group of black males. Mary and her daughter are white.

Mary spoke of how she had planned to kill each and every one of the men responsible – there – in the courtroom. She had laid it out and was ready to take action before getting hold of her mental self, the realities of the situation, and the forms of justice that would be used to resolve it.

I also met Agnes Furey. Her daughter, Pat, was killed by a man that she befriended during drug treatment and was trying to help him better his life after his release from the program. They later found Agnes' 6 year-old grandson, Christopher, beneath a pile of clothes in her daughter's apartment. He, too, had been murdered.

In my talks with Agnes I've learned bits and pieces about Restorative Justice. It is the philosophy that if one commits a crime they should be punished for it. It does not mean that they also should die.

I have battled with this concept.

In difficult moments, I have seen clearly the faces of those in and outside of Wakulla who had a corrupt hand in this case. I can see – within the targeted scope of my mental killing sight – the pupils of their very eyes.

But then, I am forced to pull back, and glance the world of faces beyond them: Their children, their grandchildren, their brothers and sisters. Faces and friends I know personally from this community. If I hate them – that much – it is better for me to stare deep into the black tunnel of the gun-barrel myself, and prepare for the blast of the pistol-ball.

I have come to the conclusion that there has been enough murder already. I do not wish to have anyone's blood on my hands, especially if I am unsure if the accused spilled first blood to begin with.

I do not wish to plead – like a petulant child – for another human being, who exists in an inhuman world, to be murdered because I, or a loved one, has been hurt. It would only prove that I have been trained to become as heartless as the unkind world that created the killer in the first place. Killers are not borne from the steel and concrete confines of death row; they are borne from us. They are fashioned, hammered, and beaten into creation by the world we have made.

I do not care to be of assistance to a public execution, or to give my consent from the shadows as a member of the silent majority. I have come to believe that those who clamor for this should: 1) Have a close relationship to the case that is in question, or is being tried; 2) That – if they wish to execute – allow the one closest to the victim; the one who seeks death the most, to pull the switch, deliver the injection, fire the shot, or pull the lever of the gallows; 3) That it should be televised and made public to all media outlets so that the world – young and old – will know that the executioner (a sweetened word for 'murderer') was equally as unforgiving, as unrepentant, as the original killer. Their loved ones, their children, should walk the earth knowing that there are others who are now victims of the second, kinder, gentler, murder.

And for the descendants of those who claim they would willingly 'pull the switch': If life becomes something of a burden for you to bear, remember that you can always ask others, like my Grandmother (if she were still alive), or my mother, my kin, or myself, what it's like to be the bearer of the scars. We've learned to live with the title of "The Mad Dog Killer's Family", for quite some time. And like us, you, too, will learn the hidden tricks of how to survive it.

Again, this is only my opinion and, surely, it will not go down well for others. But, really, what options are there when we see with our own eyes, time and time again, how corrupt our prison reform system is. When we see people released from prison because DNA findings proved them innocent. When we see people working in DNA labs deliberately contaminating evidence on behalf of wicked lawyers. When a witness finally steps forth to admit they lied, just to save face. And, above all, when there is a great deal of money to be made – already been made – by keeping a steady amount of 'heads in the beds' within our prison walls.

...

When John Mills, Jr. was sentenced to death for the murder of Lesley James Lawhon, my mother received a call on her job at the Wakulla Middle School from our county's Sheriff's department. She was informed that they did not want her brother to spend another night in their jail and was, therefore, being transferred.

Grandma Blonzie had been staying with us a few days during the week, awaiting the trial's conclusion. Before my mother could make it to our house, a Wakulla Co. Sheriff's deputy arrived on our doorstep, and knocked. Grandma answered.

The deputy stood in our doorway with a black garbage bag filled with my Uncle's belongings. Without a word, he stepped in the front door – pushed past my Grandmother – and turned the garbage bag upside down, emptying every single item onto the floor. He then turned, walked out, and left the front door wide open.

My mother walked in to find Grandma on the floor, gathering all of her youngest child's possessions to her breast. And weeping. A sound like that will never die.

To 'protect and serve'. Indeed.

...

In the many years that passed, there would be appeals, correspondences, articles, two stays of execution, and new friendships gained along the way.

On November 9, 1987, my Uncle received his Certificate of Acceptance into the Ansaaru ALLAH Community, Inc. By then, his name was officially changed to Yuhanna Abdullah Muhammad, which is translated to mean 'Allah's glorious servant who shows great gratitude'.

His artwork was featured at Khufu's Chamber, in Tallahassee, on April 10, 1993. On the program, in the section 'In His Own Words', he states the following:

"I feel that art is a means of expression. Everything I do must be a tribute to my Afrikan-ness. I am a prisoner here at Florida State Prison. I am also on Death Row for a crime I didn't commit. I'm looking for a new trial sometime soon. I'm looking to be out of here. Inshallah (if it is Allah's will)!!! After doing 10 years on Death Row, by the grace of Allah, I have found peace in a world where there is no peace."

It was my Uncle's wish that his share of his father's estate go to his nieces and nephews, to be put toward their college educations. At the time there were, I believe, nine of us in all.

Shirley Lawhon, widow of Les Lawhon, filed a civil suit and received all of it. She no longer resides in Wakulla County, and is said to have remarried.

When Gran'daddy John's property went up for sale, my father claims that, though he was the 'highest bidder', he was not allowed to buy. Even with money to give, he could not 'buy back' – not even the tiniest portion – of what my grandfather built.

Grandma Blonzie made her transition earlier this year and almost 80 years of history has departed with her. The community of Buckhorn, as we once knew it, is completely gone. The store, café, and homes have been razed. There was once a road sign erected that read 'John Mills Circle'. It has since been removed.

Buildings similar to those found along 'strip mall' areas were built and, for a while, a small restaurant and daycare functioned there. Those who bought and owned the property have now lost it. It belongs, presently, to a bank. The new buildings (those metallic models of reconstruction) sit vacant, lifeless, and utterly useless. Especially when compared to the vibrancy of the Black Americans – Wakulla County's family – that once existed there.

And still, the residents of Wakulla County are a part of us. They are forever our family for we reflect each other greatly. We coexist; swoop, sweep, and slide by each other on the daily. The skies are open, the trees are tall, and the air is clean.

But even in the midst of all this glowing loveliness, some of us, on occasion, must wipe the tears from our eyes, for we have seen far too much on the surface, and can only pray that beauty is more than skin deep; that it seeps into the porous places of the bone; springing from the soul.

Chapter Seventeen

Tallahassee Democrat
May 6, 1987

HIGH COURT DENIES STAY FOR MILLS
Wakulla killer scheduled to be executed Thursday

" *Wakulla County murderer John Mills, Jr., was denied a stay of execution Tuesday by the Florida Supreme Court and is scheduled to die in Florida's electric chair Thursday...* "

And later...

Tallahassee Democrat

CONVICTED KILLER GETS STAY

" *Less than 16 hours before he was scheduled to die in Florida's electric chair, convicted murderer John Mills, Jr., received a stay of execution Wednesday...* "

Chapter Eighteen

From the Journals and Letters of Yuhanna Abdullah Muhammad

Formerly known as John Mills, Jr.

January 31, 1989
Excerpt from a letter to his sister:

"My precious sister, Rachel. May Allah judge us with mercy and kindness, for only Allah can rescue us from this state of appalling ignorance and corruption that has plagued us...

My precious Sister, I received a letter from Mother the other day. She mentioned that you were in the hospital, and that you had surgery. I told her that I was going to write you and find out how you are doing. I pray that you are well?...

I remind myself that hardly a day goes by that if only for a moment you and your family are in my thoughts...

This week with all of the Bundy news, I couldn't help but think if anyone was thinking of me, being here. It is an old saying 'out of sight, out of mind'. I may be gone out of everyone's 'sight', but I hope there is some part of me that mingles in the hearts of those who love me...

...Back on the subject of Bundy, there was so many news reporters here, from all over the world, camping-out outside of the gates like vultures waiting on him to die. It was a major event – I've never seen anything like it, people jumping and shouting to see a man executed. I couldn't help but feel sorry for those people who have no heart; heart for human life... No matter how many times

they execute Bundy what purpose would it serve? It's not going to solve the problems with all the killing in the world today – the heaven's cry silently, life, love, success and joy to the world... while the people of the world cry loudly, death, hatred and failure to Mankind. There is so much anger in the world today. Hatred cannot be overcome by hatred, nor anger by anger. Anger is fire. Because of Satan's hatred he was hurled from heaven into the world of hell. Anyone who has that anger in him, is of Satan. If we are angry, we will see anger in others. But if we overcome Satan, anger in ourselves with compassion, we will not see it in anyone else..."

...

(Date unknown)
The mustard seed. I use it to support my logic that: If faith the size of a mustard seed can move a mountain, how little faith must it take to move a few men trying to kill me? As a result I have used and shown such dis-interest towards this death-row situation that many people can't relate to my state of mind.

Some say: He's finished. Some feel sorry. Some even say I'm creating reason to be optimistic... Sure, I am very optimistic about the outcome of my appeals. But only because I was blessed with the courage to learn the true condition of my legal position. Once I became aware of my legal position, I sought to learn the concept of the legal system and how it works.

What I learned is very simple: It works for those who make it work. The sad part, is that not many people can afford the cost of the battle if they aren't able to do it themselves. It all boils down to the/a state of confidence and faith.

Inner faith has gotten me this far. So why shouldn't I be optimistic. I feel good inside. I refuse to let my surroundings change this peace within. I've been blessed with an insight. A comfort beyond what any man has to offer. Once I've done my best at trying to help myself, it seems only wise to accept and respect the outcome.

Upon arriving at F.S.P. (Florida State Prison) there seems to be the unspoken warning of being in a "Big Boys World". F.S.P. is the last step up Florida's criminal ladder. It's not uncommon to hear guys speaking of their 200 years of compound life sentences and of course, death row.

After time you can see in the face of the next man that all of us here have a heavy load to carry. We all react to our being in different ways. There remains the rule of not looking the next man in the face too long. Or you might find yourself face to face with a man who has lost his self-control, and his ability to think properly. Causing him to act according to the direction of his uncontrolled state of mind.

Death row is unlike the free-moving population of FSP. Here we are constantly under restraints unless we're out in the exercise yard twice a week. Two hours at a time. Our cell is a 7x9. One open–bar-end concrete section, in a 17-line row on each floor, of each wing. The whole FSP is one long hallway with wings within its ¼ mile run.

Death row is at the end of that ¼ mile, barred off, with its 320 inmates. We have a television and can have a radio if we desire one enough to have it sent from a friend or family. We can have a 6-hour contact visit each weekend if we desire. I decided not to because of the distraction/element involved, for I believe that: Sometimes you have loved someone enough to push them away. Yes we all need somebody, but we must decide situations according to our needs, and/or selfishness and not confuse one with the other.

"Life is on the line"... After I was so unfairly convicted, and was facing a death sentence, a news reporter asked me how did I feel now that I was facing the death penalty. My response was: "We're all facing the death penalty. You just make sure you're man enough to handle yours."

All mankind must die from the earth at some point. None of us can truly and honestly say when and how it will take place. The way I have come to see it is this: If I die today, tomorrow, next week, or next year, my only concern would be whether I will be accepted by Christ.

Of course I would rather not be in my current situation. Yet (!) it's the very position that pushes me into finding inner confidence as opposed to going insane at the test this trial-in-life has brought about. I feel that I now have inner understanding with my inner-self so great that many people would love to be in my position for the peace-of-mind alone.

I've been blessed. And I thank Allah for my life just the way it is, full of Peace and Confidence Within... It's such a peace that the outer condition or location of the body has little or no importance... The whole affair is a make or break situation, and I'm happy to say that I've been blessed with the inner power to survive not only death-row, but any other cards-of-life dealt to me. That is, as long as I continue to have faith within/through Allah.

Speaking of Allah, I've never claimed to be a saint. I don't go around preaching of the Bible. I am still a sinner, just like the rest of Mankind. But I do believe in Allah. And I depend on Him for my inner confidence and direction. And most importantly, I accept Him as my savior.

...

Death row can be a little stressing at times. Causing a man to ask himself a wide range of questions about his present position and his possible fate with the Electric Chair. Though I'd rather not be in position at all, I still sometimes feel better about being on death row as opposed to being out in population of this place.

To hear of stabbings and killing among inmates is stressing. So far I've seen only one stabbed inmate. I can still recall sitting down by the medical center waiting to see a dentist, when all hell seems to have broken loose. There was about 30 to 50 prison guards rushing to the prison kitchen.

Next I observed nurses and medical trainees with a lawn-chair looking stretcher rushing in the same direction as the guards had. Some of the older inmates were commenting: "Somebody's got it,", "Something going down", "It must be in the kitchen."

A lot goes on in my mind. Sometimes fear tries to over-cloud me as I put too much focus on the intentions of those who conspired to get me here. Instead of organizing 'what could', concentrate on 'what is'...

Then again, it seems only wise to explore all the possibilities of any given conflict/situation if it's to be effectively dealt with. So I guess it's only natural to find some of the possibilities a little hot to the touch. Yet (!) – and YET (!) – life goes on. And it be played out to the hilt; to the end.

No matter where or what you're going through, through it all, I guess we all conduct ourselves like troopers who have made their minds up to keep the dignity it takes to make a man a Man.

...

The 'Public Officials' who seek to kill any human – or animals in some instances – for a supposedly brutal crime, are just as cold and unfeeling as they claim the person they seek to murder was in their attempt to get him/her put on death row. What is more 'premeditated murder' than an organized judicial system?

Public officials spend (according to Gov. Chiles) up to 3 million dollars in appeals on each death-row inmate, just to murder a person?

Not only that, these Judicial Murders are carefully planned over a span up to 10 years. Yet public officials claim 'premeditated murders' are what deserve the death sentence. Why aren't those who have succeeded in executing a death warrant in the same line with those 'premeditated' murderers?

'A murder is a murder is a murder is a murder'. And murder, simply defined is: The taking of another human life. Only Man added the 'unlawful' to killing. 'A killer is a killer is a killer...'

...

In my holding cell, observing it all in a way any newcomer would:

About 10 minutes after the guard, nurses, and M.T.'s rush to the kitchen, an inmate was escorted to the Medical Center. As he walked by our holding cage, one of the older inmates asked him, by name, if he was alright.

The guy looked over, smiled, and gave a proud looking wink as a response. At or about the same time, I heard someone else call to our attention the knife held by one of the guards over in the control booth.

At this point, I'm still not sure what had taken place. And I was still trying to put it all together when the final piece presented itself:

It was in the form of a 250 to 300 pound man being wheeled by in the lawn-chair looking stretcher. He was a white man. The man who had winked earlier was a P.R. (Puerto Rican) that weighed about 140 to 160 pounds. The man on the stretcher had holes in his arm and upper body.

Flesh blood must have a smell of its own. Because as the man was wheeled by, I smelled what must have been the scent of blood. The nurse and the M.T. had wiped most of it away after removing his shirt. Yet I could still see that the man was light-red as a result of blood smeared in the process of wiping him off. He's just lying there.

After the stabbed inmate was rushed on into the Medical (Prison) Center, I asked myself:
(1) Did the man stabbed seem able to recover?,
(2) Did the P.R. seem proud when he came by?,
(3) Was any blood spilled into our eating supply?, and
(4) Ain't you glad to be on Death Row all locked away from this s____t ??

My inner response to question:
(1) was D____n,
(2) D____n
(3) D____n
and to (4) Hell'yea!!

I'm not a coward. But I do expect to win my freedom on appeal, and to be in population is to be subject to the possibility of being caught up in a situation where its kill or be killed.

Some of these guys are victims of over-powered wills. They don't care about anything, anyone. A result of believing their life is over. It's sad that a man can't always walk away from trouble. It's even sadder that a man has to think of killing someone in a fight, just to avoid being stabbed in the back by the loser later on.

So yes (!), Death Row does have its good points. It's certainly a lot safer.

Still. Even on death-row you hear of one death-row killing the other as he walks by, in cuffs, with two guards... I have witnessed it many times.

Some of these guys get into word-fights. And, yes (!) – talk of killing in the exercise yard. During the times a fellow inmate has been set to die, or those with a possible 'stay' of execution, I have personally felt the weight of fear and concern for the inmate in question.

In this case, his name is Liv Jones, a man I know personally, felt closeness too, and for, him. He sat within two days of an execution, hoping for a 'stay', praying for life; trying to mentally prepare himself for Death, in case his prayers aren't part of Allah's plans for him.

Just as any person, even to have accepted death as a part of life, its only human to want to hang-out on earth a little while longer.

No! I can't be sure where Mr. Jones' thoughts were during the time of uncertain waiting. I can only recall constantly looking out my window on R-Wing, over to Q-Wing, just 30 to 40 yards from R-Wing, feet away, knowing that the electric chair is housed there in what's called The Death House. Mr. Jones was in that same wing just down the hall from the chair...

I have very serious questions as to which end is better. On one hand, you have within reach, a chance to meet The Maker. And there's the hope for longer life on earth. That's why in situations such as Mr. Jones', I simply repeat to Allah my trust in his actions.

Allah wouldn't put me through any more than I can handle. So, as a result, I simply take this death row one day at a time. As I continue to do my best to help myself to grow in soul and spirit as well as regain my freedom... One thing I do not and will not do, that is to ask Allah to get me out of prison. Of course my earthly desire is to be free in body as I am now, in spirit. But my overall desire is to be the person I am deep within. Regardless of where I am.

Chapter Nineteen

(Date unknown)
I had a few heated words with an inmate that has been here 22 years. And one of the first things I realized at the start of our word-changing was: This could be a kill-or-be-killed situation like one I've never encountered.

I knew/was told the inmate had killed other inmates during his 22 years stay here at the FSP.

At the time of our word-changing, I was speaking up for what's mine as well as putting some purpose to my manhood. Because in here, if you let a guy dog you out once, he might decide to screw you in the mouth and butt later on.

That 'what's mine' in question is my bowl and my hot water bag. Both of which I allowed him access to for his use. But instead, he wanted to heat water for the whole wing, and on top of that, he loaned my bowl to someone else who subsequently had it taken by the guard because it was being used to make wine...

I let the bowl issue slide, but when, a few days later, the Run-A-Round (22 year inmate) took my water bag down there, left it with the guy who got my bowl taken, I told the Run-A-Round that I don't want my 'bag'. He told me that he didn't want to use it anymore, and that he'd get me another bowl because he wasn't about "all that crying over the petty stuff".

I just told him that I was only looking out for my stuff and I was sorry if he didn't understand that.

This word-changing went on for about 10-15 minutes. We handled it like any two guys who knew that the other – not necessarily wanting to – would do whatever was necessary to protect his stuff.

After this time we didn't have anything to say to each other for a few days. With time, we did start to communicate on a more respectable level with each other. Yet, it was only yesterday that he (Run-A-Round), told me that I was a bug (one who is quick to get busy) for the way I went-off on him about my hot-water bag and bowl.

By the way, he replaced my bowl. Also I responded by simply saying that we're all bugs, or need to be bugs when it comes to standing up for our stuff. I never claimed to be a bad-ass, or a weak ass. I've just always stood my ground according to what I felt was right at any particular time.

Of course, that little confrontation could have gotten out of hand had either of us been unaware of how far the other would go to stand his ground. I <u>knew</u> he had killed other inmates because he told me. He only knew, since I'm on Death-Row, that I was <u>accused</u> of killing someone.

But for the most part, I carry myself in a way that tells the next man that I will treat him like he treats me. Regardless of how hard, I try to maintain an associate-ship as best I can. If two adults can't get into an argument without letting it get out of hand, we are doomed to begin with.

...

Tension seems to be in the air today. Missing is the usual laughter and conversing from cell to cell. There's the still, chit-chat here and there. But the undertones are close.

"Renegade", our Run-A-Round (trustee) the one and same 22 years inmate I mentioned previously in this log of thoughts, has somehow convinced himself that, for the most part, the guys on this wing are weaker than he is, thereby deserving the disrespect he shows for them in/by calling them 'pussies', 'whores', and other word-calling that will most likely get him into a jam if he continues.

That is, the rest of the guys on this wing know that a 'tru-blu' wouldn't sell-out about and disrespect another man, unless he was in a position to stand his turf, if the need arose.

And believe me, for 'Renegade' to talk as he does and then turn-around, go out in the yard, with everyone else, is prime example that he's either just a 'big-mouth', a 'Bruce Lee impersonator', or simply 'has a death-wish'.

I don't know Renegade's viewpoint of death-row. He has no experience that I'm aware of, of what it's like to actually be on Death-Row, other than as a trustee.

If these guys aren't in here for crimes they DIDN'T commit, some of them might have all but given up on life, and are waiting for an excuse to take someone out to prove what he might see as his 'self-worth'. So for 'Renegade', a 47 year old man, to act in such a manner, is beyond my way of rational intake and wisdom. But I observe...

For the most part, the guys on death-row play their hand close to their chest. It's like you never really know where the man is coming from.

Chapter Twenty

March 10, 1992
A news flash just report that Mr. Smith, "Tiny", has been granted a reprieve. Not really sure of its meaning myself. I was told by others on my wing that a reprieve, unlike a stay-of-execution, means that he (Tiny) will be getting off death-row and put into population. He was set to be executed 3-11-92, so he must be pretty well off with relief.

The Run-A-Round told us days ago that 'Tiny' don't feel any optimism toward winning a stay-of-execution. Much less a reprieve. He (Tiny) was said to be just ready to go with the flow...

Who's to say what's the proper conduct under such circumstances? How is anyone to know the true impact of such a complex situation? I know that I don't know. It gets kinda sad sometimes. But the beat goes on.

Each time another fellow death-row inmate is set to die, I, as I'm sure most of us do, must again prepare to combat some of the many emotional impacts/reactions to being subjected to such acts...

Sometimes I think the prison system wishes to run a boo-game on the rest of us by having the Chair so close to our cells. So close that the actual distance between the Chair itself and my bunk is only about 40 yards. Absolutely no more than 50 yards. Why else would we have to live so close to the Death House?

I don't know about the rest of Death Row inmates, but I say there's no time for tears no matter how sad it gets along the way. This whole thing, in my opinion, must be taken one day, one step, at a time. As we do our best to be our best, in firm belief that Allah gave each of us, as human beings, the necessary tools to endure all trials and confrontation in life. BUT TO BELIEVE!!

...

3-12-92
I spoke personally with Mr. Smith ('Tiny') today for the first time since his execution was stopped on 3-9-92. One of the first people I saw upon entering the yard today was 'Tiny', seeming very pleased in light of what would have taken place yesterday, if his execution hadn't been put to a stop. Who can blame him for the obvious delight on his face; even

down to the way he holds his cigar in his mouth, 'Big Boss Man' style.

Upon speaking with 'Tiny' about his ordeal over these past few weeks, I learn first-hand that his previous set execution back in 1986 came within 4 hours of being carried out and thereby letting me figure out, within myself, that those were only rumors about that particular execution coming within 30 minutes of being carried out... Although the television report stated that 'Tiny' won a reprieve, I'm not sure if it meant that 'Tiny' would be getting off Death-Row.

'Tiny' told me that if anything, he's more likely to get another trial. I can say one thing for sure: Today only put icing on the cake yesterday seems to have been. I had prepared myself for what was set for Tiny on 3-11-92. So, automatically, I was released from having to deal with its emotional impact. But, for the most part, I don't think there are cowards on death-row. I mean, whether we're guilty or not, we all, most of us, declined to plead out for a life sentence to avoid facing the electric chair.

In my case: I'd rather die as a man than to lie as a worn-out coward. I respect life, but it seems worthless if I can't have justice as a tool to use to set myself free. So! To plead-out for/in fear of death would be to show a lack of courage, or an admission of guilt. Each man must do what he thinks is best for him according to his way of reasoning.

The way I see it: Any person who lets the talk of death stop them from fighting for their rights and/or what they believe in, is a person who hasn't accepted the fact that all of Mankind must die from this earth, sooner or later.

And: later can be just as soon as sooner, since tomorrow isn't promised to anyone. That's why it's so important to me that I live my life as I feel is best; and in accordance with the way Allah makes me from within. It's not easy. It's no fun. But, at the same time, there's no time for tears.

As the beat must surely go on.

...

I write poems. So far, I have 150 that I plan to make part of my book-of-poems. The other day Mike Tyson, after sentencing, said that he had been humiliated world-wide for a crime he's not guilty of. I took 'humiliation' and wrote poem number 150, which is also an inspiration:

'Humiliation Is Inspiration'
*All through one's life
Humiliation seems a test
Defeating the weak
Inspiring a will, the rest
Only the strong survive
Is not just an ole saying
For each day, in every life
Humiliation is preying
Sometimes a little
Other times a lot
Humiliation is telling
Can you survive, or not
Can you go on
When all seems lost
Will you still stand
If loneliness is the cost
During humiliation
Some associates pull away
Concerned about other people
What they might say
Oftentimes, above
Humiliation must be endured
With an inspiration
Inner faith has assured
Only the strong survive
In joy, and humiliation
For, to those, survival
Is a life-long dedication*

Chapter Twenty-One

March 23, 1992

"Hello my precious Mother

I pray that you are well upon receiving this card. How is everyone? Please give them my love as always. My thoughts are always resting upon you with my prayers. I pray that you are well?... Mother, the reason for this letter is to inform you that my Oral Argument in my 'case' will be this Thursday in the 11th Circuit Court of Appeals. I feel good about it. I have some good attorneys arguing my issue for me. So I feel okay. I have put it in Allah's hand. And believe me, he knows what is best for all of us. He will not free me until it is his will, because of what he may have planned for me on the outside. So if the courts decide I should come home, or have a new trial, it will be all in the hands of Allah. That is who I have my trust in... Mother, this is just to say I love you. And my prayers are with you. Every day. That is all I have to say for now, I just wanted you to hear from me. And to tell you I am fine, and I love you.
Your loving son,

Yuhanna

...

April 1, 1992
Nobody likes a snitch. But a cop. So whenever there is a situation when a person's conduct is questionable as being snitching or not, that person's the subject of many thoughts by those who dislike snitches. I don't like them. I have never liked them. And I never will like them.

S___t happened today that leaves me unable to express my full opinion as to what I'd like to say about the person involved... I will say that it takes a true-chump to sell-out to a man and then go to the guards on the man. I don't/didn't have anything to do with the matter, but I d___n sure didn't like the way it went down. At the very least, the guy who went to the guard should have requested that he, not the other man, be moved off of the wing.

Not only this incident, but he went to the guard on another man not long ago after an argument. Still he claims to be a 'tru-blu'. I can't see it myself. Maybe I'm blind to the logic, if any, in his actions. But for now, I think it was a coward's way out.

...

4-3-92
Tonight the television station broadcasted a program called 'Live From Death Row'. All week I, by me being on Death Row, have known that I'd be watching this show as an attempt to get some understanding on how this environment is proclaimed to be by those who are supposedly getting a message to the public as to how death-row is run and carried out.

This show is a Joke. For starters, the show would be suitable if it was called 'Live from Hollywood." It was a big Joke from the start to the back. The program did touch on a few of the injustices involved and, in some instances, a few moral questions/issues about the Death-Row concept in relation to its need; but not enough to erase the fabricated environment and stupidity of correctional officers/staff

4-8-92
As usual, here at FSP, someone is on death-watch downstairs in cell two of the second floor.

The particular guy who's subject of this entry is in cell one of the second floor. Incidentally, cell one and two of the second floor are death-watch cells for, from my understanding, this whole prison... So, I guess by me being in cell one of the third floor, that it is fair to say that I'm pretty close – floor thickness – away from anyone who's been set to die at /on a specific date.

The man on death-watch now is known to me only as Mr. Kennedy. This is his third time on death-watch. A time in which is said to be a sure execution. But me, I never say never unless I'm telling a lie. After that, I feel that all things are reachable with the Lord.

However, that doesn't seem to be Mr. Kennedy's frame of thought at this time. Yesterday I read a kite (note) he had sent to my neighbor's cell.

In it Mr. Kennedy states that he has made peace with the world and is actually looking forward to the set execution day's potential results. He indicated that the execution would put to an end all of the emotional changes death-row can entail for those of us who take this too personally.

Does that sound wild? Or what?

Of course death-row is very personal. But it must be approached with an open-mind or it will kill your spirit long before any man would have a chance to kill the body. That's the truth.

"If people – in general – were to worry about the fact that they must one day die, every day they wouldn't feel a need to make the most of their day spent worrying about a day that will someday come anyway."

Mr. Kennedy makes it clear that he's ready for that day. That's his choice. And its only better, in a sense, that he is given time to prepare his soul for the Lord in case his execution is carried through as planned by State Officials... He could have been so unlucky that death would come out of the dark without giving him a chance – if need be – to repent and receive the Lord Allah as his personal savior. *"God can be found in any circumstance."*

Mr. Kennedy has a 30-day death-warrant which means that his execution date is within 30 days of the warrant's signing. That was about three weeks ago. And if he's moved from downstairs tomorrow over to Q-wing, that would mean that his execution date is within a week (six days)...

I used to be – when I first arrived 10 years ago – on nervous alert about this type of thing. But not anymore. I guess Viktor E. Frankl best explains why I don't: *"Yes! A man can get used to anything, but do not ask us how."* – as long as he doesn't give up too soon.

...

4-11-92
Relatives and a few semi-friends on The Outside play an ongoing role on inmates. If a guy isn't going around downgrading those on The Outside, he's walking around speaking of how glad he is for them. In any event, The Outside does play a part on inmates one way or another. For me, I don't miss a day from thinking of my loved ones. And yes! – I even think of Crystal and Yuhanna Man. A lot each day, in fact.

At any rate, Renegade found out by mail, yesterday, that his younger sister died last month (3 weeks ago). This is a guy that has a time-fashioned ego, that has burst over the twenty years he has been in this place.

By this morning he was in an unexpressive silent mood that resulted in him having lost control over the self-control as needed in here. Got him a disciplinary write-up, and he's being moved. It's kinda ironic that this is the same inmate I have mentioned previously in these writings (22 year inmate, Run-A-Round)... Oh well, life goes on – for now. Who knows what tomorrow will bring. In faith I live!

...

4-30-92
"Talk about overnight development".

It was one of those very nights last night that prompted the phrase:

"Talk about overnight development".

To know exactly what I'm referring to, its only necessary to say: Day after LAPD trial win in a no-win situation for beating Rodney King, news report indicates at least five deaths and injuries into over a hundred.

All because what seems to be the 1992 version of "Jim Crowism" regarding how a black man is viewed by an all-white jury, where the other side (Defendant) is white, or; the victim is white and Defendant is black.

In a way it's good that white America got to see how an all-white jury, mixed with testimonies of police against blacks, will overlook clearly established facts, rule against the black man, and still tell the world they did their best to be fair.

I don't agree with the type of reaction displayed out in California last night in the wake of the Not Guilty verdict, but I wouldn't try to stop anyone either. We all have to react to life and all it entails as best we know how.

If it's by/with the Mind: Think harder. If it's in fighting: Kick Ass. That's my opinion. I have a right to it. All Mankind has a right to freedom of expression.

...

Mr. Kennedy will die tomorrow (5-1-92) unless he wins his hearing before the high-courts tomorrow.

Another man, Mr. Martin, is set to die next Wednesday (5-6-92). The Gov. of Florida just last night said that he has already denied Mr. Martin clemency and that Mr. Martin will know what's happening to him. (Mr. Martin attorneys are saying that Mr. Martin is too insane to electrocute.)

I have met Mr. Martin. In fact, he was my neighbor for two years. I remember him telling me that:

"The New Death Row don't have anything to worry about because The Death will soon be unconstitutional."

Well, that still may be. But my fight is to win this thing altogether, as opposed to getting off death-row and going back into population. Even to win a sentence reversal, and go back to population, it's still within reason to seek ground for freedom.

As to Mr. Martin, what can I say? All I can do is continue to trust My Higher Power to do and be right by us all. Anything else, I just don't know what's best to pray – ask for.

We live, we live, we live; Yet (!) – one day we all die, as will human beings all over the world. There's no getting around, regardless of where you are, or what you do.

...

Since this morning's entry, I've been out in the yard for two hours of sun-n-fun. During that time I observed the Execution Chair-man staff go to the back entry of Q-wing and, according to older inmates, make sure The Chair is in good working order, in case Mr. Kennedy doesn't get another stay of execution before tomorrow's five o'clock deadline.

...

May 3, 1992
I am glad that the violence/killing, is/are over, for the most part, with the Rodney King incident – which lasted three days.

Still – I am satisfied that many people got to do something they were missing out on due to unemployment in the country. "Go Shopping".

It wasn't hard for anyone to see – unless they were like the jury on the Rodney King Beating Trials – that many of the people on and out of the streets were mom's and kids seeking food, clothes, pampers, and other basic household needs. This is a clear indication of our Country's true state for those who wait on the governmental system to help them...

Many people – far too many – don't realize that this country was designed by the type of people who came to this country disregarding its Natives as people by claiming that Columbus 'discovered' America. And went on to run the Indians off the land by driving a stick in the ground and claiming the land as theirs.

Racial undertones aside, we, all of us, must learn to work for what we want, and if the government insists on taking away jobs or allow jobs to be done by Machines, f__k food stamps "Go wilding".

Go to free shopping just as was done these past three days. It may not be right by American standards, but I don't think anyone should go hungry as long as there are steaks (food) somewhere, anywhere.

I couldn't help but to imagine the many, many men who have sat on Q-Wing, and their frame of thought as they waited helplessly as a planned murder – their own murder – was in the process of being carried out within one week to 60 days.

I say one week to 60 days because when a person on death-watch comes within one week of his set execution/murder (he is moved over to Q-Wing) and put on Death Warning.

As hard as I tried, I have no way of knowing or imagining the impact such conditions have upon a person's emotions / sanity.

And if I have my way, I won't find out.

Sometimes I ask myself if I would be more intimidated by the death-row situation if I wasn't so confident within myself as to my true legal position and outcome of my appeals. I tell myself that I'd react the same. But do I really know how I would react to a phase in life that I haven't come to experience yet?... There's a big difference between coming 'up to' something and 'into' something... All anyone can do in life is their best to be their best, in faith.

...

5-5-92
A news flash just revealed that two rounds were lost today as Mr. Martin's attorney continues to seek clemency from the Gov. of the State of Florida. Once again, Chiles – on the news flash – stated that (Mr.) Martin's arguments are without merit as far as getting a clemency.

...

5-11-92
A news flash just revealed that Mr. Martin's plea to the U.S. Supreme Court has been denied again. As previously stated, for Mr. Martin's defense attorney to have been seeking clemency from Gov. Chiles is a clear sign that the Highest Court have already denied any and all appeals concerning Mr. Martin before.

So I can't say that I'm surprised at tonight's news flash. It almost seems like someone gets a kick out of holding out a too-short hand to a sinking man... Then again, what value can one put on another day of life? Even if it is spent in confusion, isn't it at least good for the time to prepare to Meet the Maker?

I don't know! I just don't know. All I can do is try to maintain my self-control and not let this environment cause me to lose my determination to take this whole prison situation one day, one step, at a time in the same faith and inner encouragement that has gotten me this far, and still sane, and dignified; not just as a man, but as a Proud Black Man who has self-worth enough to stand up for it against what many view as an impossible confrontation.

I'm in it to win it, or try until I die... All or nothing. No in between.

Chapter Twenty-Two

5-12-92
The first sign of the type of morning we had in front of us was the fact that breakfast was started at 4:30am instead of 5:30.

Mr. Martin's set murder time is for 7:01am. The lights on the bottom floor of Q-Wing and those of the generator rooms are lit-up – unusually – this morning.

I had breakfast just moments ago. I didn't want to eat knowing what was likely to take place this morning, but I had to, in order to show myself that I was determined not to let this type of environment alter my will to survive this ordeal and those likely to come.

Again, I can't stress enough how better prepared I am for this type of thing since I have come closer to this day a little at a time.

I've been here 10 years and at least seven have come within two days, to the two hours, of a set murder time... Each of these times I have to prepare myself for emotional pressure that must surely come with this type of subjection to judiciously organized murders by State and United States Public Officials.

At this moment, I can't predict my exact reaction to what hasn't happened yet. But I hope it will be and remains positive.

6:24 am
Spectator van just arrived at back-end of Q-Wing. I would assume that the family of the victim won't come in the same van as those of Mr. Martin's. Who knows? We'll see what goes during the course of this / these events.

6:35 am
It just came into my sight. Not at the back of Q-Wing yet, but parked outside of the fence to await a closer time to Mr. Martin's murder: Ambulance.

The generators are now running loud and clear as the time comes closer and closer... I'd rather be lying down in my bunk, but I want to recall as much of these planned murders as I'm able to do from my cell / room! Not fun! Necessary! The all-white death wagon is waiting.

6:41am
I had to be very short about the van of spectators earlier – hell! There's more fully-loaded vans carrying a bunch of people – all wearing suits – just pulled up to the back of Q-Wing!!

How civil of a way to see murder? This seems to be more of a theatrical production when all the players get off work and go home at the end of the play... Hey! This is no game and definitely no show. And Mr. Martin will be on the other side of life.

7:21am
The spectators have just left. The ambulance is still outside of the fence waiting for its role in this murder.

I didn't hear, or feel, any circuits vibrating as Mr. Martin was being murdered. So I guess that eliminates the rumors I've heard about the current being felt by way of vibration, as a man is being killed in the Electric Chair... That's another positive point of observing first-hand, though no desire to experience it first-hand.

7:36am
Mr. Martin's remains were just driven back past my window. Yet! – I looked upward in farewell to his soul.

I thank My Higher Power for enabling me to be as calm as I am at this moment after being subject to such action as the well-planned 3 ½ Million Dollar Murder that just took place.

I guess I'll clean-up my cell/ room and get ready to go out to the exercise yard at 8:30 this morning.

I refuse to let this morning stop me from striving for my freedom in the same or better confidence as I have been blessed to be able to do so far. "The beat goes on even if I'm the only one that hears it."...

I don't usually go out in the mornings exercise time, but after a morning like this I feel a need to do so. I'll even go out again. Most likely Thursday morning also.

5:06 pm
Been to the yard. Had lunch. Just had dinner. And this morning's events already seem to have taken a place in the past. Which it has, if you really think about it. A second gone is a second of the past!

Everyone off my wing who were out on the yard seemed about as calm as they usually are. Then again, I have to keep in mind that: To show fear in this place is to show weakness.

I have lots of fears, but showing those fears isn't of them. I will always be myself no matter where I am. And if anyone misunderstands my ways, that is not my problem. Nor will there be a problem, unless someone plays me as weak.

...

5-21-92
The media, over the last several days, had a field-day with Coleman's (in Virginia) upcoming set execution date – which was yesterday (5-20-92). I don't understand how the press can get off with pretending to be of help to someone in such a position. They (the Press) have no power over the courts.

...

July 21, 1992 (2am approx.)
As I sit on my bunk listening to the rain outside – tv turned down – low – I can't help but call back to mind what the guy in the holding cell with me on 7-9-92, said of his night prior to his set execution morning. He told me how he had gotten no sleep, as all he could do was walk his 7x9 cell as the guard outside of his 'Phase 2' Death Watch cell sat and watched his every move.

I can't help but to, somehow, rule out the idea of Mr. Kennedy over on Q-wing right now – 5 hours before set execution time – sleeping only to wake up to be put to death in case Gov. Chiles doesn't grant a 'stay'... Somehow I picture him doing something equivalent to walking his cell. It's hard for me to even imagine what I'd be doing at this moment if I was in Mr. Kennedy's immediate predicament.

But it's not that hard to imagine how the guy from the holding cell (7-9-92) had a stroke when – an hour and a half before execution time – he was told he had won a 'stay'.

I also noticed today – as when any inmate is set to die very soon – how some guys in here seem to act out, unusually so.

The example: You hear meaningless chit-chat and laughter at things that usually go disregarded. It's all a part, I think, an attempt, to look normal even though a fellow inmate is sitting close by – on Q-wing – with death seeming imminent... However it turns out to be un-normal, in the sense that it is a form of self-deception, in an attempt to deprive reality of its existence.

...

7-21-92
6:29am: Unlike the morning on which Mr. Martin was killed in May, we haven't had breakfast yet.

I woke up to the sound of the generator that is used to juice-up the electric chair. I guess the same mode of steps will take place with Mr. Kennedy as did with Mr. Martin. It's not too late for him to get a 'stay', but d__n sure seems unlikely as time goes by.

The white station-wagon looking ambulance just pulled up outside the front fence to FSP.

6:35am: We just had breakfast. I was able to eat it by considering it as a last meal with Mr. Kennedy. Still I can't help but wonder at the nerves of the prison staff to serve breakfast so close to a set time in which a man will be killed only 40-50 yards away from where I sit at this moment.

6:50am: Two vans of spectators just arrived, as when Mr. Martin was killed. The first van I thought to be a spectator van, was very likely the van that carried the person who pulls the switch. This van had extra dark windows, and was much smaller than the two spectator vans filled with family and other spectators.

7:01am: As I looked out my window just now, an all-white seagull or dove slowly flew by our wing. It has nothing to do with Mr. Kennedy's set execution.

7:10am: Mr. Kennedy is reported dead.

7:11am: Spectator vans are leaving the prison grounds. Again there was no sound as to the exact instance Mr. Kennedy was electrocuted.

7:22am: I wonder: Could that white bird be some kind of a sign indication, a sense of freedom, for Mr. Kennedy?

The ambulance is on its way in to pick up the remains of Mr. Kennedy. Not the same one used to carry out Mr. Martin's remains... I don't think so.

7:31am: Mr. Kennedy's remains were just driven by my window. All I can say is 'Hi'.

I don't guess I'll go out on the exercise court this morning. I'd like to show respect for Mr. Kennedy.

The guards here have a way – after every execution – to try to side the mood of inmates, or what they are thinking. So I'm not going to give one of them the chance to 'read me'. This has been another extra-curious morning for me, to say the least.

10:39am: Some guys just got back from two hours of yard exercise. I heard from one of the two black guys out there today, that he was asked why the other brothers (meaning myself and others) didn't come out this morning. He was wondering the same thing, so he couldn't answer that question.

One white guy, I was told, suggested that we stayed in as to show respect for Mr. Kennedy. But one of the two young brothers in the yard responded: "We're all the same color when we're put in the electric chair."

All I can say is that this subjection to such inhuman behavior by public officials, is a sense of helplessness similar to that you see as wolves attack a heard of impalas and kill the young, the weak, as the rest stand by able to do no more than look in, full of compassion, but unable to help the ones under attack.

It's sad. But just like the surviving impalas, you must move on to gorge and drink, in order to survive ourselves... It's a little sad, but very true.

Chapter Twenty-Three

November 3, 1992
As I hoped, Gov. Bill Clinton won a seat as President today.

This is good. At the very least, in the sense, that this country – those who voted to put Clinton in office of President – will now have renewed optimism with respect to change.

By that, I mean, I hope – that Americans will do more on their own to help bring about whatever hopes led them to vote for Bill Clinton. And being that I expect to gain my freedom on appeal, my part in helping my country, is by going on to inspire many by simply showing that being subjected to unfairness (Jim Crowism) doesn't mean you have to turn cold and bitter towards the whole world.

Standing alone, my intended effects as stated above will be small. But if each individual can find cause to do a little extra to create an acceptable sense of unity, a society/humanity, I firmly believe that we as Americans/Humans will be better off later on, than our current state of existence.

Regardless of where a person might be, it's crucial that we Americans/Man/Mankind, answer Yes (!) to Rodney King's famous 'Can't we all get along' question during the L.A. riots in '92. Otherwise, it won't matter who is President. We will continue to self-destruct.

...

Three days ago a fellow death row inmate, just downstairs from me, hung himself. He's not the first inmate to harm himself since my coming here. But his applies to a 'unique' situation, due to the fact that he didn't die. He's brain-dead!

According to the grapevine, this guy Kenny is a dependent on coffee, cigarettes, and other forms of calmers, so as to stay functional in this prison/death-row environment. At any rate, he is said to have been out of any/all of these items, three days ago, when he asked the foreman (runner) down there, to sell/ trade his hot-water bag for some of these items.

But (according to the floor-man), by the time the floor-man returned with any kind of reply, he (Kenny) had hung himself there, inside of his cell. It took 10 minutes (as the grapevine goes) before the guards would even come see why all the inmates were even calling to them.

During all of this, Kenny hung by his neck. Even afterwards, when guards arrived, he hung until backup guards could come, so they could open Kenny's cell. It's said that once the guards entered the cell, it was necessary for them to shake Kenny's legs – still hanging – and ask if 'he was alright.'

Kenny is currently in an off-prison ground hospital, on a life-support system that is the only link to his living. As to how long the State will pay for such a system for a man they plan to kill anyway, is beyond me.

It's hard to say why Kenny would do something drastic, like hanging himself, after enduring this place for 10 or so years. It could be any number of reasons/excuses. Yet, it's still sad to see anyone – in or out of prison – give up on life and themselves.

I've done it in the past, only to be taken over by this superpower deep within my soul – forcing me to take a stand. I don't know why all of us don't have this backup power that kicks in quicker for some than it does for others.

I can't call the man weak, for I know that I, too, am weak without this inner power that I depend on. Maybe some of us don't have any/enough faith in this inner power, even after it presents itself. And as a result lose all hope in life.

It takes courage to have faith. For faith is actually seeing through the feeling of a soul whose only vision is confidence, and a power beyond that which can't be seen with the average set of eyes. Maybe Kenny didn't have enough of this courage. Who knows?

In addition to what Kenny went through a few days ago, it's said that the guys down there found it funny (some of the guys) and found it something to joke about. I'm more compassionate in sorrow for them than I am disgusted by their laughing at a situation that they themselves could very well be in someday. None of us, in or out of jail, can be certain as to how strong-willed and confident we will be tomorrow.

But as to those who laughed at Kenny, they most likely did so to hide their own fear at the pressure we must deal with each day in this death-row situation. I'd be willing to bet that the very ones who did the laughing are among the most scared in this place.

It's all part of their ego-trip that some find necessary in order to look tough, which is really a denial of reality. And which will eventually result in the very pressures that cause a person to wake up one morning and convince himself that he's better off dead. For this, I have compassion and sorrow for anyone who'd laugh or make fun at such a situation.

My concern goes out to Kenny. Again, this is a circumstance that I must view as part of this environment – not letting it get to me in ways that will not draw from my efforts to endure all I must endure in order to survive this phase of my life.

Though frequently sad – this place – I must continue to strive towards the next day and hope that I can use tomorrow something that I learned today, thanks to what I learned yesterday. One day, one step at a time, in hopes that I am doing the right thing – in Blind Faith!!!

...

11-12-92
Having had to live in this prison environment (much different than jail), since my so-called trials, my instincts have sharpened in ways normal street-life falls short of bringing. It becomes necessary to determine the character of a person within the first 10 to 30 seconds of an encounter.

Such practice paid off today.

While I was on call-out, seeing a doctor about my back pain, upon initially reaching the clinic area, I took in the guy in the holding cage next to the empty one I was likely going to have to wait in to be called. Even before I reached the cage, I had determined that I'd be better off not to let the guy get under my skin.

I mean, I saw all of this just by taking in this guy in within 15 seconds prior to reaching the holding cell / cage. As it turns out, I was right.

I didn't know him, he didn't know me, but as soon as I was in the cage next to his, he turned to me and, through the bar section of plexiglass, said "What's up, bruh? You got a date yet?"

All death row inmates wear yellow t-shirts so our position is known to everyone at all times.

When he asked me this, I said "What?", even though I kinda knew what he was talking about.

His reply was: "You got a date to meet the Maker yet?"

That's when I knew for sure that this guy was a fruitcake. He was wearing a green t-shirt, so that told me he was in refinement cellblock.

Anyway, I simply said 'no' to his question. After that seemingly came to his mind, part of what he said was that he had been here since 1969, or so, and that told me that this life has gotten to him, and as a result, caused him to act in a way that made him act like a fruitcake.

He was even causing the guards trouble by calling them 'Crackers'.

The guy, in question, is white.

I try my best to be civil. To understand. If my initial reaction of this guy had been other than what I said, and if he hadn't been, obviously, far out in space, I would have reacted to him differently. In a more cold nature. At one point this guy may have been twice as sane, as I think I am, today.

Chapter Twenty-Four

November 26, 1992
Who's fooling who? I often ask myself about the way racial undertones are excused. I often find a little humor in the way some people explain – by their own standards of logic – how and why certain things were done, or being done.

Today, for example, I hear AT&T has a new system that will do the job of some 3000 operators, thereby making it necessary to lay-off in the near future. I will comment on the Chrysler Corp. claim that they've lost about 600 million in sales last year (1991).

Maybe the thousands of employees they laid off for the machines would have made up for much of that loss. They'd still be working. What is the point of having machines to outwork people, and not be able to sell what the machine is producing?

The auto worker can't take his car to the car wash because he must first find another job, and meanwhile save his money. The same is so for the burger stand and any other place where the humans there were traded for a machine.

In the long run, these places suffer for not having the services of those traded for the machine. And yes the phone might even have to go.

Racial – of course! It's the Machine Race against the Human Race.

Maybe I'm just confused about the way things are. Or am I?

I'm confused still as to how anyone can talk themselves into actually believing that blacks were 33 ½ parts animal. And how a white man explains to his wife and kids that he saw fit to sleep with the black woman. Not only getting sexual satisfaction, but kids as well. Is it any wonder that the people of today are attempting to maintain such two-sided justification?

On Rodney King... I say that the racial fighting is/was a prime example, and just because this is what it sometimes takes to get a point across when pleading has failed.

"A cat will run from you as long as there's a place to run. But the same cat will viciously attack you if trapped with no place to go."

That's what took place in L.A. and what will take place all over the country unless we find a way to be a human race and not so much the divided one we are at present.

I think we must stop pretending to like, or want to like, each other. We don't like each other from / by birth. However, common respect is something we'd have to want very badly.

...

I'm often writing how I don't fear or worry about anything on earth as circumstances by Man, but today is/was an exception:

As I was lying in my bunk asleep – sleeping good (!) – all of a sudden I found myself being awakened by a noise inside of my cell. Even before my mind had a chance to register what it was, I saw sparks shooting into my cell, toward my bunk, from my vent.

As I was jumping from my bunk, I couldn't help but wonder how the f__k could this be happening! All I could figure was that some type of wire had shorted-out (odd as that even seemed) – inside of the air-vent. Therefore I was afraid to touch any of the steel in my cell.

I called out "Hey" real loud because at this time I wanted out of the f__g cell. But as I called out the Run-A-Round said (after he finished laughing) that holes were being cut into the duct just behind my vent and the rest of them (vents) on down the line. The holes were being cut with a blow-torch, which explains the sparks flying in my direction.

I guess you'd have to have been in my shoes, and been awakened, to grasp the full impact as to the scare something like that brought about. Again – and no shame about it – that scared the s___t out of me! I mean, a scare I haven't felt in many years.

Once I was calmed down, I was able to look up at the vent from time to time and laugh at myself. Which is actually very good, in the sense that, in an environment such as here, it's not often that an honest and sincere laugh makes your day as the one I've had today has done for me. Not often at all.

...

Lately I am noticing that I am having to concentrate and dictate my train of thought so as not to lose my respect and concern for humanity.

Luckily, for me, I've been blessed with a determination to accept the circumstance for what it is, and to not be discouraged from my own personal fight for survival. I guess we (all death row inmates) are expected to exhibit a strong image, or, on the other hand, be Chumps, to the max.

And, as a result, it becomes easy to lose all sense of compassion. It's a task to stay civil, but one that I am determined to take on for as long as necessary so as not to stop being as caring and compassionate as I am from within.

...

Exactly one week ago (Thursday, 11-18-92) as I was trying to encourage a brother to put more effort into his appeal process by studying case law, I realized that more of us (on death row) feel more helpless than I initially thought.

I guess this realization comes from my ability to see beyond a certain point of the 'front' the guys put up in here that seems necessary to survival.

Yet (!) – last week, as I told this guy of the self-confidence and dedicated effort he must put into his legal position, I sensed fear (him fearing his efforts) as he slowly said he was taken advantage of 12 or 13 years ago when he first picked up his death sentence.

Young and dumb to law. As that may sound sad and be true. I see no reason for him or anyone else to just throw in his fight and, as a result, be subjected to whatever those involved in putting him here wish to do.

I went on and told the brother how I, too, didn't know s__t about law. As I followed the advice of that morning that told me "Go get them Abdullah, I'm watching you."

I even told him how I got discouraged after I realized how little I knew about layman's reading and writing. I just told him how I held to that powerful force that spoke to me on that morning. I told him that I can't help but to believe an inner message so real and confident. This day I believe in myself even if I'm the only one that does.

Now to get to why I wrote of that last week:

As I sat here on my bunk doing a little case research for my attorney's use, I heard that same brother (as did the whole wing, most likely) who said he had been taken advantage of (and, even now, has no good appeals attorney). He was cheering and laughing a football game on.

At that moment, I couldn't help but ask if there was any wonder he was still on this d__n death row. It's no secret that once a man is here past 10 years – on into 12 and 13 years – its very likely that the State can't send them to the chair for one reason or another. And they (inmates) remain on death-row because he or his attorney aren't pushing the proper legal language to, at the very least, get off death row.

I read a book called 'Last Rights (Rites)' that recounted the details of 10 or so people who died in either, Florida's Death Chair, or some other nearby state. I wanted – looked for –

the common line of procedures used by state officials to get away with killing them.

Common among almost all of these cases is trials within 6-8 months, undedicated attorneys, uneducated defendants, and ineffective representation by trial attorneys.

That's what I tried to tell this brother (black guy) last week. And that's why I was a little sad to see (by ear) him, cheering on a game. I like games too. But they will have to wait until I am pleased with my own efforts to see my appeals attorney, learn all I can of my legal position, and plans to win appeals.

Chapter Twenty-Five

November 27, 1992
So, today, I listened to an inmate say he won't die until his time, and if his time was now it was just his time (standing in the heavy rain as it thundered and lightened near the watch on his arm/wrist).

I fail to agree with that set of logic.

First of all, I told him, I'd better go wait by the gate until the guards take us inside from the weather. I didn't want to be standing beside him if Allah decided to send a bolt of fire down on his ass as a result of that watch shining and flashing all over the d__n place. I don't fear death, but I respect it enough to use the common sense Allah gave me to avoid it as much/long as I humanly can.

If a person lets his own logic be based on thoughts such as those used out on the yard today, he (or she) is likely to stand in front of an oncoming train and say "If it ain't my time to go, I won't go."

Our Creator gave us each a set of arms, legs, feet, hands, and brains. Surely he meant for us to use them – all or some – to serve as common sense.

Maybe this is just another way for this person to show how fearless he is of death, as well, show others that death row sits within that same circle of concern in his life. I simply don't see any connection between Allah's will for this guy, and standing in the weather with an arm-piece that invites death.

It's another of the many indications that most of us on death row (in prison) aren't afraid of death.

Unfortunately, this very non-fear of death is sometimes overplayed to a point where it becomes easy to disregard common sense.

For that reason – one of the many I have – I try to learn from what I observe of others as I continue my everyday struggle to maintain a rational state of existence.

Events inside and outside of this place (family and friends of support) puts me, and likely everyone else in here, to and through some emotional pressure that can't help but be unique.

I'm still convinced that I haven't felt the full pressure – and don't want to – of a death-row inmate who has no idea of his legal position and chances on appeal.

I still believe in the concept of America. To be free and afforded liberty regardless of race or belief. I'm just disgusted with those who make a concerted effort to keep certain races down by and through a wide range of tactics long ago designed to create such an effect. And being as disgusted as I am, I have made up my mind to stand firm and strong so as to be an inspiration to my people.

Anyone reading this will probably think I'm a racist. Aren't we all, to some extent?

This is true. But only in the sense that I'm only able to do so much as one person. And being that my race (black) is the underdog, my natural instinct is to do all I can for my birth people.

All I ask of America, as a whole, is that my people be afforded rights as Americans. Otherwise, we have a problem – a big problem.

...

As I watch news coverage of my sisters and brothers over in South Africa, I have to feel a sense of luck to be in my current disposition, as opposed to having no food, no shelter. South Africans must go without if they aren't a part of those who are on the move, taking from the weak brothers and sisters.

Initially, I wondered what greedy and uncaring barbarian it takes to allow other brothers and sisters to starve to death. To me it was unjustifiable, and still is. And then, too, I had to remind myself that brothers – right here in this country – are doing almost as bad by selling drugs to my brothers and sisters here.

It saddens me to see this, but just today I saw a report where my brothers and sisters who were starving to death actually smiling as they received some food – something some people will laugh at, thinking it was a joke – from a force that protected the shipment as it got to them.

The moral of this issue is the fact that, as my friend Angela Thomas would say:

"No matter how bad things seem to me at times, I have to remember that – somehow – someone would love to trade places with me."

Looking at my brothers and sisters in such a state has enabled me to appreciate my life even more than I already did.

...

Even though I felt abandoned by my friends and relatives – most of them – in an ongoing sentence, the longer I remain locked up, I still didn't contemplate losing everyone. But my mother... Like I said, I'm on a mission to regain my freedom, therefore, I must count these types of situations as that of which I have no control over. Once I've done my best – and I did – on this matter.

The reason I sought a pen-pal was because of the mental outlet – writing to someone. At the same time I found it sad that – with all the relatives and friends I once felt so a part of – abandonment caused me to seek strangers to correspond with.

This is a part of all of our lives in prisons everywhere. I had heard about it but was so sure that my friends and relatives would be by my side, no matter what.

I didn't want to realize this truth, but it's become necessary to my survival that I accept this abandonment. In so doing, I am able to start anew without unconsciously depending on someone else for my own personal inner confidence and self–worth.

Now I find that I must try to not overly resent those I feel abandoned by. It would be easy to say f__k them, but to me, that would be deceiving myself.

No more than minimal with them, but I can say my love is the same. This is something – among other things – that I must learn to deal with, one day, one step, at a time. In BLIND FAITH!!

...

On a day-to-day basis I find it necessary to make certain that I have a reliable sense of purpose for my existence. As simple as that may sound, it's an everyday part of my life in this place – as I combat any potential discouragement that can result in this place. A reliable sense of purpose, I found recently, must go beyond expecting letters from family. It must go beyond the optimism which is afforded by mere efforts to do my best to BE.

As optimistic as I am about my appeals, I can't pretend that my present surroundings don't exist. Therefore, I must endure the sense of rejection I feel by those who don't have the insight and optimism of my appeal and have left me to fend for myself. That doesn't bother me any more. I've learned to rely on me, and the power my Creator has blessed me with.

...

Once again my initial brief has been sent back to the Florida court. Supreme has been denying me. By the grace of Allah, I feel I may get some play this time around. I am now waiting on a ruling. I'm confident that all will go well on the ruling...(prayer)...

It is all just a matter of time. I continue to have confidence and patience that every day I am more concerned with my brief being accurately effective as opposed to just speedy.

...

11-30-92
Every time I turn around, I hear headline reports, or t.v. programs making reference to crime and how it's seemingly on the rise. The way I see it, more and more people must be adapting to the foundation of the country (America/U.S.).

After all, isn't it true that blood, death, and force were used to take this land we call America from the Native Americans? – once claimed to have been savages – by white men – to justify their brutal takeover? Indians? – Yes! It is true.

Why then – I wonder – are there so many cries of crime on the rise. When has it been down??

All of the pretense. The very pretense that prevents races from coming to terms in unity. Even if all of us can't get to like each other. The way I see it, we have one race that stole all the marbles and now wants to lay down some ground rules that they call 'laws' and 'constitutions'.

In their shoes, I'd have created some rules also. But to those of us who were still slaves during the writings of such rules (most of us) fail to see the justification and reasoning behind the request for less crime. We're asked to adjust to the American way, and then we're called savages and criminals when we do. The American Way, is taking what you want.

A week or so ago, Oprah Winfrey did a piece on her show that dealt with early release from prison. She made me mad when she had the nerve to say 'Let's face it, these people can't be reformed."

It seems to me that when a person of color gets to talking like that, they've obviously forgotten where they've come from. If we are to believe that the white man has reformed from 400 years of everyday crime against people of color, in the 127 years from 1865 up until today – 1992, why can't we believe that a person who has committed far less acts of crime can be reformed?

It's one thing to see the white man play blind to the facts of this country's foundation, but it becomes sad when I see my people forget where they come from. And having been subjected to modern-day Jim Crowism in 1991, I know for a fact that many of our so-called 'Public Officials' are still as criminal as were the founders of this country.

Crime has always been 'up' in one form or another. And just because the press and those controlled by the white man only focus on some, doesn't mean others no longer exist.

No matter how much I evolve, no matter how I adjust to doing a particular something to endure my current position... its times like these...

Chapter Twenty-Six

12/2/92
A while back I wrote about the brother who said wearing his watch in weather that could possibly draw lightening didn't bother him, since he wouldn't die until his time. Last night I was saddened again to hear him explain why he wouldn't take a flu-shot. What saddened me wasn't his not taking the flu-shot – most of these guys don't take them for some reason or another – as much as what he said.

Throughout these writings I refer to what I call 'creating a false sense of reality', to justify a lack of self-esteem and also to protect an ego, which is no more than a cover-up of failures, to overcome the fear and doubt this environment entails.

If a person thinks in, and acts in, this fashion for a prolonged period, he or she will, sooner or later, master the art of self-deception, to an extent that their own conduct is a symbol of wisdom or power to those who are also confused and looking for excuses to justify their lack as stated above.

Many of the guys certainly complain about petty issues. Those who create a false sense of reality say anything. They talk, yet they don't say anything of, in my opinion, substance. If such energy were to be channeled toward something positive there wouldn't be a need for the continued idle gossip and/or complaints I hear.

Death row leaves the inmate confident within a 7x9 cell, 24 hours a day, except for the two-hour yard time we get twice a week, if weather is good. And this disposition can work for or against a person who must endure it.

'For' is when a person is able to maintain positive and optimistic sense of self. 'Against' is when a person allows intentions of others – those of state prosecutors, prison guards, etc – to dictate his or her sense of self-worth. If a person doesn't feel of value that person will likely have, later on, no sense of purpose in life.

What saddens still, is the fact that most of my brothers and sisters who war on each other, are actually mad and frustrated because they've been conditioned to think that what they DON'T have is more important than what they DO have: SELF.

I say declare war on the chains that keep the spirit of persons down.

That chain is only as complicated as each individual's ability to strive for self-worth and inner peace. Their ability to accept their position in life at face-value and strive to change it if it is desired. This can only be done when reality is viewed as it is, as opposed to how we wish it to be.

I do my very best to do all I can to stay up on my legal position and any legal studies. I might do so as to be of use to my attorneys. If I am going to be denied my civil and constitutional rights, anyone denying them will have to do it, obviously, in front of the whole country because I'm making certain that my position is known.

Additionally, I'm sure my knowing that I am not guilty of any of the actions against me have helped me to stand firm and fight for my rights. I am blessed with determination. I am thankful for it. And I will put it down as I get it down for a cause in which I know that I am right in fighting.

Besides, in the process I've gone through in over the 10 years since 1982 (arrest) I have had to learn how to better read and write, how to comprehend what I read, so that I can write it to my attorneys in an intelligent manner. Then, too, there is the knowledge gained while reading the legal material that I write to my attorneys from. I still have a lot more to learn, but at least I'm not ashamed of trying to learn, and subsequently, help myself as best I can.

In the county jail before I could use the law books effectively, I had to sit down and learn to spell again, learn to write again, learn comprehensive reading again, and learn how to project my thoughts and views on paper in an intelligent, legible fashion. This wasn't easy to do while under the pressure of the accusation that caused me to be in jail in the first place.

But I was determined to believe in that clear and confident voice that told me "Go get them, Yuhanna, I'm with you."

Maybe many people will make fun of this, but, so what? It was enough to get me out of my state of feeling sorry for myself, and on the ball of doing my part to help myself. S__t (!), even before this one morning I was aware of a superforce in my being that led me many times in my past.

But this time – this morning – I wasn't so naieve that I had to trick myself into thinking I would have overcome all without this force directing me at that very particular moment/phase of things. I am certain I have been blessed with a determined will that I have no intention of insulting by quiting, no matter how close I come.

...

(Date unknown)
Today a guy on my wing had to go to disciplinary court for a fight he had out in the yard last Thursday. While he was there waiting to be heard, another inmate from population (not on death-row), decided that he would stab an officer. And he did. The officer, who I was told was a high-ranking officer, was stabbed in the back.

The inmate who did the stabbing will likely get an attempted murder charge which might not mean s___t to him, since he has stabbed on several other occasions, and also has been here for over 15 years.

It's said that an officer lied on him to bring about his disciplinary write-up, and, in fact, he had already said he was going to stab one of the officers if he got some lock-up time for such bum write-ups.

The degree of f___k-up-id-ness this environment can lead some of us to take on is also why I try extra hard to avoid letting my negative thoughts dwell within me too long. For all I know, the guy who did the stabbing today could have found out that his mama, or kid, or something, had died, and as a result said "F___k it!"

In this place such conduct can happen, it seems, once such attitude is taken. It doesn't matter if the next person is an officer or inmate.

As I observe what I hear and see around this place, I try to teach myself how to evolve, either spiritually, or in plain, ole fashioned wisdom. The guys who have the hardest time from prison guards are those who display little or no self-discipline and/or self-control.

Many guys let themselves become no more than push-buttons to those who know they are easy to lose control and subsequently fall deeper and deeper in to the trouble zone on prison officials hit-list.

In a sense, that person becomes a toy to those who wish to play with him by kicking his ass, and, additionally, giving him a disciplinary write-up... I can safely say that I learned a long time ago that if you lose control of yourself, you lose control of the situation.

It may mean letting a lot pass that you wouldn't normally do, but in this type of set-up you don't have much room for a "I don't give a d__n" attitude. Unless you really and truly don't give a d__n and are willing to get stupid.

I have no idea how tomorrow will play on my self-control, but so far – thank Allah – I have been able to maintain a rational state of conduct and attitude, my current disposition, and need to do all I can to be of use to my appeals attorneys. In doing so, I go out of my way to avoid confrontation, or anything else that might work against all the effort that has gone into securing my victory on appeals. Just have to continue taking it step by step.

One of my primary concerns is that I don't unintentionally allow myself to become cold and distant toward the outside world, as is sometimes necessary to survival in this death-row environment.

I still have no idea of the full impact subjection has on the man that has no idea as to his legal position and chance on appeal. I mean, sometimes I kinda feel like a spy in the way I write about this place and its environment. As if I wasn't actually on death-row.

I'm sure such thoughts are unfounded on an intellectual level. I guess I just wish there was something I could do or say to make more of us death-row inmates display the kind of faith and inner confidence I live by each and every day.

I don't have a fear or worry on this earth, and when I see it in the eyes or voice of a fellow inmate, I only wish that person dare to have more faith in his God-given ability to meet any and all aspects of life head-on and full of vigor.

That way, no matter how things turn out, you are still a winner, simply because you tried as opposed to quitting before everything was turned out.

...

My optimism does not come easy. My faith doesn't come easy. And the only time they are easy, are from day to day. As I continue my efforts to combat negative thoughts and the many, many other potential setbacks that come with this place.

...

Still – thank Allah – I have cause for optimism – faith. Living in this 7x9 cell/room 24 hours a day – and maintaining a sense of sincere sanity – takes a little bit of time and effort to not lose touch with myself.

...

The main purpose of my starting these memoirs/notes, was for me to have a way of pinpointing some of my thoughts and opinions during my stay in this death-row system. I wanted to, should someone ask, tell how I survived day to day as I encountered different aspects of prison/death row life. So far I think I have kept about all I've wanted to keep written down for future purpose.

In my opinion, too many people don't even have the faith they are so quick to tell a sad or a low-spirited person to have. On more occasions than I can recall, I have seen doubt in the eyes of the very face that was telling me 'Keep the faith'.

I'm pretty sure it's all in good meaning, but I feel that people shouldn't advise others on something they don't know about. And by writing this line of memoirs, I'll be able to back myself up with proof that I believe in faith as someone who has experienced its powers first-hand.

This belief will be seen in my eyes and thereby show a positive note. I feel compassion for those who don't have the faith I have as they tell me to keep it – though they don't believe it, really.

...

Back in November 1991, I wrote of Mr. Leo Jones, a Muslim brother.

A news report confirmed he's receiving a new hearing, and of course, new date in court. Not 'new trial', a 'new hearing'. I'm very optimistic. I know some are more optimistic for my brother than I am, but the fact is that every other guy who has been here for a few years, have gone back to new hearings and new trials, only to come back to death-row.

I don't know the details of Mr. Jones' legal position, therefore, I won't spread what little I've heard of it. I am pretty confident that if he has something solid to work with and applies it correctly to his argument he will most likely be victor.

After all, if I didn't have some faith in the use of the legal system, I wouldn't study case laws and other legal issues in my effort to be of use to my appeals attorney.

...

12-16-92
Though our Creator has the ultimate hand in fate, in my opinion, Mankind's action, or lack of action, causes temporary fate in many instances. Today, for example, I had to question what seemed to me a suspicious turn of fate.

Leo Jones, the guy written of above, was moved into my floor/ wing today. And by me being me, and aware of this dog-eat-dog environment, I can't help but wonder if or not someone had sent Jones out to hunt down brownie-points on new trial hearings.

I mean: If the State felt Jones was likely to get a new trial anyway, they wouldn't hesitate to put him on a mission like this, to tell on anyone stupid enough to talk to him in any detrimental way.

I'm not saying that Mr. Jones is on such a mission. All I'm saying is that I have read many cases where a same or similar thing has happened.

It is important that I ponder any circumstances that possibly could have been circumvented for the sole purpose of causing harm to my person or upcoming appeals in this environment.

This environment dictates such frame of mind, if a person is to reduce the chances of being lied on outright, or have something constructed wrongly against him.

One of the most outstanding things my trial attorney told me was that in light of our solid issues to be argued on appeals by my appeals attorney, the State attorney's office (Attorney General) will likely be putting someone around me in an attempt to illicit something that can be used, detrimentally, against me.

I'm even to the point where I don't hang-out with anyone out in the yard. I converse – out-loud – up and down my wing just as I do on the few times I converse in the yard. This is done to – among other things – not allow anyone to possibly lie as to the subject of any private conversations. I'm sure I really seem anti-social as I conduct myself in such a fashion. But like I said, this is hardball. And I do what I feel I must do in order to assure my victory through appeals.

I don't know Mr. Jones, or anyone else beyond names and, quite frankly, like it that way. Even when I feel I'm getting close to someone in here I pull back because I know I will be pulling back soon anyway.

I'd like to have a down-to-earth friend, one I can hang-out with. But the whole nature of 'suspicion' that comes with this place always stops the making of a true friendship in the way that friends should be.

But back to what's stated above, 'suspicion' along with knowledge of friends turned bad in the past, works to keep friendships to a minimum. Undesirable, but a reality of this type of environment. Non-death-row inmates (population) might be able to converse without difficulty to each other.

Maybe the fact that death-row inmates, all of us, have an appeal pending in some court or another and must be careful not to do himself harm. Population, on the other hand, don't likely have as many pending appeals at once. It's hard to say for sure how death-row compares with population.

But I can say that population inmates don't have to deal with the day-to-day stress death-row inmates must combat in order to remain civil from one moment to the next.

All of this I have written to justify my immediate suspicion of Mr. Jones' being moved to my floor/wing.

Yes! – there are other guys on my wing, and Yes! – any one of them could be that person my trial attorney warned me about. That's why even now I have to conduct myself in whatever manner I feel is necessary in my effort to rationally survive this prison into a successful appeal.

At times it's sad, cold, and seemingly unfeeling. But it's the people they need to be, when on death-watch.

Chapter Twenty-Seven

1996

Early 1996
Years ago I lost my trust in the way in which my food and drinks are handled. Before today, even though I've heard it does happen, I did not think twice before accepting something to eat and drink before mealtime. Today our juice was turned around because it was somehow learned that an inmate in the kitchen took a piss in it.

That was for lunch.

But it makes me wonder why we didn't receive any coffee or milk for breakfast. And would it be better to know about the pissed-out juice that was sent back? Or even worse, did the juice that replaced the first juice have a replace shot of piss also?

It's hard to make choices in my position. I don't have access to any other way of eating unless I was able to buy food from canteen, which I'm not. Therefore, I'm forced to eat my meals and pray over them as usual without putting too much thought of the possible contents therein.

Two things I can say for sure: (1) I have stopped drinking the juice, and (2) the guy who pissed in the juice had better be glad the inmates were unaware of his actions, for some guys might do to him otherwise. Hell – I might give him a kick in the tail for a stunt like that.

All in all, life goes on, and I must eat to live. I ask Allah to bless all of my meals. I believe he does.

...

A Saturday

This Saturday there's so much noise on the tier that even my earplugs are useless. Grown men are acting like high-school girls. The guards have some kind of sport on the radio.

Everyone is happy. Emotion-filled cries of joy come from every cell. They're trying to forget their problems. Or pretend they have none. It is easier that way. Easier than grabbing the bull by the horns.

...

5:40am: All the noisemakers are asleep. They've worn themselves out for the night, making merry. Laughing. Pretending.

It is strange indeed that a man can find anything to laugh about here. But everyone in here is locked up 24 hours a day. They have no past. No future. No goal, other than the next meal.

They are afraid, confused and confounded by a world they know did not make these loud noises. They won't hear what their mind is trying to tell them. That they are not afraid. Kind of like the superstitious individual who will whistle, or sing a happy number as he passes the graveyard.

Early Sunday

It is early Sunday morning as I write this. I am using the nightlight in front of my cell. This is a rare night. A departure from the ordinary. It's quiet. It occurs to me that you are probably asleep. But then, you may not be. This is my favorite time of the night, for composing my thoughts, mediating, etc. (I was before I started this letter.) I'm doing as I've always done: Wish for five, expect three, and get nothing.

...

October 20, 1996

Greetings My Precious Sister

May Allah's blessing be upon you receiving this short note. This is just to let you know I received the stamps and the money order. All was well received and appreciated. Thank you!

My sister I have enclosed the acknowledgement slip form classification acknowledging that "H" has been added to my visiting list (Alhomodullah) Praise be to Allah...

...Personally, I am looking forward to seeing my niece. Please give her my love. And tell her I look forward to seeing her soon (Inshallah) Allah's will... I have enclosed an article regarding those klansmen guards wearing a sheet to intimidate black inmates... That is it for now. – Your brother, Yuhanna, With Much Love...

…

The Gainesville Sun
9/21/93

Guard wearing a sheet ran in Death Row halls
Union Correctional officials are investigating a report of the incident.
By David Greenberg

" RAIFORD – Union Correctional Institution Superintendent Dennis O'Neill is investigating a report that a correctional officer donned a white sheet and raced through Death Row to intimidate black inmates.

O'Neill, who would not release the name of the correctional officer...

He is looking at the officer involved in the reported incident and another who may have witnessed it and did not report it.

"It doesn't appear that anyone of a supervisory nature was involved," O'Neill said. "The incident was reported by inmates..."

...

The Gainesville Sun
9/22/93

Corrections officer faces punishment

" RAIFORD- Correctional Sgt. 'T.H.' could face disciplinary action before the end of the week if officials determine he raced through Death Row wearing a sheet to intimidate black inmates.

Union Correctional Superintendent Dennis O'Neill... was reluctant Monday to release the 'T.H.' name when he received the report, saying he wanted to review it first and determine if disciplinary action was necessary.

However, Department spokeswoman D. Buchanan released the name Tuesday, saying it was public information.

...Death Row was at Florida State Prison until this year. Most Death Row inmates now stay at Union Correctional and are moved to Florida State Prison, where the electric chair is, when their execution is scheduled."

...

October 30: Around 5:30pm, three white shirts came to my cell and informed me that I was being transferred...around 6:30p... I arrive... was escorted to the Asst. Superintendent's office and informed that the governor has signed a death warrant on me which is scheduled to be carried out

December 4 – 7. I was able to make a call to my attorney and talk for a few minutes.

...

October 31: I awaken in my new environment. I decided to write a few letters and let my friends know where I am.

... 1 o'clock, I had an attorney call-out. It was with G. Andrews. We talk about my case, what some of the ideas are that they are working on. Once she finished talking – about 10 minutes – I jump in and talk for about an hour and a half... Once back in my cell, I wrote a few letters. I felt exhausted. After writing I fell asleep. I awaken about 11:30pm. I wasn't able to sleep, trying to get used to my new environment. It was a revelation. "Death" (a cold feeling). Scheduled to die. Sitting here thinking and feeling what was going on in the minds of those who went before you, is a real revelation.

...

November 1: Today I got into a discussion about a solution to the problems of the world in which we live. After that I decided to read some religious material to get my mind out of the cell.

5:20pm: 'M' just got back from an outside hearing. He doesn't have an attorney. My concern and prayers are with him. He told me that one of the attorneys called him a nigger. So he filed a lawsuit against them. Requested another lawyer.

...

November 7: (Prayer) Another day, not really much is happening. Everything is quiet. I have meditation on Allah all morning, fasting, etc.

2:45pm: The phone rang on Death Watch. It's the Asst. Superintendent... requesting to see 'M'... Something about the U.S. Supreme Court just ruled in his case. They just pulled him – so... (prayer)... we will just have to wait and see what has happened when he returns.

3:30pm: 'M' came back just a few minutes ago. I ask him what happened. He said they are getting worse. His attorney from C.C.R. just filed appeal to reprise him. The Florida Supreme Court asked 'M' to file a motion dealing with the conflict, concerning his law-suit. As of now, he still doesn't have an attorney. I can imagine what is going on in his mind. I believe it is some kind of mess forcing the judge to change his decision which he made on Friday 11-1-96, to appoint him another lawyer. The brother was telling me about his fears, going through ups & downs, but he has got to be strong...

November 8: (Prayer)...A new day is upon me. Everything is about the same. I have a 1:00 call-out...

...I was able to talk with 'Brother H.' We had a nice two-hour discussion on religion, etc. I really enjoyed my visit with the brother.

November 9: I awakened this morning to a discussion with an officer by the name 'Chaplain', who is Christian. He told me about his family, children, his boy, 16, who is suspended for hounding another guy in the classroom... I tried to shine some light on the problems that I see in the world... people are so conditioned that they only have one move... sit...and listen to his conversation... When the Human Call, we talk...

November 10: (Prayer)... Another day...

11:00am: 'Brother H.' called again. We talked about Tyson fight... 'H.' said Tyson got his tail beaten, taken in the 11th round...

... Today I discussed religion again with one of the officers... Under a spell...

November 11: I awoke this morning cold... Yes, it is very cold down here on the floor. 'Brother H.' called... we discuss Mankind again...

November 12: Today has been very cold. I've written several requests out last night to the Superintendent trying to get some heat down here... Medina just received a phone call from his attorney. His family has come...(prayer)... Maybe things will work out for him...

Received some mail a short time ago. Life, my spirit, somewhat friends from Prison U.C.I... It was a pleasure to hear from them. Allah ...(prayer)... letting me know I am not alone.

November 13: The heat was turned on today.

November 14: ...visited me today. We kicked it around a little... He...somewhat down, concerning...trying to tell him of my thoughts, and how I see it...I think I got my point across to him ...(prayer)...

November 15: My Mother and family came to visit me today. My niece she has gotten so big I couldn't believe it!...

November 18: Today they came and got my "size" for a suit, shirt, etc...

November 19: I call my attorney. I was informed that some new evidence has come...(prayer)...

November 20: 'H.' visited me. He shared some good news regarding my case.

November 21: The Chaplin came with the oil – (prayer) – I couldn't believe it. Allah is merciful...

November 22: The Chaplin came down with the oil again today...

November 23: (Prayer)... I call my sister this morning. We talked about old times. I really enjoyed my conversation with her. We had the chance to reconnect...

...Some time ago the Chaplin brought me some oil...

November 24: ...I just got off the phone with my attorney...

11:30am: I talk to Monica. She really made me feel great (smiley face)... I kick it around with 'Brother H.'... I smile when I think of Him.

...I was telling Pedro...that I don't want to never forget this experience...I believe there is so much to learn...

November 28: Thanksgiving Day – I call my Mother... We talk for a few moments...She was glad to hear from me...(prayer)...

'Brother H.' called. We talked for about 10 minutes. The officer rushing us off the phone... 'Brother H.' got a little upset and said he was going to call back and get his other 5 minutes (smiley face)...

I have been trying to get into some studying. I have the game on, between K... and D-Lions.

6:00pm: 'M. M' ... came up to visit me. We spend a couple of hours discussing different issues... I have no idea of what his attitude is, but there is something...

November 29: Approximately 5:10, I was awaken by the... (unreadable)...on the 12 to 8 shift, calling each other 'cracker', talking about running a train on some woman – etc. I requested that he hold the noise down. He told me it's time for breakfast, it's time to get up anyway. I requested to see the Sgt. He said he was the Sgt. I requested to see the Captain... Within two minutes the 'L'...(unreadable)... was on the floor. I bring this matter to his attention, telling him to tell the officer to cut the noise down... This officer ... was very insensitive to my concern... negative feeling was generated...

...I am scheduled for attorney call-out –

12:25pm: 'Brother H.' came up. We discuss some topics about my case... Brother R.' brought some religious... and bean pies...

<u>Phase II.</u> I have someone coming to my cell-dorm every 15 minutes. If you are asleep they wake you up. I went off on one of the officers for waking me. He told me he is just doing his job. I tell him if I'm lying in my bed asleep, at night, you have no right to wake me up every 15 minutes. If you do you will lose your job for harassment because that is what it is – Harassment.

...I send out and request... to see the Superintendent about the religious matter 'Brother R.' brought up yesterday...

1:00pm: It's a funny thing. The football game is Florida State & Florida Gators. The officer wants to rush someone off the phone, but when it comes to watching the football game, they want to buy you up.

...My cellmate next to me, for some reason he don't understand what is going on. He's obsessed with the German language, as if nothing else matters. I am trying to keep a controlled environment, regarding prayer... Satan is on his job, always trying to pull someone off the path...

November 30: (Prayer)... What will it be like today?... I heard the officers talking amongst themselves, about our situation here on "Death Watch"... They are expecting an execution... The situation is real funky. So was it yesterday...

... once I was back from my visit, was telling him something 'Brother R.' had told me. The brother seemed confused. One minute he want to see the Imam and the next he is cussing up a storm... I try to tell him he is not conscious of himself, nor is he Allah fearing...(prayer)... he will be alright. 'Brother H.' ...was telling me about the number of people that would be killed concerning the football game, between Florida State & Florida Gators...

December 1: (Prayer)I begin this day saying: I seek refuge in the Sustainer of Mankind, the Owner of Mankind, Lord of Mankind, from the evil of the sneaking whisperer who whispers in the heart of Mankind, whether he be from among... (unreadable)...or Mankind

... Since Phase II, I have these officers standing or sitting in front of my cell. They aren't conscious of themselves. Everything is a JOB. Little do they know hell-fire is upon them. I am grateful to Allah for saving me from the Hell of Mad-People...

3:30pm: Call Out. Mike came up to see me. We talk for two hours. I am sure I move him to some degree...(prayer)... I came to realize he is looking for a story within me. He told me he is going to be teaching a class of about 60 students – and the subject is about ME. He talked about putting me up on phone speaker. Visit ended 5:51.

... And I sit here trying to identify these feelings... Oh, Allah, What is going to become of ME?...

An officer called out to me, "Abdullah, what is going on with your case?"

I felt compassion for the first time.

"What is your attorney saying?"

Those words brought tear to my EYE...(Prayer)...Over 3 days in this cell, a (unreadable) call (smiley face)...I smile... A sea is stormy inside of me...

December 2:
...(Prayer)

8:30am: The Superintendent McAndrew came on the wing wanting to know is everything alright... 'D.' came looking around, etc.

9:30am: Asst. Superintendent T. and his (unreadable)... wanting to know if I have any last words I'd like to read. Witnessing his demeanor, shows me all of them are subhuman. I never seen anything like this conscience in them, allowing them to know I'm conscious of them.

They ask how are you doing. What kind of question is that?... (unreadable)... He asks me was Medina bothering me. I said he is in his own world. Yes, the brother was telling me last night he was having a conversation with some people from Germany who appear in his cell. He has been talking to himself all morning...(prayer)...he will be alright...

10:40am: Trying to understand the feeling within me at this moment. Oh, feeling speak to me... What is it that you are revealing... Oh, soul, I feel Allah is with me... (prayer)... I understand your concern for asking me this question. Just be patient. Allah is with us...

11:20am: The Investigator came to my cell and asks have I heard anything concerning my case.

12:15pm: 'Chaplain' just informed me that he had some bad news regarding the religious oil the Imam left me. He said he is going to try and contact the Imam to get some more oil 'Federal Express'...(unreadable)... I just received my religious books (prayer)!

1:20pm: Medina – is going off – FREAKOUT – yelling. The Mental Health... asking is he doing alright – he's yelling, talking to himself... May Allah (prayer) blessing be upon him...

2:21pm: I hear the officer talk about get some...for Medina. Laughing and joking about the brother, his situation, as if they want the brother to do something 'stupid'... They are watching him very close. Someone is saying he can't handle it.

... The phone rang several times. Each time I hope it's my attorney, but not yet. (Prayer)...

3:35pm: Medina just had some more medical experts down here talking with him in Spanish. He is talking to them...

3:45pm: His attorney just called him in reference to a stay of execution. He said he did not want to talk with his attorney... He said someone asked him about a blue shirt in Spanish...he said he don't know who she is talking about...Is laughing, to himself. He's tricking or something...(unreadable)... That thing is getting good to him... it is funny how he started acting 'crazy' within an hour of his attorney's call, talking about a stay of execution for him!...

4:20pm: 'H.' just called and let me know everything is going well. Just as they have planned...(prayer)... it felt good to hear from him!

Medina talking to his attorney, telling them that someone was in his sink, and he couldn't drink water, so he drank out of his toilet... The officer saw this and called the physician down to talk with him... He said he is seeing people in his cell...

-I have just received my mail. I heard from my nephew Herbert Jr.!! It brought joy to my heart to hear from him! May Allah (prayer) blessing always be upon him and everyone,(prayer).

I also heard from one of my favorite Muslim brothers 'T'.

7:30pm: Here come ... wanting to know what is going on in my case.

Chapter Twenty-Eight

December 3:

Tallahassee Democrat:
KILLER'S DEATH A DAY AWAY
For nearly 14 years the Rev. Glenn Lawhon of Wakulla County has waited for John Mills' execution. On Wednesday, that wait will likely be over.
By Chris Poynter

If the script plays out as expected, at shortly before 7am Wednesday, the Rev. Glenn Lawhon will walk into the death-chamber viewing room at Florida State Prison near Starke, take a seat and stare straight ahead through the glass window.

He will watch as John Mills, Jr. is strapped into the wooden electric chair – from his ankles buckled down, then his arms and his torso, and finally a leather flap placed over his face.

When 2,000 volts of energy slam into Mills' body, Lawhon, of Wakulla County, will know that justice finally has been served...

Mills grew up in the Wakulla County community of Buckhorn. He is the son of the late John Mills, Sr., a well-known businessman who ran a general store. An unpaved road in Buckhorn bears the elder Mills' name.

Some family members still live in the area, including Clarence Mills. He is a cousin of the younger Mills, but the two haven't spoken in nearly 12 years...

"I hope they can save his life," Clarence Mills said. "I don't know how come those boys did what they did."

Clarence Mills thinks it's unfair that his cousin, nicknamed "Boone," will go to the electric chair while Fredrick is allowed to live.

Yet for a friend of Les Lawhon, fair is a relative term.

Steve Pigott, a friend of Lawhon's who still lives in Wakulla County, said it has taken too long to carry out John Mills' death sentence.

Mills has lived for "14 years after he took the life of a friend of mine," Pigott said. "It only took a matter of minutes for Les to die. That's justice? It's ridiculous."

Pigott said he has always believed in the death penalty.

"With this execution, it will be closure for this chapter in my life," Pigott said earlier this week. "It won't be closure for the memories, though."...

...

7:50am: (Prayer)... The food director came to my cell requesting to know what I would like for my last meal. I inform him that I don't need anything... He asked Medina what he would like. He said he would like a steak and ice cream. The kitchen supervisor asked him what kind of ice cream he wanted. He said "fried ice cream"... The director laughed and said I never heard of that kind of ice cream. Medina... went back to talking to himself...

10:45am: The Asst. Superintendent was just at my cell asking questions about where I wish to be buried, concerning funeral arrangements. He needed all of this information for a death certificate...

I asked how did he feel about his "job". I asked him was he conscious of himself, passing judgment on people, and the first thing he yelled was 'I'm not judging you'.

Oh but you are!! Think about what you are doing...(prayer)

Hopefully I gave him something to think about. I said all my affairs would be dealt with by my religious advisor. Conversation ended 11:05.

11:55am: The officer just told me that Medina is playing like he is in a war. He put some ketchup on his chest and fell-out like he was shot – making all kinds of sounds...

'Officer S.' came to my cell and just looked at me.
I asked 'What's up?'
He just shrugged his shoulders.
I said 'What is that?'
He said he just did not know.

I asked concerning his emotions and feelings. What he was feeling at that moment. He could not tell me what he was feeling. I told him that was his conscious Self, trying to tell him something, and that he needed to explore it.

He said 'You're right', and just walked away, and called the Lt. down to witness Medina's behavior.

12:30pm: 'Brother H.' called and let me know the argument was scheduled for 2:00pm.

1:15pm: They came to my cell asking me to try on a shirt and pants. I try them on, and ask is there anything else.

1:45pm: Everyone wants to know what they can do for me. Superintendent, Asst. Superintendent, and a new respect from 'T.'...

4:05pm: 'Brother H.' just called and let me know I received a stay...

7:00pm: Reprieved!

Today was a day I hope to never forget. Pure Madness.

I showered, my cell was shaken down, and everything was moved outside my bunk. There are some sick people.

I made me a cup of coffee – and had a soup – and have salad, then call it a night. What a day this was.
...

December 4:

Tallahassee Democrat:

> **MURDERER GIVEN A TWO-DAY REPRIEVE**
> **The Florida Supreme Court delays the execution of John Mills Jr., convicted of killing a Lester Lawhon in Medart in 1982.**
> **By Craig Poynter**
>
> *John Mills, Jr. got a temporary stay of execution on Tuesday after his attorney urged the Florida Supreme Court not to kill an innocent man.*
>
> *The justices delayed the death sentence, originally scheduled for seven this morning, until Friday. This will give the court time to take the last-minute appeal under consideration...*
>
> *Tuesday afternoon, the court heard arguments from attorney Marty McClain that Mills should get a new*

hearing. McClain works for Capital Collateral Rep., a state-funded agency that represents clients on Death Row.

McClain said Michael Fredrick, who was involved in the murder and testified against Mills at trial, lied about his relationship to Lawhon.

...according to documents filed with the court: Fredrick was a pimp and a drug dealer who provided Lawhon with prostitutes, marijuana and other drugs, attorney said.

Frederick was spared death in exchange for his testimony against Mills. He is serving a 347 year sentence..."

...

**Tallahassee Democrat:
OUR OPINION**

**Death penalty debates often in the wrong forum
Delaying sentences can be cruel punishment.**

Retributive death is even older than the Old Testament's "eye for an eye" injunction. Human history is filled with examples of such punishment.

One thinks of the guillotine, that efficient instrument of state mass murder; or the gallows at England's Tyburn, where groups of picnickers gathered to watch society's unfortunate hang.

Societal murder has long been viewed as a means of keeping the worst of us in check — or out of circulation. But as nations have moved haltingly toward what some would call civilization, there's been a corresponding re-examination of what the death penalty says about a society.

American society can't make up its mind.

Take John Mills Jr., who was sentenced to die 14 years ago for killing a Medart man, but watched and waited as his case wound through a long series of appeals.

How agonizing is it to die a slow death, to live from day to day knowing that each morning is a day beyond the legal proscribed..."

...

LETTERS TO THE EDITOR

Death for murderer a fit punishment

At the time I am writing this letter I do not know if the execution of John Mills Jr. has taken place or not. I have not talked to any reporter in years about this case, even though I was supposedly quoted in the Democrat. Les Lawhon worked for me and was a very good friend. I know he is in a better place. I do miss his friendship, but I have many fond memories.

As for Mills, I hold no grudges and I feel for his family. I knew his dad and respected him very much.

I do believe in the death penalty. Maybe it is not a deterrent to everyone, but it is to me. We have a very big problem in our country of not accepting punishment for our actions. One thing is very clear and that is once a killer is put to death, they cannot kill again.

One thing that does bother me is that the justice system and legal system were very sorry and callous to have taken 14 years to get to this point.

Stephen E. Pigott, Crawfordville

...

Death penalty wrong in Mills, Medina cases

The month of December is a time of special religious holidays for Christians and Jews. Christians celebrate the birth of Jesus Christ. Jews celebrate Hanukkah. This holiday season the state of Florida plans to kill John Mills Jr. and Pedro L. Medina.

Mills has been convicted of killing Lester Lawhon. The murder took place in Wakulla County in March of 1982. Mills has an IQ of 79. This is considered borderline mentally retarded. On Oct. 21 Florida executed John Bush. Bush was borderline mentally retarded. Now, if Mills is executed, we will have electrocuted two borderline mentally retarded persons within a matter of weeks.

There is substantial evidence that Mills did not receive a fair trial. Lawhon was a son of the Rev. Glenn Lawhon, a prominent minister in Wakulla County. There was a great deal of publicity concerning the murder before and during the trial. This publicity included newspaper articles and TV reports strongly implicating Mills in the murder. Judge George Harper, a personal friend of the Rev. Glenn Lawhon, refused to move the trial to another location. Mills is black. All the members of the jury were white.

Five members of the jury said they personally knew the victim or the victim's family. The Florida Supreme Court erred in upholding the conviction and sentence. It failed to take into account that five members of the jury personally knew the victim or the victim's family. It failed to take into account that the community was so angry at Mills that the trial judge had the first two rows of seats behind the defendant blocked off to prevent violence to the defendant...

Pope John Paul II, in his encyclical "The Gospel of Life," points out that Cain was the first murderer in human history. Yet, God did not kill Cain:

God, who is always merciful when he punishes, "put a mark on Cain, lest any who came upon him should kill him" (Gen. 4:15).

Both Mills and Medina should never be released from prison. They should be incarcerated for the remainder of their natural lives, but they should not be executed. Gov. Lawton Chiles should immediately hold a specially called meeting of the Clemency Board to commute the sentences.

Thomas A. Frederick, Jr., Meridian Road

...

(Prayer)! Allah... has blessed me to live on this day that I was scheduled for execution. I am sure a lot of people are upset. A lot of money. With all the officers coming down here yesterday, it was...(unreadable)...

8:00am: ...an officer asked me was there some hope now. I said there has always been hope. They were so sure it would be my execution this morning. That is just to say they don't run nothing. Allah is the Master of the Day of Judgment.

9:25am: I was informed that I have an attorney call-out and religious from 10am to 11am.

9:30 am: The Superintendent asked what could he do for me. I told him I requested to see a doctor a few days ago, by him. I still haven't seen anyone yet, so I decided not to burden anyone...(prayer)...I will be alright.

He said he was sorry, and that he didn't realize that no one had seen me. Now he is on the phone to a doctor...I will just wait and see what happens.

12:05pm: 'Brother H.' was back in the visitation room to see me. The Florida Supreme court denied me, so...(prayer)...Allah's will be done...

2:40pm: The Superintendent came to my cell with a message from 'Brother N.' of 'B. Fellowship'. May Allah's blessing be upon them.

3:00pm: 'Mike R.' came to see me. We talked for a couple of hours, about different things concerning a stay, etc.

Once back to my cell, someone had been in it. Moved my stuff, etc. If it ain't one thing it's another. I pray that I overcome. (Prayer)...

...

December 5, 1996:
10:15am: (Prayer) I ask Allah for a special blessing today. I am waiting on him to answer.

10:10am: The Assistant Superintendent was just here concerning my contact visit from 12pm-1pm.

11:20am: 'Brother H.' called. He just informed me that the 11th court turned me down. So I guess this is it. Allah, call me home. (Prayer)...

3:00pm: 'Muhammad L.'... we had a beautiful conversation (prayer)... he asked did I want my body to be moved there. I haven't –

Chapter Twenty-Nine

The Wakulla News
Reporter's Notebook:
ON MILLS' EXECUTION
By William Snowden

Those of us on the list to witness the execution of John Mills, Jr. are told to be in the field across the street from the prison at 5:30a.m.

The fog is thick, and adds to the damp chill as several reporters stand around in the darkness, waiting for the van to come pick us up.

None of us slept last night, we had to admit. The exception is the reporter from the Associated Press, an old hand at this, who has witnessed all the executions since 1984. He admits he slept some, but not very well. "It's an unpleasant thing," he tells us in obvious understatement.

***At 5:45a.m.**, the prison van shows up, the officials verify our credentials, and we load up for the short drive over to the prison.*

***By 6:15a.m.**, we are through the security checks. Each of us has to produce photo identification again and pass through a sensitive metal detector. We are not allowed to bring in anything – cameras, recorders and notebooks are forbidden.*

***At 6:20a.m.**, we are in a staff break-room for a briefing with Gene Morris, a spokesman for the State Department of Corrections. We have been provided with legal pads and pencils to take notes.*

Morris reports that Mills made no last meal request and was so served the standard last meal of steak and fried potatoes and eggs. "He ate none of it," Morris says.

Mills met last night with his attorneys from Capital Collateral Representative, and visited with his family, including his mother and sister, and his spiritual advisor.

"He did not sleep much at all last night. People who were in charge of cell front security described him as unusually calm," Morris says. "I saw him yesterday evening and he was in a very pensive mood, reading from the Koran and very peaceful."

He then describes to us what will take place inside the death chamber, when the chair was built, that there had been 37 executions since the death penalty was reinstated in Florida in 1979.

Just before 7a.m., we are led out to a van to drive us over to the Q-wing of the prison, where the execution will take place.

Just after 7a.m., we enter the observation room. There are four rows of six seats; reporters sit in the back two rows.

Rev. Glenn Lawhon, the father of the murder victim, Les Lawhon, sits in the front row center, perhaps 4 feet away from the electric chair, separated by Plexiglas.

When Mills is led in by two officers and as he is being strapped to the chair, he looks only at the Muslim cleric Imam Rabani Muhammad, who is seated in the front row in the observation room. Mills smiles at the Imam, nods, indicates he is prepared.

Asked if he has a last statement, Mills recites a Muslim prayer. His shaved head, which glistens with a gel to aid *in conductivity, is fixed with a headpiece. A black leather face mask is then attached to cover Mills' face, and the electrodes are attached to the cap.*

The superintendent goes to the telephone to ask the governor if there is any reason the execution should not take place. He leaves the phone and nods to officials in the death chamber.

There is a loud clang as a switch is thrown at 7:11a.m. For two minutes there is the sound of an electrical hum. Mills' fists are clenched tight. At 7:13a.m., the switch is turned off and Mills' hands unclench.

Two doctors checked the body for vital signs. We are told the execution has taken place.

The citizen witnesses file out, leaving reporters to sit here until they clear the prison. For the few minutes it takes, we sit there in silence, Mills' corpse still strapped to the chair a few feet away. The prison officials in the death chamber are waiting for us to leave before removing the corpse, they all stand there patiently at parade rest.

***At 7:20a.m.**, we have been loaded into a van to be dropped back off at the field where we started.*

The AP reporter jumps out and grabs his cellular phone to file the story with his bureau; the TV crew sets up for a report; other newspaper reporters gather around as the Lawhon family holds an impromptu news conference in the parking lot.

It's first light. Still foggy, the ground is wet with dew.

I walk over to where the capital punishment protesters stand, most of them wrapped in shawls, some candles half-burned out on the ground. I count the number of people, write down what some of the signs say. They stand there silently.

Back to the field where the Lawhon family is holding their news conference, Rev. Lawhon, prepared for a photo op, has a portrait of his son in his arm. He had told one reporter that he would confront protesters with his son's portrait.

Before I left my motel room this morning, I re-read the description of the gruesome murder that Mills committed, wanting to be sure that I kept the perspective of what the victim suffered while I observed the execution.

To me, the only noble actor in this sordid play is the Imam Rabani Muhammad, who was with the condemned man all night, talking and praying with him, preparing Mills to face his death.

I have the feeling that there will be a reckoning for all of us who took part in this. Whether to our conscience or to our God, each of us will need to answer for our role.

...

In the book, 'Last Words of the Executed', by Robert K. Elder, with a forward by Studs Terkel, Yuhanna Abdullah Mohammed's last words were:

"I bear witness that there is no God but Allah, and I bear witness that the prophet Mohammed is the messenger of God."

...

He was quickly prepared and buried according to the Muslim tradition. He requested that his body go nowhere near Wakulla County, the place of his birth. Everyone agreed to this, for there were threats that his remains would be dug up and further desecrated by certain members of our larger, second family, of Wakulla citizens.

A storm hit the county that night with wind gusts of up to seventeen miles per hour, and just under two inches of rainfall.

...

When asked if she wished to say anything regarding the death of John Mills, Jr., a woman replied:

> "I have no comment. Another family is suffering."

These words were among the most compassionate ever spoken by a Wakulla County resident in regard to this case.

It was in my moments of rage, when recalling this incident, that these words humbled me. It was when I felt despair upon viewing the world and how cruel it could be, that these words filled me with hope, and pierced my mental darkness with the tiniest light, letting me know that there was still kindness to be found in the heart of man.

These words were spoken by the mother of Lesley James Lawhon.

Epilogue

On Friday, December 6, 1996, after a sleepless night in Brooklyn, New York, I went to my next-door neighbor's apartment to ask if I could watch the *Today Show* on their television. Jeremy and Tim were still very much asleep when I sat on the floor beside their highly elaborate bunk-beds, waiting for Katie Couric to give any news about my Uncle's death that morning. There was none.

I gathered myself, went to classes at American Academy of Dramatic Arts. Chekov, Ibsen, O'Neill, Shakespeare, nor August Wilson meant anything to me in that moment. Not anymore.

After class, I went to my part-time job at the Helmsley Hotel. It was a menial coat-check position that gave me time to write when the dining room was slow. I tried to jot down all I could remember about my Uncle, as if to not capture it now – in that moment – meant that I would never possess the strength to recall his name or pull his face to the forefront of my memories ever again. But the words trickled in slowly, and often came out wrong. I began to see my mother's face, my grandmother's, and how I'd left them in such hostile territory to bear it all alone.

I stood behind my gate watching that peculiar mix of New York's people, the world. The glitter on their wrists, fingers; their smells, like a fantastic, high-priced garden, consuming the senses as they walked past and throughout the room. All were smiling as our hotel piano player (whose name I can no longer recall, but who often gave me cd's of his work), played their favorite yuletide classics.

It was the beginning of December, after all, and the holidays were preening themselves day and night, ready to burst into full bloom. These people had no clue, I thought, of the deadly gift the State of Florida handed my family and I earlier that morning. And, furthermore, they wouldn't have cared.

For, the only thing of importance that chilly December day, with its freezing sun, was the pending arrival of Santa, and whether or not America's children would be found worthy of a holiday prize.

I arrived back to my apartment, lay down, cried, and fell asleep in my work-clothes.

The next day, Saturday, December 7, a day after the State and taxpayers of Florida used all manner of spiritual and mental detergents to wash away what remained of blood-red spots and splatters, I received the following letter:

" In the name of Allah, most merciful and compassionate.

My Precious Nephew... Alhamdulillah!

It is said: Our feet are example. We must walk in the direction they are pointed. When we walk on our heels, going backward, we will be subject to so many accidents.

May He cause us to rush to divine, luminous wisdom that dispels the darkness.

Bismillahirrahmanirrahim... ("In the Name of Allah, Most Gracious, Most Merciful")

"As salaam alaikum" (Peace be upon you) my precious Nephew. May Allah's blessing be upon you receiving this. I received your letter 12-2-96. I was deeply moved by it. Moved into a state of grace. Alhamdulillah.

You have no idea how proud I am of you. As I write this water rests in my eyes, Alhamdulillah...

To answer your question concerning the crime that I am in here for, No, I didn't do it, nor did I have anything to do with it.

You may ask 'Well, what are you doing on Death Row?' Nephew, as I started this off by saying, Our feet are example. We must walk in the direction they are pointed.

I say that to say this: Allah alone knows the meaning and the mystery of our lives. We belong to Allah and to Him we shall all return. We own nothing; everything belongs to Allah. We are His Creation. He can leave us here or take us back to Him. It is not our job to worry about where Allah will keep us. But our duty is to keep Allah within our hearts. Within our thoughts. Within our love, and within our intention.

Nephew, we must do this no matter what difficulty we face or hardship we must endure. We belong to Allah, and to Him we shall return.

This world does not belong to us. Where we live does not belong to us. This is a school to which we have come. Nothing belongs to us. We have come to this school of the world to study. We have come to study birth and death. We have come to study.

We have come to study the good and evil in this world. The hell and heaven here. We have come to see what God is and what Man is. To study the difference between Man and Beast. We have come to study Creation. The beautiful and the ugly. We have come to see what happiness is and what sadness is.

We have come to study all of this. And then the goodness and the evil that we collect, will all be counted in the end.

We have to learn before we die, and die as true believers, so that we can answer the question in the grave, before the angel of the grave. Maker and Make-e. Ask us... We have to be able to answer their question. We have to understand each quality of (Allah) God. We have to work it. We have to plant it. We have to reap the benefit and get those qualities so that we can answer for ourselves.

Because everything we do is written.

Nephew, I didn't mean to bore you with all this, but I think it is something you need to know. The lesson is not easy.

My Holy Book, the Holy Quran says:

"Do men think they will be left alone on saying "We believe" and that they will not be tested?"

"We did test those before them and Allah will certainly know those who are true from those who are false."

Footnote: Mere lip profession of faith is not enough. It must be tried and tested in the real turmoil of life. The test will be applied in all kinds of circumstances in individual life, and in relation to the environment around us. To see whether we can strive constantly and put Allah above Self.

Much pain, sorrow, and self-sacrifice may be necessary. Not because they are good in themselves, but because they will purify us like fire applied to a goldsmith's crucible to burn out the dress.

Precious Nephew, Allah has blessed me to write you these words.

Everything is 'inshallah', Allah's will... Inshallah, I shall see you again, if not in this world, inshallah, the next one.

I was given a stay of execution until 12-2-96. Allah is merciful.

So upon closing, I leave you with these words:

O My God Allah. My father. The only vehicle which carries my love to You from this world, is tears. They flow from the depths of where You exist, penetrating the cold stone shell of my heart, and reverberates back to You. They flow from the depths of where You exist and speak back to You. They are Your reflection, from my soul, my love, You.

P. S. Yes my beloved Nephew, I enjoyed your letter. It brought true blessing to my heart. Thank you for not forgetting <u>ME</u>.

Look at me... Tears are resting in my eyes again. A reflection, from my soul to you. Alhamdulillah (All praise is due to Allah).

That is it for now... You take care. My love, you, always.

Your Uncle,
Yuhanna A. Muhammad

As-salaam alaikim

About the author...

Playwright, Herb Donaldson's first play 'At a Time Like This' was featured by NBC as part of their PSNBC Festival at HERE Theatre. It went on to the National Black Theatre Festival and was later produced by Arcos Communications as part of its Downtown Urban Theatre Festival (DUTF). His play 'Brighterburn' launched the Fifth Annual DUTF at the Cherry Lane Theatre.

Another work, 'A Matter of Seconds', was produced by the Urban Pop Theatre Festival and later the Walnut Theatre (Philadelphia, PA) by BanjiGirl Productions.

He was also a writer for the short film, 'Love Aquarium'.

He's worked with New Federal Theatre, Public Theater/New York Shakespeare Festival, and was Director of Interpretive Programming for The Schomburg Center for Research in Black Culture.

He is one of the original founders of The Palaver Tree Theater Co., and currently serves as Artistic Director for the southern branch of the company in Wakulla County, Florida.

His first book, 'Southern SHOCK Americana', is the account of his Uncle's life on Florida's Death Row. Formerly known as John Mills, Jr., and later, Yuhanna Abdullah Muhammad, he was executed by the State of Florida on December 6, 1996, for a murder of which he is believed to have been innocent.

Palavertreetheater.org

Herbdonaldson@live.com

Acknowledgments...

If you were looking for the perfect book with no typos or grammatical errors, you have not found it here. And, in a way, I am glad for that.

This book would have never gotten this far if not for the people who actually knew Yuhanna (John, Jr.), my family, or me. 'Kickstarter' provided an opportunity to raise $2000 to write this book, format it, publish it – you name it.

Each and every dollar came from these people listed below and it was given with love, trust, and a belief that I could actually do it, when I had very little belief in myself.

Also within this list are those who, though they could not give financially, read rough drafts of the piece and either inspired or challenged me. Actually, I think they did both:

The Estate of Blonzie Mae Booth Ransom Mills Carter; Rachel and Herbert Donaldson, Sr.; Jennifer and Robert Monroe; Mary, Rachel, Lakeshia Monroe; Kevin, Lena, and Kelton; Alexander Ransom; Lloyd Ransom; Floyd and Pauline Ransom; Eunice Donaldson; Ka'ramuu Kush; Kaci Fannin; Mark Olkiewicz (MarcO); Elinor Elfner; Michael A. Olden; David Lennemon; Conswalia Green; Shirley Howard; Glenda Webster; Giancarlo Gonzalez; Johnathan Craig; Ayanna McMichael; Hope Harley; Chuck Robinson, Molly, and the 'rebel kids'; Brett Allbritton; Alex Ubokudom; Bayard Stern; Petra Shuff; Woodie King, Jr.; Jessie Sampson; Clayton Lewis; Byrd Mashburn; Nikki; Butch; Shane; Grace Rosier; Solomon Mills (hang in there, cousin. We'll see you soon); Murray and Helen McLaughlin; Layne Davis and Family; Scott Joyner, Tawanna Williams; Alice and Sylvester Williams; Cheryl and Charlie Creel; Margaret Thomas;

Stephanie Thomas; Julie Monin; Louise Reid Ritchie; Agnes Furey; Kurt Wadsworth, Jr.; M.J. Harrington; Sherrall Jackson; Tonya Price and Family; Debbie Dix Bishop; Rachel Sutz Pienta; Leigh O'Berry Key; Pat Chamburs; Sammy and Sandy Tedder; Colleen Skipper; Judith Harriss; Mary and Clarence Gavin; Tim Jordan; Judge Mike and Andrea Carter; Anne and Howard Kessler/Van Meter; Alan Brock; Laura Taff; Brian Burke; Michael O'Connell; Preston; Doug Jones; Joan Hendrix; Palmer Carr; Freeman Pigott; Betsy D. Smith, Markly Ceaser; David Roddenberry; June L. Noel; Dina Davis; Mimi Jones; Steve Adams; Sheila Meehan, Mark Elliot, Tammie Barfield, Mary Katherine Westmark, and William Snowden.

If your name is not listed, please know that it was not intentional. You now have an open door to attack me about it in the near future.

Thank you again, Everyone

A note on resources...

For the last 14 years I have collected information regarding this case. For the most part, it has been catch as catch can. Many trips to our local courthouse, the local papers, browsing the internet, email and handwritten correspondences, and of course, my Uncle's binder that he kept with him in his cell, tied together by two orange pieces of yarn.

I list here as much as I can find:

Florida Dept. of Corrections; U.S. District Court Middle District of Florida (my Uncle's personal correspondence); State of Florida Inmate Request forms (personal correspondence); Tallahassee Democrat; The Wakulla News; Capital Collateral Representative , CCR (personal correspondence); Death Penalty Information System (DPI); The Corrections Offender Network; Incident Report-Narrative Forms; Wakulla Co. Sheriff's Office; Wakulla Co. Courthouse; Wakulla Co. Public Library; Circuit Court of the Second Judicial Court, in and for Wakulla Co., Florida (Lisa Gainey); Affidavit for Search Warrant (Wakulla Co. Sheriff's Office); Florida Dept. of Law Enforcement; The Florida Flambeau; Supreme Court of Florida, Nov. 15, 1983, appeal (Roosevelt Randolph); Supreme Court of Florida, May 5, 1987, appeal (CCR); Appeal from Denial of Post-Conviction Relief, Motion for Stay of Execution, and Motion for Stay of Execution pending petition for Writ and Certiorari, May 4, 1987 (CCR); Petition for Extraordinary Relief and for a Writ of Habeas Corpus, November 15, 1989 (CCR); Reply to State's Response to Petition for Writ of Habeas Corpus, January 15, 1990 (CCR); Supreme Court of Florida, response, November 8, 1990; U.S. Court of Appeals,

Eleventh Circuit, No. 88-3945, April 15, 1995; United States Court of Appeals, Eleventh Circuit, August 15, 1995; Case No. 89434, Emergency Motion: Capital Case, Death Warrant Signed; Execution Imminent, Initial Brief, December 3, 1996(CCR); Supreme Court of Florida, Corrected Opinion, No. 89,434, December 4, 1996; Appendix to Petition for Writ of Habeus Corpus, Volumes II and III; Excerpt from the Oral Argument of Mills v. State on Direct Appeal Before the Supreme Court of Florida, May 9, 1984; Uniform Commitment to Custody; Judgment and Sentence, Michael Fredrick, Case No. 80-C7; FDLE Investigative Report (Mary Turner); Psychiatric Treatment Records from Apalachee Community Mental Health Services and Jail Medical Records for Michael Fredrick; Interrogation of Fawndretta Galimore, May 17, 1982 (Kerwin); Transcript of Hearing (on change of plea in Fredrick v. State), October 4, 1982; Transcript of Hearing (sentencing in Fredrick v. State), January 7, 1983; School records of John Mills, Jr.; Psychological Evaluation by Harry Krop, Ph.D.; Psychiatric Commitment Records of Blonzie Mills; Affidavits of Fifty-One Wakulla Co. Residents at the Time of Trial; Insurance Application for Glenn Lawhon, March 13, 1978; Carlton's, Claxton's, Lawhon's, Landrum's and Sheriff's Jury Selection Charts; The Gainesville Sun (newspaper); and the journals, compiled paperwork, and letters of John Mills, Jr., (1987 - 1996).

Made in the USA
Charleston, SC
13 January 2014